THE SAN FRANCISCO
CHRONICLE READER

THE SAN FRANCISCO
CHRONICLE READER

Edited by **WILLIAM HOGAN**
and **WILLIAM GERMAN**

McGRAW-HILL BOOK COMPANY, INC.
New York   Toronto   London

THE SAN FRANCISCO CHRONICLE READER

CRIME AND PUNISHMENT

LIVELY ARTS

WAR AND PEACE

NEWS IS WHERE YOU FIND IT

OUR VERY OWN

THE FRONT PAGE

TRIVIA UNSHAKEN . . .

Introduction

The San Jose jail is crowded.
Smallpox has disappeared from Stockton.
Trout are now abundant in the Russian River.
Wheat is growing finely in Sonoma County.
Woodland is in need of a new fire engine.
The Navajo Indians are at war with the Apaches in Arizona.
The new horse railroad between San Jose and Santa Clara is doing a rushing business.
The lamplighter of Virginia City has deserted for White Pine, leaving Virginia City in darkness.
The editor of the Woodland Mail, Yolo County, fears assassination by the Democrats of that place.
The Sacramento Union persistently says that San Francisco is not a fitting site for a city. Perhaps Sacramento is.

> —Pacific Coast Brevities, from the
> *San Francisco Daily Morning Chronicle*,
> January 17, 1869

The intelligence in 1869 was brisk and to the point. The variety and scope of coverage were admirable. For sheer economy of language it was close to perfection. And, until that last item, it was a model of objectivity. That last, nasty item—that's where the model ends and *The Chronicle* begins to show through. The news, pure and unadorned, might have been anybody's standard. Add that barbed aside and you have the glimmer of the attitude that has grown into a *Chronicle* trademark.

From the beginning the *San Francisco Chronicle* has been an audacious instrument of journalism. The audacity has persisted over the range of a century, sometimes rampant and sometimes merely dormant. Some years it has bent with the styles of the time. On occasion it has dipped into cuteness or soared into ultra sophistication. There were even long periods at *The Chronicle* when the traditional restraints of the trade were scrupulously and rigidly respected. But always these arid stretches were broken with a renewed faith in the principle that the rules must only be established by the news itself. Each awakening was marked by the bold return of comment, criticism and free expression to the news columns. The sacred tenets may have been violated, but the interest of the reading public was vigorously assaulted.

The *Chronicle* cult of personality is the recurrent theme in the vaudeville show of journalism that follows here. The most memorable jobs of reporting seem consistently to be those in which the reporter never quite gets off the stage. He may establish his presence with a phrase or a thought or through the whole concept of his report, but what is crucial is that his point of view must somehow lend extra meaning to the event itself. This may seem like a dangerous flirtation with prejudice and imbalance, and it is. So long as writers and editors maintain an honest regard for basic truth, why shouldn't the creation of a daily newspaper be an exciting and dangerous enterprise?

That *The Chronicle* has been able to indulge in this sort of adventure and continue in the public esteem has been due largely to a rare and fortunate chemistry—a blending of astute coaches and talented players.

The happy chemistry was there in the nineteenth-century dispatch which reported that a minor western outpost called Los Angeles "has a velocipede school for ladies where the *dear creatures* are induced into the mystery of the bicycle free of charge."

The chemistry was there in the 1930s when editor Paul C. Smith was arming every *Chronicle* typewriter with a machine gun, and even charging personally down to a Salinas newsfront to rescue his embattled troops from "power-mad deputies, some of whom were, in addition, glazed by the glow of too-free indulgence in alcohol."

And the chemistry was still there, more potent than ever, in the past decade, when reporter Tom Mathews could stare down a shameful assignment—shepherding two teenagers on a visit to

Hollywood and Elvis Presley—and turn it into a warm and important analysis of the girl-of-the-species;

Or when George Draper covered a murder trial in Downieville by ignoring the trial itself and reporting the story of the tiny Sierra community, still basking in the glow of its gold-rush history;

Or the evening Art Hoppe courted disaster in his account of the first television debate between John Kennedy and Richard Nixon. Under the meanest of deadline pressures, Hoppe chose to brave the pitfalls of a trick device, adding dimension to his story by playing it against a backdrop that was set one hundred years before.

Let no one, however, get the notion that this book is a collection of mighty reporting, or mighty editing, or mighty anything. Earlier we called it a vaudeville show. In its enjoyment, we hope it to be exactly that. It is not a history of *The Chronicle,* nor a history of San Francisco. Yet a good deal of the material is plain and unrestrained nostalgia. The collection does not represent the best of *Chronicle* writing, nor the worst. Yet some of the stories are splendid examples of writing skill while a few are noteworthy for their lack of it. Certainly it puts no premium on the importance of the communication, even though some of the least serious efforts may be laden with inherent sociological import.

What has been sought out is a sampling of *Chronicle* copy that remains fun to read *today*—for whatever reason may apply to each piece. Some prizewinners qualify by this criterion and many do not. Some great events fall flat in the retelling and they do not appear at all. Several such major stories were best represented, not by the big account, but by the sidebar report which remained in sharper focus. Few of the stories are scoops. Those seem to die the quickest.

We must admit partiality to exhibits that represent the vast areas of nonsense in newspapering. We justify that partiality on the simple ground of truth. Like it or not, that's how it is much of the time in the homey business of written information and entertainment. And *The Chronicle's* eminence in the fields of horn-blowing, trivia and characters cannot be denied. From Pierre Salinger to Count Marco to The Last Man on Earth is a combination unique in American journalism.

There are fine memories, enjoyment and strong reading matter in the pages of a great metropolitan newspaper. This book is an attempt to rescue some of that local literature from the garbage pails it has lined so well and so long.

We are indebted to *The Chronicle*'s management for the opportunity of opening the newspaper's files to the light, and delight, of today. We also pay homage to the reporters and writers who performed the original work involved in this collection, and to their natural enemies, the editors and copy-readers who harangue and guide and paste and polish. Our particular thanks to city editor Abe Mellinkoff, ringmaster of the local scene. It was under his direction and guidance that much of the modern material here was gathered and written. City editor Mellinkoff has this to say about the craft and his staff:

"Writing a story for a daily newspaper is creation, and all creation is formed of fragile ideas and feelings. The reporter can at times be lightly guided but he cannot be directed. Rigid memos on how things will be done can be posted on the bulletin board in the city room, and constant flagellation of the reportorial mind and psyche can create a corporate style of writing. But the results will not be creative. The stories will be acceptable—safe at first base. None will ever clear the fence for a beautiful, easy home run.

"In the many uncertainties of journalism, there is one certainty: The reporter is the single indispensable ingredient of a good newspaper. Many a paper—God knows—is duller and less perceptive than its staff. But no paper can rise very far beyond the competence of its reporters."

And so, enough. On to the *Chronicle*'s dog and pony show.

—William Hogan
—William German

San Francisco Chronicle

THE FIRST BIG ONE

This is how it all began for *The Chronicle*—with a sensational scoop on the assassination of Abraham Lincoln. The scoop sent the new publication winging on its way toward becoming a real newspaper and a power in San Francisco.

It was all due to a prodigious feat of alertness and memory by Charles de Young, who, with his younger brother M. H., had recently used a $20 grubstake to establish *The Daily Dramatic Chronicle*, a tabloid-sized throwaway concerned mainly with theater news and programs.

The nineteen-year-old Charles was in the habit of stopping by the telegraph office to gossip with the operators and glean what intelligence he could for free. On the morning of April 15, 1865, he struck a bonanza. As he entered the telegraph office the news of President Lincoln's assassination was being tapped out from the East. De Young, who knew Morse code, eavesdropped, not daring to take a note. He didn't need to. When the tapping stopped, the intrepid Charles rushed back to his newspaper and wrote the whole story from memory. What matter if there was a contradiction about the fate of Seward? What if Wilkes Booth was accused in the headline and not even named in the story? Who could carp if the narrative itself seemed to be missing an important chunk right out of the middle? As a matter of fact, later comparison with the official telegraph report proved Charles was accurate even in his errors.

Charles not only had a scoop, but he had one with all the details. The story remained *The Chronicle*'s exclusively in San Francisco for the entire day because the other papers had already gone to press and were reluctant to gather up their staffs for an extra. And in the excitement the question of the telegraph story's "ownership" was never raised.

Charles and brother M. H. continued to publish *The Chronicle* together until 1880, when Charles died, himself the victim of an assassin's bullet.

M. H. de Young carried on alone for another half century until his death in 1925. The paper remains today in the hands of the de Young descendants.

Assassination of President Lincoln

LATEST DISPATCHES

Washington, April 15, 1865

(First dispatch)

Gen. H. W. Carpentier: His Excellency President Lincoln was assassinated at the theatre last night.

(Second dispatch)

President Lincoln died at 8:30 this morning, and Secretary Seward a few minutes past 9.

(Third dispatch)

Reports are contradictory. It is reported that President Lincoln died at 7:22.

DEATH OF THE PRESIDENT

MURDEROUS ATTACK ON MR. SEWARD

Wilkes Booth Supposed to be the Murderer of the President

Washington D.C.
April 14, 1865

President Lincoln and wife, with other friends, this evening visited Ford's Theatre for the purpose of witnessing the performance of the "American Cousin." It was announced in the papers that General Grant would also be present, but that gentleman took a late train of cars for New Jersey. The theatre was densely crowded, and everybody seemed delighted with the scene before them.

During the third act, and while there was a temporary pause for one of the actors to enter, a sharp report of a pistol was heard, which merely attracted attention, but suggested nothing serious until a man rushed in front of the President's box, waved a long dagger in his right hand, exclaiming, "Sic semper tyrannis!" and immediately leaped from a box which was in the second tier to the stage beneath, ran across to the opposite side of the stage, making his escape, amid the bewilderment of the audience, from the rear of the theatre, and, mounting a horse, fled.

The screams of Mrs. Lincoln first disclosed the fact to the audience that the President had been shot, when all present rose to their feet, rushing toward the stage, many exclaiming "Hang him!" The excitement was of the wildest possible description. Of course there was an abrupt intermission of the theatrical performance. There was a rush toward the President's box, when cries were heard of "Stand back," "Give him air," "Has anyone stimulants?"

On a hasty examination it was found that the President had been shot through the head above and back of the temporal bone, and that some of the brain was oozing out. He was removed to a private house near by. The Surgeon-General of the army and other surgeons were sent for to attend him. On the examination of the private box, blood was discovered on the back of the cushioned rocking chair on which the President had been sitting, also on the partition, and on the floor; a common single-barreled pistol was found on the carpet.

About 10 o'clock a man rang the bell, and the call having been answered by a colored servant, he said he had come from Dr. Viede, with a prescription, and at the same time holding in his hand a small piece of paper and saying, in answer to a refusal, that he must see the Secretary, as he was entrusted with particular directions concerning the medicine, he insisted on going up. Although repeatedly informed that no one could enter the chamber, he pushed the servant to one side, walked heavily toward the Secretary's room, was met there by Mr. Fred Seward, of whom he demanded to see the Secretary, making the same representations which he did to the servant. What further passed in the way of colloquy is not known, but the man struck him on the head with a billy, badly injuring the skull, and felling him senseless.

The assassin then rushed into the chamber and attacked Mr. Seward, a paymaster in the United States army, and Mr. Hunsell, a messenger of the State Department and two male nurses, disabling them. He then rushed upon the Secretary, who was lying in bed in the same room, and inflicted three stabs in the neck, but severing, it is thought and hoped, no artery, though he bled profusely. The assassin rushed downstairs, mounted his horse and rode off before an alarm could be sounded and in the same manner as the assassination of the President. It is believed the injuries of the Secretary are not fatal, nor those of the others, although both the Secretary and Assistant Secretary are very seriously injured.

THE SAN FRANCISCO SCENE

In the wonderful world of San Francisco journalism Herb Caen is the champion. It's no contest. Caen outdraws anything in the paper. Caen is the best known man in town. You must read Caen to be in the know. You find out what's doing, who's who, how it is, and where it happened. Caen's column is enthusiasm and jive talk and a love letter between you and him and the city. It's a guide book and a gossip sheet and a laugh riot. It is also honest and sensitive and as smoothly finished as a fine piece of Danish furniture.

It would hardly be possible in a brief example to demonstrate the powerful appeal of Herb Caen's daily effort. The effect is cumulative, and, even then, often inexplicable to the outsider.

What follows here are two of the columns that fall into the "Baghdad-by-the-Bay" category, in which the writer paints and repaints the image of San Francisco. The columns were written twenty years apart. There is much similarity between them, but if you look carefully there is also much that reflects the passage of twenty years in the bigtime column business. For the "modern" Caen it is still Baghdad, but the rose-tinted lenses have begun to smudge just a little bit.

Baghdad

October 1, 1940

By the dawn's early light Coit Tower standing starkly silhouetted against the first faint flush in the east. . . . A sun-and-windswept corner on Montgomery Street, where you can look west and see a wall of thick, dirty fog rising genii-like from the Pacific, while a finger of whiter, puffier stuff feels its way into the Bay, twisting this way and that till it conforms to every contour, snugly and coldly. . . . And the poor man's perfume of Skid Road—a melancholy mixture of frying grease, stale beer and harsh deodorants that clings to your clothes and your thoughts for hours.

The smug majesty of City Hall's famed dome, higher (and dirtier) than Washington's, and so far above the conniving that goes on beneath it. . . . The few surviving little wooden houses of Telegraph Hill, clinging together for mutual protection against concrete newcomers slowly pushing them out on a limbo. . . . And

Fisherman's Wharf at 7 A.M., with its tiny fleet of tiny ships lined up in neat display, and proud seagulls strutting past to review them.

The aged hangers-on outside the Public Library in Civic Center, singing an *a cappella* chorus of futility against the roaring backdrop of a metropolis in motion—Market Street. . . . That occasional white ferryboat drifting over from the Oakland mole and dipping respectfully beneath the aloof bridge that doomed so many of its side-wheeling sisters. . . . And block after block of flatiron buildings along Columbus Avenue—sharp edges of a city that grew in too many directions at once.

The incongruity of a lonely foghorn calling somewhere in the Bay as you stroll hatless down a sun-swept street—and the grotesque sight of this jumbled city from Twin Peaks, a sardonic, hysterical travesty on the dreams of those who stood there after the Great Fire and planned the Perfect City. . . . Long-forgotten cable-car slots wandering disconsolately and alone up steep hills that are now flattened, with a contemptuous snort, by high-powered, twin-engined busses. . . . And the Saturday-night symphony audiences arriving breathlessly at the Opera House from streetcars, on foot, in shabby automobiles—a far and enjoyable cry from the Friday-afternoon trade slinking slowly up in limousines that actually look bored.

University of California's Medical Center (where they discovered vitamin E) rearing up like a spectacular movie set against the darkness of Mount Sutro and Parnassus Heights, while in the pre-dawn hush of Golden Gate Park, far below, squirrels sit unafraid in the middle of the silent roads, and ducks waddle importantly along the bridle paths. . . . The full magnificence of the Pacific bursting into your consciousness as you swing past the Cliff House. . . . And the monumental mechanical madness of the Kearny, Geary, Third and Market intersection, where traffic, honking the horns of its dilemma, squeezes painfully through a bottleneck with a "Stop" sign for a cork.

The too-bright mask of Chinatown's restaurants and bars, sometimes standing half empty, while upstairs, in the tenement-like apartments, live six Chinese in one room. . . . The glittering Golden Horseshoe during opera season, a constant reminder that there are Upper Classes even in a building paid for by the masses. . . . And the eye-bulging sight, from atop the Fifteenth Avenue hill, of the little white new houses marching through the Sunset District toward the Pacific like stucco lemmings that decided, just in time, not to hurl themselves into the sea.

St. Francis Wood, Pacific Heights, and Sea Cliff, where the homes have room to puff out their chests in the satisfaction of success; and the ornate frame buildings just west of Van Ness—before 1906 the mansions of the mighty, today living out their long lives as boardinghouses for those who are merely existing. . . . The two distinguished neighbors, the Mark Hopkins and the Fairmont, staring blankly at each other across California Street in the silence of 5 A.M., when even the cable slots cease their friendly gibberish. . . . And the corner of Jackson and Kearny, a one-worldly blend of China, Italy and Mexico, where, all within a few steps, you can eat chow mein, top it off with chianti, and then step into a Spanish movie.

The inner excitement of Stockton tunnel, as the jampacked F cars wiggle noisily through, autos somehow squeeze past, and school kids run excitedly along the inside walk; and North Beach, with its 1001 neon-splattered joints alive with the Italian air of garlic and the juke-box wail of American folk songs. . . . The dismal reaches of lower Market after midnight; the city within a city that is the deep Mission District, and the bittersweet juxtaposition of brusquely modern Aquatic Park against the fortresslike jumble of red brick where Ghirardelli makes his chocolate.

The crowded garages and the empty old buildings above them, the half-filled night clubs and the overfilled apartment houses, the saloons in the skies and the families huddled in basements, the Third Street panhandlers begging for handouts in front of pawnshops filled with treasured trinkets, the great bridges and the rattletrap streetcars, the traffic that keeps moving although it has no place to go, the thousands of newcomers glorying in the sights and sounds of a city they've suddenly decided to love, instead of leave. . . .

This is Baghdad-by-the-Bay!

December 3, 1961

IT'S SAN FRANCISCO, city of a saint and a pirate, where the garbage trucks are yellow and the Yellow Cabs are more like orange and the De Soto Cabs are Plymouths and the graceful church spires yearn toward the heavens, almost as high as the rooftop saloons. . . .

BLESSED CITY of St. Francis, with the pigeons huddling under the benches in Union Square to escape the rain. An old lady is trying to coax one out with a handful of peanuts. "I love 'em," she rattles. "The little devils. I like to swat 'em with my umbrella." She goes cackling off into the misty haze, toward Maiden Lane, dear Maiden Lane, once the street of the prostitutes, now so chic and sleek, with its Frank Lloyd Wright, and a few would-be Wrights gone wrong, and all the time the bird-legged models pattering along, laughing at the crazy old woman swinging her umbrella at the pigeons. . . .

WESTERNMOST city of life and death and the many imitations thereof, city of sirens and siren songs, open your Golden Gate and throw yourself off its bridge—and out there in the night, Alcatraz, Isle of the Dead, a black blob of rock under the nervous searchlight that tics around and around, looking for a way out when there is none. . . .

SAN FRANCISCO (not Frisco), the red plush seats in the Opera House, caviar and sour cream on blinis at Alexis', chilled Pouilly Fuisse at Monroe's, candlelight dinners on glass balconies overlooking the Embarcadero (the miners arrived in '49, in '61 they're doing fine) and the limousines lining up in chauffeur-driven droves outside I. Magnin's; for 'tis the season to be. . . .

And the parties. A particularly fine one is going on in Mr. Melvin Belli's ornately precious law offices on Montgomery—an old mahogany bar as central motif, chandeliers glittering over old law books, old cronies, crones young and old. Judges are there, properly sober and hoping to remain so. Mr. Ehrlich is there, exuding immaculate white linen from every pore. Pretty girls and thick slices of turkey and your glass never allowed to become empty.

Outside two automobiles come together in the sickening sound of the times: grinding metal, splinter and spray of glass, an awful hush broken by a hubcap clattering free down the street, slower and slower and then the brrrrrrr-clop as it comes to rest.

The lawyers make jokes. A few pull out their business cards and head for the crash, laughing, still clutching their highball glasses. The president of a big insurance firm shoulders them aside. "For once," he guffaws, "I'm gonna get there first."

Outside the two smashed cars are locked together, like fighting bulls. The driver of one is unconscious. The other, an attractive girl, is in shock, sitting behind the broken steering wheel, her eyes staring sightlessly, her broken arm angled crazily. From the walls and nooks and crannies, up from the sewers, come the gawkers, some with flash cameras. She gazes unblinking into their exploding bulbs.

An ambulance crew tenderly pries her out of the car. She is wearing a black dress and pearls, and a stole is strewn on the front seat. So she was on her way to dinner, to meet her date. The lawyers stand and watch, still sipping their drinks as the ambulance pulls away. Through the crowd walks a Chinese boy, a wooden box under his arm, and he is chanting, "Shine, shoeshine, who wants a shine," and you wonder who was waiting where for the girl in the black dress and pearls. . . .

OLD TOWN and new, bay windows sagging up the sides of Russian Hill and a cable car limping past as though its feet hurt, and meanwhile the great glass skyscrapers glisten coldly in the rain. A seagull screams past the Ferry Building in perfect marriage, an instant microcosm of The City That Was. If only you weren't viewing the sight from the Embarcadero Freeway. . . .

YOU WALK ALONG Kearny, once The Street of Adventurers. Now the sole adventure is finding a parking space, or crossing an intersection. The cops blow their whistles, but only at cars and pedestrians. At Mr. Tiscornia's miserable cluster of buildings, you stop and peer through a dusty old window that still bears the legend, Cohn's Coffee Club, and inside you can make out the counter and the chairs.

Who are you, Cohn? Where are you? Remember the day you opened, so many years ago. Flowers from well-wishers and your friends saying, "Cohn's Coffee Club, a clever name; you'll make a fortune." And Mrs. Cohn beaming proudly as she contemplated a long, rich life ahead, serving people, making people happy on The Street of Adventurers in the City of San Francisco.

Well, Cohn's Coffee Club folded a long time ago, so the front door has grown over with the mold and grime that are a big city's weeds. The windows have not been washed since Mrs. Cohn washed them last, decades ago, and you remember how she liked to make those windows sparkle. How now, Cohn? Where did you go, you and your wife and the floral horseshoe that said "Success"; where did you go, leaving behind your name to fade in the dust of Kearny street? . . .

DON'T CALL IT FRISCO. Call it San Francisco, call it beautiful and bright, dirty and ugly, watch the neon elevators rise in the new towers, see the funny lady hit the pigeons with her umbrella, hear the cars crash and the Christmas carols floating out over Post street in the Year of Our Lord. . . .

★   ★   ★

You get to Sausalito by driving north across the Golden Gate Bridge and turning to the right and downward almost as soon as the bridge makes contact with the hills of Marin county.

It is an unlikely suburb. It is peopled largely by successful types from San Francisco, business executives, advertising men, big city lawyers and doctors. Its cliffside real estate brings enormous prices. In almost any election it is a cinch to vote Republican.

But its women shop in leotards and Bermudas. Its children are sent downtown on weekends to shuck stones at tourists. And its social outlook is so liberal that its public houses are classified openly according to their degree of heterosexuality.

This account of a morning's events in Sausalito attempts in no way to probe the mysteries of this quaint, upper-middle-class community. Reporter Tom Mathews merely accepts and observes. If it should happen that the reader understands any more about Sausalito after he has read the story, that would be highly unlikely.

Renaissance at Dawn

October 16, 1955

"Does everyone have a wand?" asked the grand marshal. "Let us go forward then."

And at 5 A.M. yesterday, in the darkness and fog, the Save-Sausalito-from-Banality parade began.

At the head marched the marshal, Dame Enid Foster, painter, sculptress, the Edith Sitwell of Sausalito's Bloomsbury set. Behind her in loyal concert wavered Val Bleeker, who works at murals and the local distillery; Serge Trubach, a graying painter of a decaying world; and Elizabeth Enquist, a blonde with non-conforming ways.

Burly Swede Petersen, a wand in one fist and a cigar in the other, drove the village fire truck to light the way.

All had listened to the call of Miss Foster, who became so appalled by the dark ages of practicality last month she took vows to start a renaissance.

It was this fall that the muses died. Before then the artists joined every year to show their works, in a festival known for great cultural achievement and monumental hangovers. But a malaise of spirit (some did all the showing and others all the working) killed the movement.

Miss Foster was as shocked as the day they built the bridge and took the ferry boats away. She asked for a parade Saturday afternoon, just herself, suitably costumed—perhaps a plumed staff and a mask.

Nope, said the City Council. Tie up traffic.

How about 5 A.M.?

Be quiet, stay on the sidewalk, and keep the crowd down, said the City Council.

Thus it was that she appeared at 5 o'clock with masses of bright cellophane furbelows, a number of short bamboo sticks and some long poles dangling paper fuchsias. "The fuchsias are symbolic," she said with sweetness. "Few—shshsh."

"I'm delighted at the response," said Miss Foster, handing out poles, sticks, strings and furbelows. All but Serge tied things on themselves, even Swede.

"Serge, you have nothing on," Miss Foster said.

"I have my clothes on."

"Don't be improper. Does everyone have a wand? Let us go forward then."

The procession started, but stopped when a couple in red night-shirts tagged on. Miss Foster asked their names.

"Carol Potter."

"Gottlieb Schmekinlipp."

"What an interesting name," said Miss Foster. Schmekinlipp had a Chinese hat on with ribbons hanging thickly to his knees.

Everyone started up again, going from the Plaza south along Bridgeway. The route took them past the Sausalito Bait and Tackle Shop, crowded with fishermen waiting for party boats.

Miss Foster trained her eyes firmly forward. No barbarians were going to interfere with the renaissance. "What an exquisite morning," breathed Miss Foster. "Revel in that air. It's like champagne."

Serge, who tends to irony, turned up his coat collar. "Hurrah for Fog Day!"

In the gathering light, an occasional passing car showed startled faces at its windows. "People don't understand. They think we're coming home," said Elizabeth, stopping to stare back.

"You want to break the spell," said Serge. "Get in line."

At Richardson street, which makes a right angle with Bridge-way on the water, everybody turned around in a tangle of poles. Fog and water met in a luminous backdrop as they walked along the seawall toward the Plaza. Cars became more frequent. One stopped and a woman jumped out with a camera in her hands.

"It's a tourist," said Val. "Don't stop the parade for tourists."

"Long live Fog Day!" Serge shouted at the woman. "Long live Leash Your Dog Day!"

Two young men, with very red eyes, but a respectable steady gait, asked if they could join. Miss Foster handed them wands.

It was light enough now to inspect the windows of the downtown shopkeepers. In some of them were the work of artists Miss Foster had persuaded to exhibit. For herself, she had hung a monotype pen drawing in the Bank of America window. It was titled "The Rich and the Poor."

There will be a winner-take-all judging today for prizes donated by the merchants up and down Bridgeway. The prizes include a haircut, five stingers, five martinis, five bourbons-and-soda, $3, a box of handkerchiefs, a shoe soling, a T-bone steak, a banana split, a can of rum babas and a fish net. All these were rounded up by Miss Foster, who has decided that the artists will do their own judging. If each votes for his own work, then they'll flip coins.

"I don't think that will happen, though," she said, as her parade reached the Plaza and disbandment. "Gracious, I hope whoever wins will take his friends on the collection tour."

"Not me," said Serge. "See you next year, same station, same pogrom."

★   ★   ★

Two generations passed between the writing of the two stories that follow. In those 60 years the Big Game, a football contest between the University of California and Stanford, assumed a ritual importance incomprehensible outside of Northern California.

The report on the first Big Game was unsigned, probably composed by rewrite from facts gathered by a number of reporters. The 1953 story, which was merely the non-sports, page-one color account of the great event, was both legged and written by Edd Johnson of the city staff.

It is interesting to note how rich and similar both stories are in the social comment department. Watch closely.

The Big Game

I

March 19, 1892

One did not need to be an astrologer to discover in the signs of yesterday morning in San Francisco early and abundant evidence of their being something unusual in the air. The bulk of the testimony presented itself in the form of a tide of humanity coming from diverse points of the compass, each delegation sufficient in itself to leave a visible impress on the aspect of the busy city.

These cohorts, coming down like the wolf on the fold, were clad —one division of them at least—in the blue and gold raiment that has come to be locally known as the war paint of the students of the University of California. And up from the south, by special train from Palo Alto, came a cardinal-garbed delegation, full half a thousand strong, representing the young ladies and gentlemen who enjoy the advantages of Leland Stanford Jr. University.

There was no outward evidence of the direct cause of this marshaling of collegiate cohorts, but it was evident there was to be an intercollegiate contest of some kind. There was a rumor afloat that the game was to be one of football, but subsequent events proved that this fact came very near being lost sight of in the assiduity and enthusiasm of the collegians.

As a matter of fact, however, the day had been set apart for the first intercollegiate football contest between the two leading universities on the Pacific Coast. It had been long talked of and eagerly looked forward to, and never has there been aroused such enthusiasm as that manifested in both institutions when the eventful day dawned. Professors and their families joined the throng of travelers citywards, and if there was an undergraduate left behind he must have been hopelessly ill.

The young people from over the bay made their headquarters at the Palace Hotel. The earthquake-proof building was severely tested all the morning. "Ha! ha! ha! Cal-i-for-ni-a, U.C. Ber-ke-ley, gip, boom, ah!" was the burden of the song of the hundreds of stentorian shouters who congregated in the rotunda and trampled ceaselessly along the corridors.

Over at Lick House the same scenes were being enacted with a different setting. Here there was nothing visible but red. Cardinal red the Stanford boys called it, but every conceivable shade of the lurid color was brought into requisition and "everything went."

There is no need denying the fact that the Berkeley boys thought they had a walkover, and it is quite as much of a fact that the Stanford boys had but small hope of winning. Whittemore, the captain of the Stanfords, said to a *Chronicle* reporter at the Lick House: "I am afraid that our boys are too green for the Universities. They have never played an intercollegiate game and I don't know how they will behave."

In the Universities' camp, however, there was little thought of defeat. One of the Berkeley team, in conversation with a *Chronicle* reporter before the game, characterized the Stanford boys as a "kid team." "They play fair football for boys," he said, "but they can't do anything against us."

Just then a coachload of Palo Alto boys drove by, making the welkin ring with their tin horns and devil's fiddles, and shouting their war cry, "Rah! Rah! Rah! Rah! Rah! Rah! Rah! Rah! Stanford!" "That's all right," said the U.C. man, "but see what we've got for them. We've fixed up a take-off that will kill them dead. Just wait till after the game and you'll hear us shout 'Ma! Ma! Ma! Ma! Ma! Ma! Mamma! Mamma! Stanford!' "

The betting was 5 to 3 in favor of Berkeley before the crowds began to move parkward, and the Berkeley contingent seemed to have the best of it in the racket line.

Seldom, if ever, has the Haight-street ball ground accommodated such a crowd as yesterday. The inclosure may have held more people on the occasion of one or two baseball games, but never did the surrounding hills re-echo such a pandemonium of sounds. Long before 3 o'clock the grandstand was full and the seats on either hand were nearly so. The front of the grandstand was draped with blue and gold and blue and gold floated from the flag poles on the roof.

There was only one reason why the game was not called promptly at 3 o'clock, but it a most excellent one. Both teams were ready for the fray, and were just about to march out onto the field when someone casually asked: "Who's got the ball?"

The query went around the entire assemblage and the ridiculous fact was presently established that not a soul had thought of providing that inseparable adjunct to a football game, and that there was not a ball on the grounds. There was nothing to do but to telephone down into the city for a ball to be sent out as quickly as possible. Meanwhile the word went round that patience must be the order of the hour, and the crowd forthwith proceeded to enjoy itself. Squads of wearers of the distinctive colors of the contesting parties marched up and down before the grandstand to give their friends a chance to cheer them, and manipulators of different engines of ear torture took advantage of the interval to make all the noise possible.

Thrice glad were those who had nothing but their ears to amuse themselves with, when the cry went round, "The ball has come."

During the first ten minutes of the game the advantage was immaterial. Presently the ball had been forced down nearly to the Berkeleys' ten-yard line and the blue and goldites were getting ready for a grand cheer. All at once a sturdy Stanfordite was seen to break out of the bunch with the ball in his arms and to be making his way around the end of the line. The air was full of red banners up on the bleaching boards and an ominous hush pervaded the Berkeley cohorts. The man with the ball was Clemans, Stanford's sturdy left half-back. His friends yelled his name lustily and cheered until no other sound could be heard, but there were half a dozen Berkeleyites hanging around Clemans' neck by this time, and he was finally pulled off his feet, but not until he had carried the ball well over the ten-yard line on his own side of the field.

From this time on, in the first half, the ball never got back on the Berkeley side of the field. Little by little it was forced eastward. There was some terribly tough tackling done, and a lot of hard falls were sustained, but every once in a while the redoubtable Clemans would get hold of the leather and make another break around the end.

Finally Clemans made a great run through the line, toppling two men over as he ran and, cheered to the echo by the wearers of the red, got a touchdown south of the goal.

Stanford stock was way up. Berkeley couldn't understand it, and when Whittemore kicked the goal that gave the Palo Alto boys the first six points there was great gloom in the house of Berkeley.

A few minutes later, when Clemans secured another touchdown, it seemed as if the Stanford boys would go wild. It was the third Stanford touchdown, however, that broke the Berkeley camel's back. Fourteen to nothing was a terrible dose.

In the second half Clemans was again conspicuously alert and made two magnificent runs, but the Berkeley team had learned to keep their eyes on him above all his associates and Stanford was not allowed again to score. The two touchdowns and the safety scored by the U.C.'s in the last half were won by the hardest kind of work. The team gained its ground inch by inch, but, do their best, they could not tie the score.

Before the second half was finished it had begun to grow dark and the grandstand was quite deserted when the teams were all bunched up in the northeast corner of the field for the final effort with only about two minutes to spare. Hunt had the ball passed to him and made a desperate effort to get the tying touchdown, but the Stanford team stood like a brick wall before him, and the wall had not been scaled when the referee's watch said 6:40 o'clock and all was over. Score, 14 to 10.

The boys met again in the evening at the Bush Street Theater and everybody around for blocks knew it. How they did yell and stamp and whistle and abuse their din-creating instruments.

The students and their friends crowded the theater long before the curtain rose and kept up an unearthly hubbub. It sounded as though a certain gentleman who resides underground somewhere between here and China had turned loose all his imps.

"What's the matter with Stanford. She's all right, you bet! Ha, ha, ha! Fizz! Boom! Ah! Who's all right? Stanford!"

"What's the matter with Berkeley? She's in the soup! Rats, rats, rats! Scat! Boom! Bah! Who's in the soup? Berkeley!"

"Ha, ha, ha! Californi-a! U.C., Berkeley! Fizz! Boom! Ah!"

"Rah, rah, rah! Rah, rah, rah! Rah, rah—Stanford!"

II

**Stanford Stadium,
November 21, 1953**

As you read these lines in the cool of the morning after, you may find it difficult to credit that only yesterday you and I and all of us were a little dippy, and loving it.

It was Big Game day, of course, and unless you are an incurable square or have just come out from under an anesthetic, you know how this one ended. (For squares and convalescents, let it be recorded—University of California 21, Stanford University 21—a football game played in Stanford Stadium.)

But such a game. Such a crowd. Such a television audience. Such a fine pagan folk festival.

And, let's face it, such a debauch.

They gave out the attendance figures at 92,500. Those whose job it was to watch that 92,500 can assure those others who merely fainted beside their television sets that all 92,500 were near the end of their emotional resources in those last four excruciating minutes.

Up to those last four minutes it had been a real good game played in the excellent tradition of all the other Big Games in all the other 55 annual meetings of these rival teams.

The schoolboys down there on the field were exhibiting praiseworthy strength, courage and finesse. The student athletes from Berkeley were doing a little better than had been expected of them and the Stanford scholars were doing a little worse. That made it nice and neat, and the score was tied with just those four minutes of playing time left.

Of course, a tie game meant that the Stanford team would be eliminated from election to represent the Pacific coast in the Rose Bowl at Pasadena on New Year's Day. But that sort of thing has happened before in the Big Game.

Up to those last four minutes the pageantry of the folk festival had proceeded with orthodoxy and elan.

The day dawned fine. Recent rains had made the playing field springy, but left the highways, over which the assembling multitudes would for the large part pass, dry and relatively safe.

The traffic jams, as they always manage to be, were just a little more curdly than anyone expected. Sly motorists contrived to go by unaccustomed routes, to outwit others who likewise went by unaccustomed routes.

As a result, some people found it took them an hour to detour the Bay via the Dumbarton Bridge, and other sly ones inched along the secondary route of the Skyline boulevard at eight miles an hour.

So, in the fine tradition, guests failed to show up for luncheons at the appointed time, and anxious hosts finished the whole pitcher of martinis in their anxiety, and policemen scolded those who tried to make up for lost time either on the road or at the sideboard.

As the warm and lurid sun passed its zenith, the great earthen bowl of Stanford began to suck up the sly, the anxious, the drunk and the tardy, and soon it was almost game time.

For all the exacerbations of the journey, and the pain of rising after the traditional excitement of the Night Before Big Game, it was a pleasant and expectant crowd that meandered toward the bowl. Some came in cotton dresses and shirtsleeves. Others came in fur coats and carried blankets. All looked livelier and more alert than the dull-eyed gainseekers you see downtown on workaday.

With the rooting sections in their places at midfield, but the stadium not yet filled, there was enacted another rite in the tradition of the Big Game. The ax, that symbol of the sublimation of aggression that has been stolen, hidden, restolen and returned more times than anyone need remember, was returned to California's care.

The missing ax was discovered minutes before the kickoff in the parked car of Stanford football captain Norm Manoogian.

The ax was rightfully California's by virtue of the U.C. victory in last year's Big Game. Someone, no one was saying who, had stolen it from its resting place in Cal's Stephens Hall last winter. Its return brought forth a roar of approval from the more than 20,000 U.C. students present.

Then the California band marched out, cutting their bright blue figures and tootling enthusiastically on the green. Then the Stanford band, in suits of flashing red, assembled, covering something less than half the acreage, because Stanford, after all, is a smaller school, although not to be discredited for its size.

The color guards assembled beyond the goal posts, the bands blew in unison, the colors were presented and the Star Spangled Banner got itself played, while 90,000 stood at attention and no more than 2500 latecomers struggled up the stairs.

The bands left and the teams came on the field and began to play, fumbling and falling in their nervousness. As football, the first few minutes were ragged and inconclusive. Then it settled down and we got through the whole first quarter without serious damage to the aspirations of anyone.

The second quarter tensed things up a bit. But the cheering still was mannered and mannerly. At the bidding of their leaders, the rooting sections cried out: "We want a touchdown," "Throw 'em back," "Hold that line," "Get that ball," "First and ten, do it again," "Roll on, you Bears," "All the way," and similar appropriate things.

When Don Whyte, of the California boys, dived under a Stanford man for the first touchdown, he struck the turf of the end zone very hard indeed. He bounced up as from a trampoline, flung his arm into the air, kicked his heels and broke into a wide, circular trot.

The California rooting section, with less room to maneuver in, tried to imitate him. But by half time when Stanford had tied the score at 7 to 7, the stands had settled down to normal hysteria.

The half time pageantry was, in the words of a former coed in our neighborhood: "Just wonderful, all those things they think up." The sun was shining almost full power by now, and it reflected prettily the flashing colors of the massed rooting sections, holding up their glistening cards of many hues to make images of pride in self and mockery of their fellows across the way.

The bands marched again, in symbolic patterns. One pretended it was a rocket, and the other spelled the name Sousa while it played the tunes a man of that name had composed.

A boy dressed like a bear and another dressed like an Indian cavorted. Some of the 92,500 joined in the singing of some songs, occasional seatmates roaring out contradictory themes, according to their convictions. Old grads, sure that no institution of learning that had once had the good judgment to include them in its student body could ever be bested, debated in gravelly voices the outcome of the half of the game ahead.

And so the second half began, and the schoolboys played as expected and the score became Stanford 21, California 7, and it was just another Big Game with the better team winning and the Big Game dances ahead.

True, on the last play of the third quarter, Paul Larson of California unexpectedly skipped down the sidelines for another touchdown and the score became Stanford 21, California 14, but that, too, could have been expected.

For another 10 minutes it was sporty, clean-fought and pleasant to watch. It was only after the next moment when California suddenly tied it up that 92,500 persons were seized for four minutes with spasms, loss of breath and the screaming meemies.

By the time the surging fortunes of the game had carried the California line within field goal distance of the Stanford uprights the clock showed only 10 seconds to go. The seizures seemed almost unbearable in their intensities.

Then Larson, the California schoolboy, kicked the football from the rubber tee (and, oh, the unworldly importance that tee had acquired) and the ball went straight and upward, but not far enough and the game was over.

Thousands of persons who had flung themselves from their places in the stadium to glot up in an unruly mob outside the Stanford end zone surged forward. The goal posts on both ends of the field were in splinters seconds later.

Within an hour the stadium was cleared. The great earthen bowl of Stanford, having boiled over, slowly cooled and was quiet.

★   ★   ★

All of us old fans of Anna May Wong know about the olden days in San Francisco's Chinatown. We know that the dimly lit alleys abounded with hatchetmen and opium dens and runaway slave girls. We can even guess that its sinister tentacles extended in sinister fashion into all the sinister laundries of Salt Lake City, Buffalo and Des Moines.

Strangely enough, there were such things as slave girls and highbinders and tong wars. And, if not exactly sinister, they were still a cause for public concern. We flash back first to November of 1909.

CHINATOWN
Tong War

November 11, 1909

The honor of the abased and humiliated Yee family, which has lost two members as a result of the fierce tong war waging in Chinatown was avenged last night when Ow Lum Gum, member of the On Yick tong and cousin of Ow King, acting Chinese consul, forfeited his life to the unerring aim of a Yee gunman at Jackson street and Sullivan alley.

Dear was the price paid by the Yees for the first blood of the Yicks, for hardly had the victim fallen upon the pavement before Yee Yum, the boldest of the wealthy but timorous family whose name he bears, was seized by a policeman, who claims to have seen him fire the fatal shots. A score of persons saw Yee Yum dart from the crowd at the scene of the shooting and run across the street.

Closely pursued by a policeman he dodged into a basement hallway at 737 Jackson street, and a few moments later was found snugly enfolded in the blankets and coverings of a bed in the darkened room. As the policeman entered he was apparently slumbering peacefully, but beside him lay an almond-eyed infant whose wide and startled eyes belied the feigned repose of the wily Yee Yum.

His capture last night was bemoaned as a calamity by the Yees, whose consternation and woe was even deeper than the grief of the Yicks at the death of their cousin. Without Yee Yum, further vengeance by the Yees is difficult, they assert, while the death of Ow Lum only fans the seething fury of the Yicks, and strengthens their purpose.

Yee Yum had been released from the City Prison only yesterday morning. On Wednesday last, the day following the slaying of his two family members, he armed himself and vowed by all the spirits of his ancestors that a hated Yick should die. Policeman Hurley of the Chinatown squad, however, learned of his sinister oath and arrested him for carrying a concealed weapon. The charge against him was dismissed in the Police Court yesterday morning, and forthwith he hastened to fulfill his vow.

There were many witnesses to the tragedy last night, although none but Policeman Saemann, saw Yee Yum wield the revolver. He had no weapon when found in the room or in the street, although a thorough search was made. A woman from a neighboring window claims to have seen the shooting and says Yee Yum positively did not fire the shots.

With the death of Ow Lum, three lives have been forfeited to the implacable enmity of the On Yick tong and the Yee family. Until last night the Yees were bowed with humiliation, for eight days had elapsed since two of their cousins had fallen at the hands of the Yicks and no Yick had fallen in atonement.

War was declared by the Yicks because of the refusal of the Yees to meet the demand for indemnity for the elopement of Bo Gue, whose comeliness has been the pride of the Yicks since she has grown from childhood. None of the other maidens of China-town was as charming as she; none had such a wealth of smooth-combed tresses, and the glances of no other Celestial damsel aroused such a storm of jealousy in the hearts of the youths of the Pagoda quarter.

Suddenly she disappeared, and great was the consternation of the Yicks when no trace of her could be found. That was a month ago. Through the lavish expenditure of money it was discovered she had eloped, and the fury of the Yicks was violent. But their anger knew no bounds when it was discovered she had gone with a miserable Yee, a man who would not fight, it was said; one whose only attributes were an oily tongue and ways that appealed to women.

The elopers were traced to Santa Barbara, and Sergeant Mc-Mahon, armed with a warrant charging the girl with grand larceny for having taken away jewels that had been presented to her by admiring Yicks, was sent after her. On her return she was given into the care of a home in Oakland, and indemnity in the sum of $1300 was demanded of the Yees. That was refused and called blackmail by the Yees.

A meeting between the heads of the Yees and officials of the Yicks was held. The demand was reiterated and again refused. Three hundred dollars would be paid, said the leader of the Yees, and not one penny more. The meeting ended abruptly.

An hour after its adjournment Yee Fun Wah, member of the family of the Yees, was ambushed and killed at Church alley and Washington street. Four hours later Yee Gee, also a member of the family, was assassinated in his home in Oakland. Last night the Yees retaliated.

Further tragedies are expected momentarily.

Three months later the war was on the verge of being ended. The peaceful Yees had fought the highbinder tong to a standstill.

More important, they held firm on a matter of principle—and when peace was at last made it was on the terms of the gentle Yees.

Tong Peace

February 7, 1910

After almost four months of guerrilla warfare, the expenditure of about $50,000 in actual cash, a loss of $100,000 owing to the demoralization of business and the killing of nine men, the war which has disrupted Chinatown came to an end last night with the announcement that the sum demanded by the On Yick tong as indemnity for the theft of one of the society's slave girls had been paid.

Articles of peace were drawn up and were signed by the thirteen Chinatown tongs, but the Yee family has not yet put its official signature to the document, and will not do so until it has been carefully examined by the clan's attorneys.

Yee Hong, a by-no-means prominent member of the Yee family, eloped with the On Yick slave girl, Bo Gue, several months ago. The On Yicks demanded the sum of $1300 indemnity from the Yee family, threatening to take the lives of some of the clan if satisfaction was not given in the sum demanded.

The Yees are the most peaceful family of all the Chinese, devoting their attention to laundry work and merchandise. The On Yicks, headed by Tong King Chong, apparently thought their demands would be at once granted, and it was believed in Chinatown that the Yees would not attempt to fight the powerful highbinder and gambling tong. But at a meeting of the head members of the Yee Family Association it was pointed out that the day of blackmail had passed and that it was now time for the peaceable Chinese to resist the demands of the highbinders.

When the On Yicks were notified that the Yees would not pay the indemnity of $1300, Yee Fun Wah was shot and killed in Church alley by a member of the On Yick tong. The murder was a particularly cold-blooded one, for Yee Fun Wah was a member of the On Yicks and believed himself safe from their vengeance. The same evening another member of the Yee family was killed in

Oakland, and so it went until six members of the clan had been murdered.

In the meantime one of the On Yicks also met his death and two men were killed who did not belong to either the tong or the Yee family. It is believed that these latter were shot in mistake for members of the warring factions.

In spite of the number of deaths and the terror under which they were forced to live, the Yees remained steadfast in their determination not to yield to the blackmailing tong. Tong King Chong and Gee Hong On, two of the leaders of the On Yicks, were indicted by the grand jury for murder, together with two minor members of the society. Tong King Chong and the tong's interpreter were arrested and are now in the County Jail awaiting release on bail, while the other two highbinders are in hiding.

Finally the On Yicks said they would grant peace terms provided that the Yees agree to withdraw from all prosecutions of the members of the highbinder tong who were under arrest for the various shootings and would also assent to Tong King Chong's release on bail.

A tentative truce was signed two weeks ago, which was to last until after the Chinese New Year holidays, ending March 1. Last night the merchants of Chinatown called another meeting in the directors' room of the Six Companies' headquarters, and it was then announced that Yee Hong and Bo Gue, the couple who eloped, had raised the $1300 demanded by the On Yicks and were ready to pay it.

The peace agreement was then signed by the Chinatown tongs to the number of thirteen, but the Yee representatives did not affix the seal of the family. In explaining this, Yee Sing, president of the Yee Family Association, said last night:

"We have refused from the first to pay the $1300 demanded by the On Yicks and would have kept to our resolution even though every member of the family had paid for it with his life. The money was paid by the two people concerned and the Yees had nothing to do with it. The On Yicks declare themselves satisfied with the money, but now they want us to agree not to oppose the release of Tong King Chong and to withdraw from the prosecutions of the men under arrest for killing our members. This we will not do. We did not sign the agreement last night because we want to examine it very carefully and see that it does not bind us on these points in any way. We did not start the war, if such it can be called, and we do not wish to continue it, but we will not compound a felony by withdrawing our witnesses from the prosecutions now under way.

"We are fighting the fight of all Chinatown, and, in doing so, we have expended nearly $50,000 in actual cash for guards and in attorneys' fees. The various business houses owned by members of our family have suffered to the extent of over $100,000 and we have lost six of our men, who were killed in cold blood. In spite of all this, we have remained steadfast in our position and we would suffer ten times the loss in money or men before we would consent to yield to the On Yicks or any other highbinder tong. If the Yicks are through with their killings we are satisfied, but if this depends upon us dropping the cases against the men now under arrest, the war is not at an end, for on that point we will never give in."

According to the understanding in Chinatown last night, the agreement will be lived up to by the On Yicks. The $1300 will be used in defending the men under arrest and efforts will be made today to secure the release of Tong King Chong on bail. The stand of the Yee family in the whole matter is generally commended and it seems to be the general opinion of the better class of Chinese that the clan's action has done much toward destroying the power of the highbinder tongs of Chinatown.

But other tong wars continued to flare violently and end inexplicably. The inscrutable Caucasian, fresh from a four-year bloodletting of his own, apparently felt that Chinatown was in an unreasonably constant state of killing. In 1921, a *Chronicle* editorial offered this unrealistic and ungracious expression of distaste.

An Editorial

March 29, 1921

There is another tong war on and more work in prospect for the Chinese undertakers. The Chinese as a people have many admirable qualities, one evidence of their wisdom being their ability to export great numbers of their undesirables. They have plenty, however, left—piracy still continuing as one of the extensive industries on the Chinese rivers.

That we should endure the presence of the tong-warring Chinese is evidence of our political imbecility. Every member of every tong should be rounded up into the most unsanitary ship we can find and delivered anywhere on the Chinese coast. Care should be taken to load at least two tongs on each ship and see to it that both are well armed. There will be fewer to unload when the ship reaches its destination. The fewer there are left alive the better for the rest of mankind.

And when we speak of tong men we do not mean merely the gunmen. They, possibly, are the least troublesome. They will not kill anybody unless they are paid for it, for they practice only commercialized murder. The Chinese whom we have specially in mind are those who contribute money to hire the gunmen. Deportation of the officials of the fighting tongs, and everyone who has ever been such an official, is the primary requisite. If any American-born Chinese are concerned in this business we suppose that we cannot lawfully ship them to China. But we must have some uninhabited islands on which we can deposit them with a supply of provisions calculated to last as long as the gunmen last.

That we should permit these Chinese undesirables to continue to live and fight in our midst is conclusive evidence that our democracy does not amount to shucks. It has no gumption.

There is little evidence that the real causes and cures for the violence in Chinatown were ever sought out by the press or by the city authorities. Eventually, it took self-policing measures by Chinatown's own citizens to turn that community into a crime-free model.

But before that happened, the law-abiding Chinese, deploring every moment of the tong troubles, suffered in outward silence. One of the brief exceptions was this discerning letter received by *The Chronicle* as San Francisco prepared for the International Exposition of 1915. It was published in its original form, probably for laughs. It scored a few other points as well.

A Letter to the Editor

January 25, 1915

PROTECTED THE FAIR CITY

Mr. Chronicle,

Big News Paper Co.,

Gentlemen.

I know your paper is good, so I send you this letter to put on the paper. Will you fix it good and put in for me. We thank you very much. Will you excuse me, I gone to tell you all about it, long times ago.

More Chinaman in Hongkong, they have no tong war, because he catch the murder he hang them; money cannot buy him out. We all like to have peace. You no can stop the Europe war. But the Police Judge can stop the tong war all right all right.

The head man cheat some, the interpreter cheat some, the Lawylor and Judge get some, is all. Sometimes other case the poor highbinder get twenty years or lifetime, not enough five years. You see him come out again, because the money fix it all right.

If you caught the murder, hang him. If you caught the highbinder with gun, send him back to China, take his picture, make him never can come back. If nobody pay for the fare, make him work hard for his own fare, no matter how big piece money can't dismissed. By and by the tong war vanished and the tong war have peace forever.

I think the Lawylor and Judge like the fight very much, they know plenty money comeing in. I shouldn't worry.

This 1915 year the Lawylor and Judge don't do the straight work, send the tong man to China, it will put the Fair in bad. Not the Chinaman fault, is you people fault.

I knew our people dem fool to have the tong war, die and hang is Chinaman, shoot to dead is Chinaman, but the money is for Lawylor and Judge.   (signed)

HOW SOME YEN

AH LEE SING

Oakland, Cal.

★   ★   ★

The year was 1952. Time had brought politeness to the "Chinese problem." With calm and restraint, reporter Bernard Taper let the facts of the Sing Sheng case tell the story. Its message came across.

Southwood vs. Sing Sheng

February 17, 1952

Residents of the Southwood District of South San Francisco were triumphant yesterday in their efforts to keep their neighborhood 100 per cent Caucasian.

They achieved this object by the use of one of democracy's most fundamental instruments—the secret ballot.

By a vote of 174 to 26 they told Sing Sheng, a former Chinese Nationalist intelligence officer, that they did not want him, his pretty wife and his small son as neighbors.

They did not want the Shengs as neighbors for a lot of reasons which added up to one big reason: the Shengs are Chinese.

The ballots were counted in a garage in the neighborhood. The long narrow building was crowded with some 100 homeowners and spectators.

Sheng, a young man of 25, dressed in a double-breasted blue suit, sat at the balloting table. His Chinese-American wife sat in the front row. She is pregnant. Her baby is due to be born February 22, Washington's birthday.

The suggestion of putting the matter to a ballot came from Sheng himself after he received numerous objections to his purchase of a house on West Orange avenue last week. Most of the objections asserted that his presence would depress property values.

"I didn't know about any race prejudice at all until I came to Southwood. I was sure everybody really believed in democracy, so I thought up this vote as a test," he said at that time.

Before the counting of ballots began, Edward Howden, executive director of the San Francisco Council for Civil Unity, told the assembled homeowners he had learned of a scientific study recently made in the Bay Area analyzing the actual effect of non-Caucasian residents on property values. He asked if the group wanted to postpone counting the ballots until they had a chance to consider and discuss this study.

Voices from the back of the garage shouted this down:

"Let's get on with it. Let's not fool around any more."

Each ballot was tallied aloud, read by South San Francisco City Manager Emmons McClung. The ballots were phrased so that the homeowners were asked whether they objected to the purchase of a home in the neighborhood by this Chinese family.

The Shengs heard McClung read the phrase, "I object," 174 times as he tallied the ballots. By the end of the balloting they looked crushed.

A silence followed the final tally. Then Sheng stood up and let it be known that he would abide by the vote.

"We'll have to sell the furniture we bought and go somewhere else to live. I hope you people will be happy in your community and that your property values will increase every day."

The meeting broke up. The homeowners exchanged jubilant remarks as they drifted out of the hall.

Many of them were articulate to this reporter about their reasons for not wanting the Shengs in their district, but not one would permit his name to be quoted in connection with these explanations.

"What do you want to do, put me on the spot?" one of them demanded.

The homeowners were indignant at *The Chronicle* for reporting the story in the first place.

"We have a quiet, respectable neighborhood here and we don't care for publicity," one said.

If Sheng had wished, he could have ignored the vote and insisted on his legal right to move into the house. The U.S. Supreme Court has ruled "restrictive covenant" agreements unconstitutional.

Despite this ruling, the American Homes Development Company of Burlingame—describing itself as "developers of this representative American residential area"—sent a letter to all homeowners in Southwood last week urging them to hold fast to the principle of restrictive covenants in their housing transactions.

"These covenants set forth salutary and beneficial restrictions on the land for those purchasers desiring ownership in a community where they could welcome their neighbor and live in equality."

The Shengs also wrote a letter to the Southwood homeowners before the balloting. It read:

"We wish to express our gratitude for the interest you showed in the welfare of our purchasing the house at 726 W. Orange avenue.

"Before you reach any decision as to how you will vote in the ballot, allow us to tell you our opinion. The present world conflict is not between individual nations, but between Communism and Democracy. We think so highly of Democracy because it offers freedom and equality. America's forefathers fought for these principles and won the Independence of 1776.

"We have forsaken our beloved China and have come to this country seeking the same basic rights. Do not make us the victims of false Democracy. Please vote in favor of us."

Southwood's homes are in the $10,000 to $12,000 price range. Of the 253 homeowners eligible to vote, 31 did not return ballots and 14 expressed themselves as having no opinion in the matter. Six ballots were void.

The owner of the house, Jack Denson, said after the meeting he would return Sheng's $2950 down payment. The Densons said they had been subject to "considerable pressure" ever since the sale to the Shengs was announced.

"We were given to understand that if the sale went through people would see to it that we would have a hard time buying another piece of property anywhere on the Peninsula," Mrs. Denson said.

Sheng came to the United States in 1947, intending to study for the diplomatic service. When the Communists took over China, he decided to stay in this country. He is employed as an airline mechanic. He and his family live in an apartment in colorful—but congested—Chinatown, at 47 Eagle avenue.

This week the Shengs will resume their efforts to find a home. They hope to meet with better success, because this is Brotherhood Week.

★   ★   ★

The love affair between San Franciscans and San Francisco is ever fanned by words of courtship in the newspapers. Sometimes in rather unlikely directions. Glamorous garbage, for instance.

This short essay by reporter Robert de Roos appeared origi-
nally as a text for a series of sketches on San Franciscans at work.
The happiness of garbage collection in San Francisco is apparent
even without illustration.

No Gnomes Here

July 24, 1949

Why is it that San Francisco's scavengers operate with such
noticeable vigor? In other cities the garbage men are sad, gray and
black—gnomes at gnomes' work. Here for some wonderful reason
the garbage guys have a flair—black-haired charioteers flinging
their great green and red trucks across intersections, bouncing and
jolting with their loads.

Since 1921, two companies, the Sunset Scavenger Corporation
and the Scavengers' Protective Association, have handled the bulk
of the city's garbage load. Before then it was every garbage man
for himself, chaos among the clanging cans. It is still about as
noisy as ever, but the two cooperatives have eliminated overlap-
ping routes, and systematized the business. Now almost every garbage man is part owner of his enterprise—required to buy a share
after he has shown he can do hard, dirty work.

At about four o'clock every morning rain or shine—and how
they hate the rain—these scavengers, men of Genoan descent for
the most part, go to their important work. The other dawn *The
Chronicle* sent a man along on these dark morning rounds. These
are the notes he wrote:

"A trip with S.F. scavengers. We started at 4 A.M. I was rider
on truck 47 of the Scavengers' Protective Association. Crew chief
Anthony Solari nosed it toward Nob Hill. Bunches of keys dangling
from the dashboard. 'There are 300. You got to remember them
all,' he said. Keys to basements and porches entrusted to scavengers. Crews disappeared into tradesmen's entrances, their flashlights piercing the blackness. I followed James Scopel into the
Residence Club (mostly milk containers). He gathered them in
his blanket (blanket term used by garbage men, means their burlap
strips).

"I trailed Solari into Fairmont Garage, innocently crossing a light beam which set off a bell signal. A lone taxi cruised by. A woman in bandanna, green coat and hostess slacks ran out of apartment house entrance and nervously hailed the cab.

"I followed E. V. Jones into Pacific Union Club (duck feathers, wild rice cartons and wine husks). A nurse, a paperboy and milkman passed. Metropolitan Life Insurance Company (vegetable soup cans).

"Day began to break. Worker passed by carrying lunch pail, warmly wished all of us a good morning. Turned into Stanford Court Apartments. Harold Barsted gathered the stuff in his blanket (champagne and liquor bottles, lots of food, nibbled at). Streets filling imperceptibly with office workers. Eight o'clock. I left crew of truck 47 as they stopped for lunch."

That's just the way it is.

★　　★　　★

In 1958, "Beatnik" was still a new and uncertain word. San Franciscans knew it through the gossip columns and television jokes. To most, it was somehow synonymous with the Beat Generation, which was a movement written about in a book by a writer called Jack Kerouac.

To San Francisco, Beatniks meant people who lived, or at least were in evidence, in certain parts of North Beach. The male of the species wore a beard. The female wore black stockings.

Who they were and what they wanted wasn't clear. If you thought for a moment, you guessed that lots of Beatniks were poets or jazz musicians and maybe got high on marijuana occasionally. But you weren't really sure about this—or any of it.

This was the basis of the assignment given to reporter Allen Brown. Tell about the Beats, who they are and why they are and how they live. It was an assignment that called for arduous leg work, for obtaining the trust and honest convictions of people who had no faith. It called for reading their writings, the works of the obscure, the prophets and the critics. Most of all it was an assignment that called for understanding, in an area dangerously susceptible to overstatement and sensationalism.

The two-part report turned in by Brown is a monument in sensitive journalism. Seldom has a news story—for in its essence it was just that—done a better job of explaining man to his fellow men.

The Beatniks

I

June 15, 1958

The Beat Generation, an unorganized group of men and women that has brought national attention to San Francisco's North Beach, is not a generation at all.

It includes people from 15 to 55. They are not beat in the sense that they are tired; they don't work that hard. They are not beat in the musical sense; they are too cool, too indifferent, too pseudo-intellectual to care about foot-tapping jazz.

They are Beat because they feel battered by life. They have lost faith in nearly everything, and they refuse to conform to the ideals in which they no longer believe.

Being Beat is leaning on the dusty bar of a bistro and saying softly: "I don't believe in God or in Billy Graham, either. Today's messiahs are all in the loony bins." It's getting high at marijuana parties or deliriously intoxicated anywhere and everywhere with a sharpened awareness of sights and sounds and smells. It's having sex as often and in as many ways as you can. It's shacking up for weeks at a time with a Beach chick or picking up homosexuals in gay bars, or bumming all the way to New York just to see if that Greenwich Village chick is just as good as the memory.

It's using the monosyllabic, hopped-up language of the bop musician. It's "walking tall" as a non-conforming individual. "Man, I say to hell with togetherness." It's wanting—sometimes desperately—to die.

Beat headquarters, lying on Grant avenue from Vallejo to Filbert streets, has been dubbed by one of the beats as "an open-air, come-and-go mental hospital three blocks long."

Its sagging, unpainted buildings house small family-style Italian cafes, Chinese laundries and sewing subcontractors, art shops, grocery stores and spaghetti factories as well as the tiny bars that are the meeting halls of the Beat Generation.

The area is San Francisco's historic home of youth in revolt. It sheltered the Lost Generation of the Twenties, the speakeasies of Prohibition, and the intense, politically-minded rebels of the Depression Years. The Beat Generation—mixing mysticism with its Bohemianism, caring nothing for politics—is something else again.

But you won't find out what makes the Beat Generation that way simply by visiting the bars. The Beat will give you what they call "a complete turnon." Explained one bearded Beatnik: "Of course, I give these tourist squares the turnon, man. They can't dig the Beat anyway, because they ARE square."

You push through the Dutch door of the Coexistence Bagel Shop at Grant avenue and Green street and find a small, 16-table delicatessen serviced from a meat case, coffee urn and beer cooler. One wall of the Bagel Shop's single room is papered with announcements of dance festivals and poetry readings, travel posters and a huge photograph of Henry Miller, the Big Sur author revered because about certain Beat men he wrote:

"These individuals are not concerned with undermining a vicious system but with leading their own lives—on the fringe of society.

"These young men have discovered . . . that the American way of life is an illusory kind of existence, that the price demanded for the security and abundance it pretends to offer is too great."

At the Bagel Shop's window table is a young man with a wispy fringe of blond beard who lives on his wartime disability check of $50 a month. He has just come from a marijuana party where he "went very far out on pod." But he won't tell you about it. You probably won't even know that marijuana used to be called "Tea," then "tea pot," then simply "pot," and now simply "pod"—all to confuse the squares. Ask Blond Beard what he thinks of life and if he answers at all, he is likely to repeat only what his idol, author Jack Kerouac, called his philosophical final statement: "I DON'T KNOW. I DON'T CARE. AND IT DOESN'T MAKE ANY DIFFERENCE."

Walk up Grant avenue to a sawdust-on-the-floor establishment near Filbert street called simply "The Place." It features 25-cent schooners of beer, bartenders who sport beards and Blabbermouth Night. This Monday evening event, just over a year old, packs The Place to its capacity of about 30 people. A yellow soapbox on the ledge of a small balcony over the bar is used as a lectern by Bohemians and tourists alike who deliver three-minute speeches on almost any subject in competition for a prize bottle of champagne.

The black walls of The Place are covered with modern paintings of the daub-and-swab school. The walls, between the paintings, are chalked with expressions of Beat wit:

"What did Christ say at the Last Supper? 'Who's going to pick up my check?'"

"Herb Caen Go Home."

"What a Day for an Auto da Fe!"

Go through the leather-padded, swinging doors of a restaurant-bar just off Grant avenue, and you'll find dozens of young men enjoying their $1.35 full-course dinners. You could stay for hours without realizing this is the hard core of a Beat Generation group that practices its own peculiar protest against the conforming American ideal of home and family: Homosexuality.

At the Cellar, you walk down a flight of old wooden stairs, through an art gallery and into the subterranean improvised, timbered, rectangular room where the reading of poetry to modern jazz was born in San Francisco. Four men—two of them bearded, one mustached—are playing instruments. But because you're square you don't get the angry, spiteful message of their music.

At the Coffee Gallery and Tea Room, you find your first North Beach character. He wears a plumed cavalier hat and boots, and he says his flowing hair and beard have encouraged others in North Beach to call him "J.C." for short. His real name is Padraic Seumus O'Sullivan. He is a native of Greenwich Village, a full-time janitor, a part-time poet, a part-time song writer.

"I'm not Beat," he tells you. "In fact, my book of poems, 'Weep Not My Children,' is really an answer to the Beat Generation. I say the only time a man is Beat is when he's lost his sense of humor."

Seated at the bar near O'Sullivan you find a young couple willing to talk about the Beat Generation. But they are "week-end Bohemians" who have driven in from their tract home to find out what the Beat has to offer. They hope to find a real, live poet. They probably won't. The serious poets and authors of the Beat Generation are too busy creating to mingle often with the Beatniks.

The part-time poet leaned against the display of literary quarterlies in the City Lights Book Shop on Columbus avenue, lit a cigarette and declared: "There's just one thing that makes the Beat Generation. It's being written about. It's building its own literary tradition. It's being written about by critics like Kenneth Rexroth and Herbert Gold and Norman Podhoretz, by authors like Norman Mailer and Henry Miller and Eugene Burdick. It's being written about in the Saturday Review and the Reporter and the Nation and Partisan Review and New Republic."

He reached over to a nearby shelf to a paperback novel called "Go." "It all started with this," he said. "John Clellon Holmes wrote this novel six years ago. And almost in passing, he referred to 'this beat generation, this underground life!'

"The ball started rolling. Then the Beat got headlines when the police tried to suppress Allen Ginsberg's poem, 'Howl', here, and Jack Kerouac's 'On the Road' made the best seller lists last year. Suddenly, everyone was writing about us and we were a Generation. Address: North Beach. Well, it's true. This generation IS different. And everyone gives a different reason for the difference.

"Miller talks about our 'thorough-going nonconformity' and says we're the spiritual descendants of the nonconformists who settled America. This is true.

"Ferlinghetti says we're all hung up in a 'dissent against the ideals of America's upper middle class.' This is true, too. And it is a 'dissent.' It's not a revolt because it's passive. Almost condescending.

"The Beat man looks at the guy who works in an office from 9 to 5 so he can support the trappings of his middle-class life—the well-dressed wife, the cocktail parties—and the Beat man only says, 'Oh, you poor, silly sap.' "

The poet ground out his cigarette with his heel. He left the bookshop and cut across Columbus avenue toward upper Grant avenue, talking as he walked:

"You know most of the people writing about the Beat Generation are so hung up with the marijuana and the sex and the homosex that they don't see the Big Picture. They don't realize that most of the Beat are existential, that they want to die. It's true. The Beach chicks surround themselves with death symbols. They wear black shoes, long black stockings, black skirts, and black sweaters.

"Some of the experts who have written about the Beat Generation say we are divided into only two big groups: the heterosexual and the homosexual. Actually, we're divided even more by our attitude toward life. There are the 'loners', the people Kerouac wrote about in 'On the Road', the ones who storm back and forth across the country and live on a high pitch of awareness and spend all their time digging life. They are the ones who say, 'I'm here, and I wish I weren't, but while I have life I'm going to really live it.'

"Then there are the real Beatniks, the do-nothings who sit around the Coexistence Bagel Shop or lie in the sun at Aquatic Park all day and talk. They aren't hoodlums because they don't CARE that much about life. They might make it with a Beach chick once in a while, but they make it to relieve their boredom. They say, 'I'm here and I wish I weren't and to hell with it.' "

He entered the Coffee Gallery and Tea Room on Upper Grant avenue and nodded toward a white girl sitting with a handsome young Negro at a corner table. "That's different here, too," he said quietly. "You don't see much of the interracial bit in New York. You don't see it at all in New Orleans. But it's big in North Beach.

"It's all tied up with the death wish, of course, but also with the Negro's desire to be more like the white and the Beat white's desire for the primitive. It's also very closely tied up with music. Herbert Gold, you know, says the Negroes a few years ago tried to break away from their jazz past by imitating the coolness of the whites. Then the whites started imitating the new coolness of the Negro, and jazz got cooler and cooler. Norman Mailer says the Beat hipster is really a 'white Negro.'

"I should write a poem about that. Maybe some day I will."

He lit another cigarette and walked off into the night.

The 33-year-old "loner" named Max shifted his chair on the floor of The Place so he could lean back against the black wall. His girl, Nel, cupped her chin in her hands and gazed out of the dirt-streaked window while Max talked.

Max scratched the stubble on his chin and said: "I haven't had time to shave. I was making the scene in Denver with some cats early yesterday—very early, very early in the morning, man—and we stopped for gas and this guy in the station said he was anxious to get to Frisco. So I switched cars and drove him out—straight through.

"Got here and cut out for Nel's pad and we were too busy making it. So I haven't shaved. Not that I'm putting down the bearded Beatniks. They've given the turnon to the stuffy ideals and all that Madison avenue crap. More power, I say. But the Beatniks are really bugged by life. They're afraid of it. They just want it to end.

"Well, maybe I do, too."

He brought his chair down hard to the floor and leaned forward: "But here's the difference. The loner recognizes the fact of life. He looks it in the eye. Squarely. And he tries to get everything he can out of it.

"Like this ride. I could dig that, man. Every minute of it. The ache in my back when I sat the same way too long. The crazy new blue color on the gas pumps. The wild hunger when we drove over Donner Pass. That's the difference between the loner and the Beatnik. The loner is aware."

Max scratched his chin again, then sipped his beer before he said: "I've felt this thing—this need to be aware, this hunger for sensation, this urge to be on the go—since my high school days. I hitchhiked all over the country and into Canada, just to see and feel as much as I could. Then, after college, I made the same scenes in an old jalopy. All the time I told myself I was looking for the place I wanted to settle in. Now I know I was looking for a place or a thing that I could believe in.

"I'm still looking. Everyone I know is looking. Some guys find it in Zen. Some find it in monasteries. Some find it in creativity or self destruction. There are plenty of guys today—you'd be surprised how many—who have decided that creativity is the key to the meaning of life and they say they have to be on junk or juice to create and who are killing themselves.

"Now, I smoke pod—tea, marijuana, call it anything you want. But I'm not on pod to slow things down. There are so many things to hear and to see and pod slows it all down so I can dig everything."

Nel interrupted: "I've been told I wear black clothes because they're death symbols. Well, I don't know. I wear black because it's cheap and it's practical. But, of course, existentialism is very real for me, too.

"When did I start making the Beat scene? Not very long ago. I was in my smart sorority in a smart little midwestern unviersity and I was studying Oscar Wilde's 'The Picture of Dorian Gray' for English Lit when I read some things that really shook me up."

Her unplucked eyebrows bunched with the effort of remembering Wilde's line: "Ah! Realize your youth while you have it. Don't squander the gold of your days, listening to the tedious, trying to improve the hopeless failure, or giving away your life to the ignorant, the common and the vulgar. These are the sickly aims, the false ideals of our age.

"Live! Live the wonderful life that is in you! Let nothing be lost upon you. Be always searching for new sensations. . . . To be good is to be in harmony with one's self. Discord is to be forced to be in harmony with others. One's own life—that is the important thing."

She shrugged. "Well, I never got back to the English Lit class. I bought a bus ticket the next day and told my family I was coming out here to do historical research. They send me money."

Max nodded. "Okay. Wilde did it for you. Kerouac told me what kind of man I wanted to be. Here."

He pulled out his wallet, carefully unfolded a page torn from "On the Road," and shoved it across the table. The underlined paragraph read:

"The only people for me are the mad ones, the ones who are mad to live, mad to talk, mad to be saved, desirous of everything at the same time, the ones who never yawn or say a commonplace thing, but burn, burn, burn like fabulous yellow Roman candles . . ."

II

June 22, 1958

Members of the Beat Generation who spend their days and endless nights in North Beach bars and delicatessens wear no watches. They don't care what time it is. They have no place to go. Nothing to do.

They are pale shadows of the loners. The sitters and squatters of Upper Grant avenue don't care enough about life to dig it, to understand it or be excited about it.

They were characterized by critic Thomas J. Albright, in the preface of a pamphlet of poems recently published in North Beach, as "a group of individuals, psychologically ageless, living individual existences, confirming one another's presence from time to time, waiting not for Godot but for the time to run out."

Most of all, the Beatnik wants to die. But next to death he loves talk. It is his chief occupation. His talk is endless and almost inarticulate. Its main theme is one of destructive criticism of everything except the Beatnik way of life. All else is "put down" in the slang of the bop musician, a form of expression in which, it has been said, it would be impossible to leave a note for the milkman.

"Life is a drag, man," said a 24-year-old Beatnik in the Bagel Shop. "Really a deathly drag."

Asked why, he replied: "Oh, man! I mean like. . . . Well, a drag, man. . . . Well, if you don't KNOW. . . . Everything's all hung up, man. . . . Rugged, you know? Well, you gotta feel it, man. You gotta feel that it's a drag to know it. Then, when you know it, you're cool. And it's a drag and doesn't make any difference."

More than one critic of the Beat Generation has suggested that life is only as boring as the Beatnik makes it.

The Beatnik's day begins each morning in his North Beach "pad," a cheap room or apartment usually fitted out with little more than a single chair and a mattress on the floor. The improvised bed is seldom made up, and the sheets are dirty.

The Beatnik, after arising, may or may not brush his teeth. He probably will not wash and almost certainly will not shave. From a heap on the floor, he pulls the limp shirt and baggy trousers he has worn for several days, dresses, and slouches up the street to the Coexistence Bagel Shop. The Bagel Shop opens about 11:30 A.M. daily, and it is then that the Beatniks—most of them in their 20's and early 30's—begin to take stock of themselves.

"Lemme have 15 cents for coffee, willya man? Sure, I'll pay you back. Next week. Soon as my unemployment check comes through."

"Mad Myrtle cut me in nicely last night. This tourist, this square told her he wanted some pod. He called it 'tea.' Well, Myrtle told him I had a connection, so he slips me $10 and I cut out. Now I suppose she'll want half."

"Here's the 65 cents I owe you, Ajax. Mom sent me $10 from

Chicago so I could pay for my 'art lessons.' Dig? Well, now my bills are paid. No, man, not ALL my bills. Just the money I owe PEOPLE. The stores and the corporations can go to hell."

"Hey, anyone seen Don? He's been drunk ever since he rode in from New York two weeks ago. Drunk and out on pod and trying to make it with every chick in the Beach. Didn't see him all day yesterday. Yeah, maybe he's cut out."

The talk goes on and the day wears on.

Some talk about the novels they are going to write—someday. "This cat cuts out to his little tract house from his Montgomery street office, see, and he finds that his wife has changed into a big-lipped Ubangi. It's very symbolic, see? The big climactic scene is when he tells his psychiatrist about it, but the psychiatrist won't believe him."

Poet Lawrence Ferlinghetti, who calls such Beatniks "illiterate Bohemians," says most of the day-and-night sitters and talkers of North Beach are too ignorant to read, let alone write.

Norman Podhoretz comments on them in Partisan Review: "This is the revolt of the spiritually underprivileged and the crippled of soul—young men who can't think straight and so hate anyone who can; young men who can't get outside the morass of self and so construct definitions of feeling that exclude all human beings who manage to live, even miserably, in a world of objects."

Podhoretz sees a close connection between what had been described as the Beat desire for primitivism and the "illiterate Bohemianism" mentioned by Ferlinghetti:

"The plain truth is that the primitivism of the Beat Generation serves first of all as a cover for an anti-intellectualism so bitter it makes the ordinary American's hatred of eggheads seem positively benign."

And Herbert Gold, writing in The Nation, offered this diagnosis of the Beatniks' sociological sickness: "They have carried their rebellion from society past the end; existing from their innards the cant of a mass culture, these fierce surgeons have also badly cut up their humanity.

"They are cool. Now they blow nothing but the miseries."

"Welcome to my pad."

The slightly built man holding open the door to his "pad," a two-room clapboard cottage on Potrero Hill, was credited by fellow members of the Beat Generation with knowing all about sex, marijuana and music.

He led the way into the kitchen-living room and dropped into an unpainted wooden chair. Paint, flaked from the walls and ceiling of the small room, had been left to mix with rolls of dust beneath the few furnishings—an improvised bookcase; a single, lumpy overstuffed chair; a battered range; a scarred drop-leaf kitchen table.

He hadn't shaved for three or four days. The buttons were broken from the button-down collar of his rumpled Ivy League shirt.

"It's true, true," he nodded slowly. "All true, what they say about me in the Beach. All true. It was more true a couple of months ago, though. I only make it with a girl, oh, occasionally. I'm living here alone now. No chick to do the dishes for me and take care of me. I'm trying to get to know myself and make some adjustment in my mind between myself and the world.

"Really, you know, until I started making the Beach scene in San Francisco a few years ago. . . . Well, until then, I never really had a chance to be promiscuous. In college, you know, you take a girl out and send flowers and you buy dinner and maybe you get a goodnight kiss.

"But these Beach chicks—well, they don't want flowers. They're putting down the stuffy middle-class ideas about pre-marital virginity, and they're putting down those ideas the best way they know how.

"Also, for a long time I've been hung up with this Wilhelm Reich idea that all happiness depends upon the perfect sexual experience. I had to find out if it was possible to have a really fine, a really long-term relationship with a girl based only on sex. I had one chick living with me for six whole weeks, and sex was almost the only thing we had in common, and we balled here with sex and pod for six weeks and then I decided that Reich was wrong. There has to be more than sex.

"Pod's done great things for me. GREAT things. And it has made me so AWARE. Aware of little things like colors and textures and odors and sounds. Everything was on a high, tingling level, and I could really dig it. But the contrast was too much.

When I came down from the pod cloud, I came down hard. Pod took me very, very far out, but it was hell getting back.

"I came, finally, to the place where I could do just one of three things: Go to junk (heroin), kill myself, or just get off pod. I quit pod. Just like that. I quit it, and now I'm trying to set my own consistent level of awareness without it."

He stood up and walked over to the range to prepare his lunch of canned soup and dry tortillas. He nibbled on a tortilla as he continued: "Not many of the musicians around town can be very articulate about the Beat Generation. They can blow it, but they can only say, 'like WOW, man! Gone!' But you can talk with jazz. You can blow hate or anger or the miseries. Like when the fuzz (police) tried to suppress Ginsberg's poem, I thought: They'd try to suppress me, too, if they could hear what I'm saying with my bass."

He sipped his warm soup from a cracked coffee cup. "I'm 34 now, and I've been making this Beat scene for about six years—three here and three in New Orleans. I got with it in New York. Went there after graduating from Yale—oh, I'm good family, very Boston, very Back Bay—and got a job doing publicity for the movies. It was very white collar and very square, and they all said I had a very good future.

"But then I started thinking. I remembered what the old 9-to-5 did to my father. He worked like hell and came home at night so pooped that he couldn't do anything but eat and go to bed. He had no joy, no fun, no life. He'd work like this for 50 weeks so he could have maybe two weeks of fun during vacation, but then, maybe, he couldn't take a trip because he had to pay his income taxes.

"And, as I say, I was in New York. We were worried about The Bomb. I didn't want to be in New York when it landed. And I wanted to ball a little before it did.

"And there was this terrible, dragging conformity. Everyone getting married and moving to the suburbs and tithing their lives to General Motors. Everything in group. All 'we' and no 'I'. So I cut out.

"I went to New Orleans to make the scene at the French Quarter, and I dug out my bass that I hadn't used since college days and

I started to play. It was good. It was cool jazz because it's withdrawn and unemotional, and you can say things with it. It's think music.

"New Orleans got to be a drag, though, because of the race thing. Everyone was all hung up with it. So I cut out for San Francisco, because everyone said things were different here. How do I really feel about cool jazz? Well, it's like. . . . Look."

He shuffled through a stack of papers on the drop-leaf table to find a tattered clipping of an *Esquire* article by John Clellon Holmes. It said:

"Modern jazz is almost exclusively the music of the Beat Generation . . . because jazz is primarily the music of inner freedom, of improvisation, of the creative individual rather than the interpretive group. It is the music of a submerged people, who FEEL free, and that is precisely how young people feel today."

He replaced the clipping and said: "That's pretty much it."

The Beat Generation is being kept by the squares.

And this, according to the poet-philosophers of North Beach, is the true social significance of Beatism. Said one poet: "These squares usually are highly literate, thinking people. They've held steady jobs all their lives, making payments on their new cars, getting all hung up with child psychology and income taxes and fancy clothes and bills, bills, bills, doing their best to live the kind of lives someone else says they SHOULD live.

"And now suddenly, they've begun to wonder whether the rat race is really worth it. To a Beat nonconformist, this growing unrest is encouraging."

To the economy of the Beat Generation, the interest of such squares also is essential.

Their purchases have put Beat novels on national best-seller lists. Their interest in the "cool" music of the Beat Generation provides work for the Beat musicians and has enhanced San Francisco's reputation as a jazz center. Their regular forays into North Beach have made commercial successes of a half-dozen Beat bars or delicatessens. Their interest has earned for some of them the status of "week-end Bohemians."

Ferlinghetti has written a poem in which he urges such people on: "Let's go. Come on. Let's go. Empty out our pockets and disappear. Missing all our appointments and turning up unshaven years later, cigarette papers stuck to our pants, leaves in our hair. Let us not worry about the payments anymore. Let them come and take it away, whatever it was we were paying for. And us with it."

The week-end Bohemian is not quite willing to make such a break.

"I'm a nurse," said one recently at The Cellar. "I like nursing and I'm going to keep on nursing."

She smoothed her black skirt. "But I don't like being told by Madison avenue what I should think and what I should buy and who I should vote for. Sometimes it's hard to be independent when you're living on Pacific Heights. There are times when you feel the pressure they are putting on you to make you like and think like everyone else. When that happens, I come into North Beach.

"After a few hours listening to the Beatniks—they're against EVERYTHING, you know—it's easy for me to go home and live with my little protests.

"But I won't go all the way with the Beat Generation. I'm too moral for all this crazy sleeping around. I have no desire to even try marijuana. I like to date men, not women. Still it's good to know that there are nonconformists who go all the way."

Homosexuals are among the week-end Bohemians who come to North Beach to find conformity for their nonconformity. Said one: "Some guys hang out all the time in gay bars. Looking for new friends, mostly. I can't. I can't risk it. I have a good job and I don't want to lose it.

"So all week long, I'm straight. I talk baseball and I take girls out for dinner and maybe even dancing. But by the week end the masquerade gets to be too much. I want to be with my own kind. So I pull on an old sweater and come into the Beach and have dinner in one of the gay little restaurants and just look around and realize that I'm not alone."

The week-end Bohemian, seeking to conform, dresses to conform. Said one stenographer from Sausalito: "It takes me almost as long to get myself ready for North Beach—to be properly sloppy in my smart little black outfit and to comb my hair just right over my eyes—as it would to get ready for a date on Nob Hill."

The tourist in North Beach, as opposed to the week-end Bohemian, has no desire to conform to the nonconformity. He comes to watch the Beatniks, not to join them. Some old-time Bohemians claim these tourists are ruining North Beach as a Beat Generation stomping ground. And some even say that to the tourist will go the eventual victory in the Beach.

"They have too much money," complained one Beat regular. "And they are respectable people. So the police are in here thick to protect the monied, respectable people.

"Some of them decide that the Beach is so quaint that they should live here. I think I can see what's coming. In a few years, North Beach will be just like Greenwich Village in New York today: A few tourist Bohemian bars in the middle of a middle-class, high-rent district."

★   ★   ★

Critic Alfred Frankenstein's regular assignment is music and art. Occasionally, as in this instance, he turns his eye upon more pedestrian pursuits.

Critic on the Pavement

October 26, 1953

Much of the life of ancient cultures has been reconstructed from inscriptions on old pavements, like the famous "Caveat Canem" found, if my memory serves, on a street mosaic in Pompeii. On the basis of similar evidence, archeologists of the Twenty-Sixth century are likely to report some rather strange things about the people who lived in California in our time.

ENTER
NOT
DO

is a rather thought-provoking slogan which appears with increasing frequency around town as more and more streets are restricted to one-way traffic. It might perhaps, be the inscription over the gates of Nirvana, just as

RIGHT

TO

KEEP

might go over the doors of some conservative club for the proper-tied.

ONLY

TURN

RIGHT

seems to embody the message of many a Sunday sermon. On the other hand funny signs

XING

CHILDREN

DEAF

conveys frightening implications of nameless mayhem committed by a Charles Addams ghoul.

This epigraphy-in-reverse arises, of course, from the conviction on the part of our State highway authorities that every motorist keeps his eyes rigidly fixed to a point on the pavement about 60 feet ahead of his radiator cap, so that warnings and directions must be painted backward on the streets in order that the words may glide into the path of the driver's vision in the proper sequence. The Authorities know perfectly well that anybody who did drive that way would be dead inside of five minutes, and that our life-time habits of reading produce an automatic reaction whereby, as soon as we see print, our eyes jump to the top line. Nevertheless they keep right on painting everything upside down.

Some of these inscriptions, to be sure, make equal sense either way. Everyone knows what

STOP

BUS

means, and

TURN

LEFT

NO

merely transforms a command into a question and an emphatic answer. The latest and oddest, however, is one I recently found at the corner of Market and Fell. It reads

CROSS
NOT
DO
PED

These words are painted very close together, and there is every reason to believe they are intended to prevent pedestrians from crossing the street at that point. They now think we read upside down when we walk as well as when we ride.

PERIOD PIECE

On Tuesday, the 11th of May, 1869, *The Chronicle* joyously announced receipt of the following dispatch:

"Promontory Summit, Utah, May 10. To the Press East and West: The last rail is laid—the last spike driven! The Pacific Railroad is completed to the point of junction, 1080 miles west of the Missouri river and 690 miles from Sacramento."

A *Chronicle* reporter was aboard to record the engineering marvel of the first train trip from Sacramento to Salt Lake City. Astutely, he also found time to look out the window, as witness this bit of intelligence on life in the western mountains. It was filed from Gold Run, on the California slope of the Sierra.

The Iron Horse

May 8, 1869

Speeding on by Rocklin, where the granite comes from, to Newcastle, remarkable for only some dirty children, who peered at the passers curiously, we arrive at grades which tell of those to come. Steadily we wind among the low hills, where once upon a time the ancient miner, with pick and pan reaped wondrous harvests of the yellow metal. Here and there a cabin remains, and with it a hermit-like remnant of early days, clad in a tattered red or blue shirt and with his unmentionables branded with "Warranted of Superior Quality—49 lbs."

Now and then one came from his cabin, and with an effort gazed dreamily after the train, as though he felt a mild sort of anger against the daring men who had sent the iron horse snorting through his shady hollow, disturbing his Rip Van Winkle sleep.

A few little ranches cluster among the ravines, with clumps of fruit trees and vines. The whitewashed cottages, with smiling female faces peering from within the doors, seemed to be a rebuke to those who, like the ones just spoken of, still adhere to the pick and cabin, poor clothes and celibacy. . . .

★ ★ ★

The field of California finance following the Civil War was one of frenzied speculation. One of the most powerful financiers was William C. Ralston, president of the Bank of California, who held vast interests in Nevada. Ralston was a trusted, if colorful, titan of San Francisco's business life. So was his associate, William Sharon. Both lived on a grand scale, even after the bottomless treasure of the Comstock Lode began to take on some semblance of financial reality. But, then . . .

There had been a financial depression two years before in the East, and it finally was felt in the West. Business was bad all over. The rumor was that the silver crowd was going to open a new bank in opposition to the Ralston-Sharon enterprise. So Sharon began dumping silver stocks. The plan backfired—and on August 26, 1875, the mighty Bank of California closed its doors. Panic spread—and it eventually cost Ralston his life. *The Chronicle* reported the disaster in enormous detail, from which the following is extracted.

The Crash

I

August 27, 1875

A great misfortune, scarcely paralleled in the history of San Francisco, occurred yesterday. This was the failure of the Bank of California, one of the most important moneyed institutions in the United States and one of the greatest in the world. Rumors affecting its solvency, and also the credit of William C. Ralston, one of the wealthiest men of the coast, have been current for the last six months. Whenever they have become too frequent they have been quieted and the public have been led to believe that everything was right in that quarter. All persons interested in the prosperity of the coast have been glad to believe in the stability of an institution which they have come to regard with pride and affection. The causes which led to the tightness of the money market, which induced the suspension of the bank, have been fully rehearsed in the newspapers of the city for many weeks past, but nowhere more fully than in the columns of *The Chronicle.*

Among such a variety of conflicting statements, emanating from a large number of intelligent persons, the reader can select such as suit him best, taking his own knowledge of the subject into consideration. The interviews with James C. Flood and Mr. Ralston, the two principal actors in this scene of local excitement, will be perused with no ordinary interest. *The Chronicle,* in its extended accounts of the troubles, has given the views of intelligent brokers and bankers—in other words, has repeated the best information to be gathered in the best informed circles. With what has been already said upon these grave topics the reader has sufficient matter for his consideration.

It is said on authority which can hardly be considered doubtful that the Bank of California has been painfully straightened for the last three days. Its customers have been scarcely accommodated at all, and large depositors have entered it with doubts regarding its solvency. It has made extraordinary efforts to call in its loans, yesterday morning sending peremptory orders to creditors to come forward at once with their ready money. A few more wary customers have been for two or three days past taking out their coin and placing it where they deemed it more secure. The withdrawal of deposits began at an early hour yesterday morning and continued through the forenoon, but so moderately as to attract little attention from outsiders, the timid ones outside the counters forming a very slight addition to the regular routine of daily customers.

It was not until 1 P.M. that the officials of the institution became much alarmed. About that hour several checks for $100,000 or $200,000, or similar amounts, came to be cashed from depositors not usually disturbed by rumors of financial trouble. All these were paid without a murmur, but they kept on increasing. The scattering drops became a quiet patter and the patter became a heavy shower. By 2 o'clock the steady withdrawal of funds had quickened into a "run" which attracted attention and drew a crowd of spectators about the doors. The news ran along the street like a prairie fire, causing the greatest commotion among brokers and operators, who rushed toward the center of interest, some with bankbooks in their hands, others simply inspired with a desire to join in the excitement. As the news spread to adjoining streets, and into the quarters of the city devoted to heavy business, it aroused everywhere the same attention. Stores and workshops were emptied of their occupants, either to see the excitement or to enable a withdrawal of deposits before the hour for closing the banks, which was now at hand. The people thus led by curiosity or interest streamed from all quarters toward the corner of California and Sansome streets, filling the space in that locality for a square in every direction. At half-past 2 the excitement culminated in a scene of extraordinary interest, which could be taken in at a glance from an elevated position. The streets were thronged as far as the eye could reach, the crowd being quiet in certain places, in others alive with motion. The steps of all banks and offices were packed with spectators. A pale face was seen at every pane of every window. Wild men were rushing in all directions, papers fluttering in their hands, and among them the inevitable bank book. Pale women, with disordered hair and dresses, began to appear, giving the scene a little variety of color, and striving vainly to reach the narrow entrance at the door of the Bank of California, besieged with crowding, struggling, obstreperous white-faced men.

All sorts of rumors flew about like wildfire. One garrulous individual loudly proclaimed having heard that Mr. Ralston had committed suicide by hanging himself in a rear ante-room of the bank, and that his corpse, guarded by a squad of policemen, was surrounded by his frantic family. Other reports gained credence among the credulous class, that several depositors had blown their brains out in despair, and that one stock broker, having failed, had gone stark mad, and was dancing a maniacal hornpipe among baskets of stock certificates in his back office. It is, perhaps, necessary to state that a most assiduous search by a *Chronicle* reporter failed to discover that insane devotee of Terpsichore, and he is without a doubt a myth.

After the bank had closed its doors, a woman having evidently crossed the Rubicon, but ghastly with paint and rouge, vainly endeavored to climb into the bank through a closed window, declaring she would have her money, every cent of it, and if her John wasn't out to sister Abigail's in Amador, he'd see that her hard-earned savings wasn't stolen, you bet your life he would. Only desisting after finding that entrance was entirely out of the question, the frantic woman departed, wringing her hands and protesting, amid torrents of tears, that never again, no never! would she put her money in strange folks' hands to keep for her as long as there was a spade to dig a hole in the ground to bury it, there! And so the perturbed female departed and was lost to view from California street.

While the run was as its height, an old Californian, having the highest faith in the Bank of California, struggled vainly for entrance, declaring that he had $40,000 which he would deposit if the crowd would open its ranks and allow him admission. But the throng, drunk with excitement and alarm, paid no attention to the protesting individual, who struggled and shouted until he was exhausted and speechless, when he strode away breathing husky anathemas upon the "D——d cowards who thought the bank was going to bust!"

II

August 28, 1875

The light of yesterday morning broke upon a disturbed and feverish city. People were early astir. The truce of the night was dissipated like the fog-clouds that hung about the crest of the surrounding hills, and long before the ordinary business hours the streets leading to the spot where the stirring scenes of the day before were enacted were fairly alive with crowds of nervous, hurrying pedestrians, all anxious to see the beginning of the struggle they knew to be inevitable. The excitement was not only universal but intense. California street presented an appearance thrilling in the extreme. At 8 o'clock the whole space between the curbstones was a mass of swaying, sweltering humanity, to say nothing of the sidewalks on either side, where it was utterly impossible to gain a footing. Montgomery Street was about as impassable, and little Leidesdorff looked like a huge ditch filled with squirming bodies. The windows and balconies of the Merchants' Exchange swarmed with spectators, and on even the tops of the surrounding buildings were to be seen huge clusters of the curious perched on chimney tops and gables of dormer windows.

The objective point of all eyes seemed to be the corner where the London and San Francisco Bank was located, and here the crowd was so dense that some of the unfortunate humans composing it fairly gasped for breath. And now look! the hands of the clock in the tower opposite point to the hour of ten, and the crisis is at hand. Open fly the doors of Latham's stronghold and in squeeze the long line of depositors, struggling with the police inch by inch for the right of way. As fast as they reach the counter they are met with the glittering coin, loaded down till they fairly stagger, and passed out by the side entrance. Here drays and express wagons were in waiting to carry the treasure of heavy depositors to a place of safety. And so the run continued for an hour and three-quarters, during which time $900,000 in gold had been passed over the counters and still the usual stock in hand of the concern had not been exhausted.

While the run on the London and San Francisco Bank was at its height the Anglo-California Bank, on the opposite corner, was busy entertaining a crowd similar in temper and complexion to the one over the way. Here the rashly importunate were met with the same glittering provender, and as an encouragement to continue their feverish work, a telegraphic transfer from the Sub-Treasury of the United States in the sum of $150,000 was flaunted in their astonished faces. This and the news that the London and San Francisco Bank had received a telegraphic transfer from the same source for $500,000 completely broke the back of the panic movement, and the crisis had passed. At 12 o'clock matters had quieted down in an astonishing degree: the crowd began to thin out; there was little or no excitement and people began to congratulate themselves that what in the early morning seemed to an inevitable "Black Friday" had assumed so satisfactory and favorable an aspect. At one time the run on some of the different savings banks wore a threatening appearance, but they all succeeded in weathering the storm without any signs of weakening.

★   ★   ★

A news story of equal sensation broke the following day. Ralston's body was found floating in the bay. Was it suicide? Again, *The Chronicle*'s coverage was enormous. The lead story:

August 29, 1875

As an extraordinary and unexpected finale to the gloom and excitement of the last two days, William C. Ralston, the dethroned bank king, was drowned yesterday afternoon while bathing at North Beach. No one who was present while the run prevailed at the bank, and saw him pale, but resolute, sweep around within the counters, and stay the trembling hands of his clerks and tellers from further disbursements, could have thought such a catastrophe even remotely possible. His appearance was simply that of a hero, conquered but undismayed. But great natures, nerved to great crisis, break suddenly, and are gone, the victims of accident, or subject to eternal laws. Yesterday Mr. Ralston transferred all his property to Senator William Sharon for the benefit of his creditors, and Mr. Sharon, in receiving the trust, pledged his honor to stand by his old friend to the last dollar of his own magnificent private fortune. All day long the great bankroom, not excelled in the beauty of its proportions and its ornamentations by any room in the United States devoted to similar uses, saw strange sights. Anxious clerks and book-keepers, from whose nerveless hands the pens had dropped never to be there retaken, were scattered about at desks and counters in all sorts of picturesque attitudes. The doors of the great bank were swung back and bank directors were peering inside, taking out and returning coin securities and all kinds of paper evidences of wealth, or the lack of it. The back rooms were occupied by stockholders, officials, disinterested capitalists, with here and there an officer in gray uniform, seeming to notice nothing but seeing everything.

About mid-day there was a meeting of the trustees, at which there were present besides Mr. Ralston, George H. Howard, D. J. Tallant, John O. Earl, D. O. Mills, William Morris, William Alvord and Louis Sachs. Nicholas Luning was not present, because not in the city. Mr. Ralston promised the meeting that if the management were left in his hands he would pay dollar for dollar to every depositor and fifty cents on every dollar to every stockholder. His life had shown that he was not given to idle boasting. There was an exciting discussion over the proposition, and the sentiment expressed was that since the bank had failed while in charge of Mr. Ralston and many remarks had been made to his prejudice, such an arrangement would not be advisable. Mr. Ralston tendered his resignation, and it was accepted. A Committee, consisting of George H. Howard and William Alvord, was appointed to examine into the affairs of the bank, with instructions to prosecute their labors last night and to report to-day. It seems hardly necessary to say here that the tragedy of the afternoon will defer that report for a day or two. Pending the arrangement of these details Mr. Ralston went out into the banking-room and while seated there in a dejected attitude, with his head bent forward, Jas. R. Keene, the wealthy broker, entered. He came up to Mr. Ralston, touched him on the shoulder and said pleasantly: "When we get the affairs of the bank straightened up I am going to get together a capital equal to that which it has been swinging, and we'll start another." To this bit of king-hearted facetiousness Mr. Ralston simply replied: "I shall never be engaged in another banking enterprise." Matters dragged on listlessly in the bank until 3 o'clock, when Mr. Ralston left the building and was not thereafter seen alive by any of his friends.

Oscar Meysel of the Niagara House, 331 Bush Street, told the following last evening to a *Chronicle* reporter: "I was bathing at the foot of Larkin street at North Beach, at about half-past 3 this afternoon when Mr. Ralston arrived there. He went into a bathing-house and divested himself of his clothing and then took a shower-bath. He ran briskly down the beach in his bathing-suit and plunged into the bay. I saw him swimming toward the old steamer, about two hundred yards from the shore. He was about half way between the smelting works and the old boat, when he turned on his side, and in a few minutes afterwards he made two or three dives. He was under the water an unusual length of time, and the bathing-house keeper rowed swiftly out to the place where Mr. Ralston went down and secured the body. I hastily put on my clothing and called three or four men. We sent for physicians and rolled Mr. Ralston on a barrel. A physician arrived in a half an hour afterward, and we tried to restore Mr. Ralston to life. I put my mouth to Mr. Ralston's lips and breathed in his mouth, at the same time the physician pressed against his stomach. For the first half hour we thought that we were surely bringing him to life, but his lips began to grow cold, and after an hour and a half's work the physician pronounced him dead.

A slight case of earthquake and sex, vintage 1872. Reason for the three-week delay in reporting this particular tidbit of news was that it took a while to establish the quake's center; then it was a six-day trip for the *Chronicle*'s man to get to Lone Pine, after which it could hardly be expected that the honest details could be obtained and verified immediately.

Coward at
Lone Pine

April 21, 1872

The earthquake which occurred at half past 2 o'clock on the morning of Tuesday, March 26th, was the greatest convulsion of nature that has taken place in the United States since 1812.

Although it was felt from Oregon to Central America and Mexico, it seems to have spent its force in the Owens river region, distant from this city hundreds of miles, and lying on the opposite side of the Sierra Nevada on the line of the state of Nevada. Independence and other settlements in the locality suffered from the disastrous effects, but it was the fate of Lone Pine in Inyo County to be marked for destruction as the center of the earth's convulsive action.

The first great shock laid in ruins all the adobe buildings in the place and caused the death of 30 persons. During the ensuing week it was computed that more than a thousand shocks were felt—in other words, the earth was almost constantly trembling.

One of the tragic deaths was that of Antonia Montoya, a misguided young Mexican woman, who on the fearful night shared her couch with a paramour. Of this, our correspondent at Lone Pine writes:

"The shock startled them out of their sleep—the woman to scream and pray, the man to bound out of bed and at once leap clear of the building, with its treacherous roof and crumbling walls.

"She had been caught in the bed by a mass of adobes and screamed vainly for help. Had the man not been one of the basest of the devil's creatures he might have lingered a couple of minutes and released his paramour from her terrible strait; but the coward heard only to disregard, and in his mighty selfishness the craven creature fled alone, leaving the poor woman to perish miserably in the ruins."

★   ★   ★

A major social event in San Francisco often becomes a matter of great civic importance. The Opera Opening, the Debutante Cotillion, the Important Wedding are sources of great joy and pride for the populace. Some say this is a fiction of the local press, which treats such affairs with all the solemn detail of a war or a world series.

Here is evidence that such newspaper practice is at least well-grounded, and, in this case, perhaps well-deserved. The occasion was the stopover in San Francisco of General and Mrs. Grant after a world tour. In their honor a ball was held at the Belmont mansion of Senator William Sharon.

The Chronicle covered the ball with teams of reporters who were sent to Belmont in carriage relays. The next morning, the entire front page of the paper, as well as column after column on subsequent pages, was devoted to this social tribute to San Francisco's eminent guests. The following is merely extracted from the middle.

A Ball in Belmont

October 9, 1879

The first train arrived at half past 8, and the guests which it contained were rapidly transferred to the Belmont mansion. The great house absorbed them and scarcely felt their presence. Soon after 9 the second train deposited its living freight at the depot. The pressure now became inconvenient.

Those leaving the dressing rooms met those entering from the train on the stairway, and so dense was the throng that passage up and down was for a while almost impossible. Fortunately before the third train arrived the guests of the other two were already distributed in the various rooms.

Invitations had been very generally accepted, and among the guests were to be seen every person of social, official or military distinction in San Francisco and Oakland.

The past week all of San Francisco society has been in a state of intense excitement. In the short time for preparation it seemed at first impossible to prepare costumes equal to the occasion; for San Francisco, always notable for its elegant attire, wished to excel all that it had ever before displayed. Our leading dressmakers and designers would have gone daft in the hurry and whirl were it not that money was pouring into their coffers in such abundance as to compensate them for weariness of fingers and brains.

Many ladies designed their own costumes, and new and elegant effects were produced. Among the richest dresses a predominance of white and pale ivory tints was noticeable, and a new departure, in the shape of heavy garniture of richly-hued flowers, was characteristic of many of the newest costumes. Many dresses in their perfect arrangement of color and detail, graceful draperies and thorough rapport with the lovely faces and forms of their wearers were poems in themselves.

The house never before contained half so many visitors. The press was everywhere. Promenading was difficult, and dancing next to impossible. Still, however, the service of Terpischore continued and dancing was persevered in against all obstacles.

A band of 15 pieces were stationed in the main hall and discoursed a well-selected programme of popular airs under the sway of Ballenberg's baton. The following is a list of dances:

Lancers, Waltz, Schottische, Quadrille, Waltz, Galop, Lancers, Schottische, Waltz, Quadrille, Waltz, Schottische, Lancers, Galop, Waltz, Lancers, Waltz, Medley.

General Grant received in the inner drawing room. At his left stood Senator Sharon, and near him Colonel J. P. Jackson, who introduced the guests as they descended the stairs. Mrs. Grant stood at the General's right. At her right was Mrs. J. D. Fry, who, as the guests passed on from the General, presented them to Mrs. Grant. They then passed on to the dancing room and mingled with the other guests. The General exchanged a word or two with each when it was possible. When no opportunity to speak was given he simply shook hands with them, and they were crowded forward into the general mass beyond. The throng swayed back and forth in the main rooms, swept in long processions from one apartment to the next, crowded one another, jostled the dancers and became inextricably entangled.

General and Mrs. Grant continued to receive until nearly 11, when they disappeared, probably to recuperate. After an absence of about half an hour they returned.

The supper banquet came from the kingdom of the prince of caterers, Jules Harder, chef-de-cuisine of the Palace Hotel. All day long the billows of war thundered from the kitchen below to the supper room above. A small army of cooks, stewards, waiters and underlings filed in endless march and countermarch around and about the kitchen, up and down the stairs. A glance through the kitchen was a picture for the illustrator of L'Isle des Mirmidons.

In the main room the tables bore probably the richest, most diffuse and costly burden of delicacies ever gathered for the delectation of hosts and dancers. The chef-de-cuisine triumphs in the shape of boned capons and turkeys, ornate with all the various decorations known to the profession, rose in pyramids, arches and various architectural shapes unknown to any era, side by side with cathedrals, churches and structures of unique character in the richest of confectionery.

The lavishness of the spread was the subject of universal comment. Every delicacy known to an occasion of this kind was served in a style as original as possible, and whether salad or capon, ice or ice cream, the delicacy was lingered over and chatted over. A raised stand at the end of the room held a band of musicians, and mastication was made all the more pleasurable through a variety of digestive melodies ranging from the fifth symphony to "The Turkish Review."

The following is the menu:

Chaud

Huitres a la Soulett.
Petits Pates a la Talleyrand.
Bouchees a la Cumberland.
Huitres Frites.
Terrapines a la Maryland.

Entrees Froides

Aspic de Crevettes a la Morghan.
Cotelettes de Foie Gras a la Kalergi.
Galantine de Perdreaux en Belle Vue.
Hure de Sangier en Poulade.
Pain de Volaille a la Chantilly.
Salade de Langoustes aux Oeuf de Vanseaux.
Salade de Volaille a la Moderne.

Grosses Pieces Froides

Trouphee de Galantine a la Richelieu.
Filet de Boeuf a la Renaissance.
Bastion Rustique et Fantasie.
Grand Piece Oriental sur Rocher.
Chateau Fort en Pain de Gibier.
L'hermitage Bourguignonne.

Plats Froids Decoupes

Dinde a la Gelee.
Caille Piquee au Cresson.
Filet de Boeuf et Langue a la Gelee.
Poulets Gras Glacee.
Assiettes de Sandwiches Varies.
Petit Pain a la Francaise.

Grosses Pieces de Patisserie

Rafraichissement

Punch au Champagne.
Orangeade.   Groseille.   Orgeate.

Chaud

Consomme de Volaille en tasses.
Bavaroises au Lait d'Amande et
Mexicaine.
Cafe.   Vins.

★   ★   ★

James J. Corbett of the Olympic Club was the first of the national sports champions home grown in San Francisco. These
two reports on his activities tell first of the unusual fight on the
barge against Joe Choynski, in which Gentleman Jim proved
himself before the home folks, and then of the moment three
years later when he won the heavyweight title from John L.
Sullivan.

If there is a lesson in these stories for modern sports writers
it is to mock not the ancient scribes. How often these days must
anyone row to ringside at 5 A.M.? How often does anyone come
up with a dressing-room quote that tops the little old lady at the
head of the stairs?

Battle of the Barge

June 6, 1889

The Corbett-Choynski fight, which has been the absorbing topic
in sporting circles for months past, was decided yesterday in a
manner which settles thoroughly a long disputed question of fistic
supremacy.

Corbett won in 27 rounds, through which he showed himself
much the cleverer boxer.

On Tuesday afternoon it leaked out that the referee, Patsy
Hogan, had ordered the boxers to be ready on the next morning
to resume the battle which was interrupted on Decoration Day, near
Fairfax, by the Sheriff of Marin County. Everybody known to be
connected in any way with the arrangements for the fight immediately became an object of deep interest to the circle of ardent
ring-goers who desired to witness the contest without the formality
of invitation. The plan of campaign had been skillfully laid, however, and only a limited number of those whose presence was not
desired discovered that the fight was to take place close to Benicia,
and that the tug Sea Queen would convey the spectators to the
scene. The last hack to arrive with a party of invited spectators
contained the redoubtable Jack Dempsey, himself, who had been
engaged to aid Choynski.

The Sea Queen headed straight for Benicia, and when about

half a mile from that town turned into the cove under the headland known as Dillon's point. Several small stern-wheel river steamers and a couple of long grain barges lay at anchor in the cove. The barge nearest to the steamer was the chosen spot for the fight. A hack and some buggies were seen hurrying down from Benicia, and fears were expressed that the Sheriff was coming to stop the fight, but the apprehensions were groundless.

While the crowd on the Sea Queen was surveying the scene of the battle at long range the tug Richmond, which had chased the Sea Queen up the bay with a party of politicians on board, arrived. Both tugs tried to steam up to the grain barge, but stuck in the mud, so that the remainder of the trip had to be made in small boats. This was a hazardous proceeding, as the crowd fairly leaped into the frail crafts from the decks of the tugs.

Every boat was laden clean to the water's edge. All managed, however, to reach the side of the barge without floundering, but in the excitement of getting on board several spills occurred and one boat capsized completely, nearly drowning Phil Crimmins, and J. J. Kenney, the well-known San Francisco politicians. The Sea Queen arrived off Dillon's point at 4:30 A.M. and at 5:30 A.M. all of the voyagers were on board the barge. A number of salmon fishers and a dozen boatloads of Benicia people added to the crowd of spectators, who numbered about 200.

At 6 A.M. everything was ready for the fighters. It was then discovered that Choynski had not brought his gloves. Corbett had his on, but Choynski's had been forgotten. Some bloodthirsty individuals suggested that the boys should fight with bare knuckles, but Dempsey shook his head. "We don't all want to go to prison, do we?" he said.

The Corbett side at length gracefully conceded a point to their opponents and let Choynski take any gloves he wanted.

The referee announced that when the men clinched he would order them to break away and step back without striking, and if they did not do so he would call it foul. This innovation proved a remarkably good one, and led to a most scientific stand-up fight, entirely devoid of the slogging which marked the first match.

Then, after a round-by-round description:

The right-hander sent the game lad down for the last time, and Choynski rolled over on his back beaten and disheartened, a bloody, disfigured and pitiful object. He struggled to regain his feet, but had only got on one knee when the ten seconds of grace lapsed. He got to his feet however, and struggled to his corner, where his victorious opponent shook hands with him while the excited clubmen who had hung with breathless interest on the ropes jumped through them and nearly shook Corbett's damaged right hand off.

A rush was immediately made for the tug boats, and the scene of the first embarkation was repeated. The fight ended at 8:40 A.M. and at 9:35 the Sea Queen had taken the principals in the fight aboard and had started on the return trip.

A large crowd was waiting for the tug at the Vallejo street wharf, and the pugilists were fairly mobbed as they tried to force their way to a couple of hacks that were in waiting for them. The damaged condition of Choynski's face convinced the crowd that there had been a hard fight, and as the hacks rolled away the mob scattered to spread the news along the city front.

Champion Jim

New Orleans
September 7, 1892

By Special Dispatches to *The Chronicle*

John L. Sullivan, for 10 years the mighty champion of the world, was knocked completely out in 21 rounds tonight by James J. Corbett, the young San Francisco pugilist.

For the first time in a brilliant career Sullivan was whipped. The reason was proclaimed from his own bruised and bloody lips. Staggering to the ropes after regaining consciousness, and raising his great hands into the air with a gesture more dramatic than he could possibly portray on the stage, full of the realization that his time had come at last, John L. Sullivan, the fallen idol of pugilism, exclaimed in a loud but choking voice:

"Gentlemen, I have only one thing to say, once and for all, and that is this: This was to be, and is, my last battle. I have lost. I have stayed too often with a young man, and to James J. Corbett I pass the championship."

As he spoke Sullivan was the picture of awful despair. He reeled through the sand, knowing what he was about, but still weak from his adversary's terrific blows. His nose was split, his mouth puffed from blood vessels severed inside, his ponderous breast bloody and heaving, and his lips set with determination that showed he understood the serious position in which his last fight had placed him.

The famous man staggered into his dressing room and, sinking in a chair, wept like a child.

John L. Sullivan was really beaten into insensibility as thoroughly and artistically as any pugilist that ever lost a battle. He was outsparred, outwinded, outpunched and outgeneraled. He was the toy for an opponent who was lighter than he by 20 pounds.

The San Franciscan put up the greatest battle against long odds known to the ring in this country, and honestly earned the title of heavyweight champion of the world, and was clearly entitled to the $45,000 that depended upon the issue.

When Sullivan fell under the terrific fusilade of blows delivered by Corbett, pandemonium broke loose and no victor was ever cheered as was Corbett. While the young champion was being kissed, hugged and fondled, Sullivan's limp form was laid into the chair. Corbett came to him, but the beaten man was like the dead.

Meanwhile, that same night back in San Francisco:

A City of Lunatics
September 7, 1892

"Zip! Whizz! Boom!"

They backed Jim.

"Well, I'll be hanged! How did it happen?"

They backed John L.

"Whoop! Boom ta-ra-ra boom da-ay!"

That was the Olympic Club.

"Pop! Fizz! Here's to the champion. Let 'er go. Drink it down and have another."

If a roof had been placed over San Francisco last night it would have been the largest insane asylum in the world, for it was bedlam turned loose.

When the telegram which contained the account of the last round arrived the crowd was still as death.

"Jim lands good right and left, Sullivan groggy, falls upon the floor unable to respond to the call of time."

If ever words bore a charm to make men lose their heads, these did.

A gray-haired old lady stood on the top step of a brilliantly lighted house at 307 Hayes street. She was surrounded by a group of smiling young ladies and brave-looking young men. On the sidewalk the crowd that had temporarily ceased prancing around a fire whooped themselves red in the face. An elderly man with a broad grin on his face broke away from the crowd, and running up the steps, caught the gray-haired lady in his arms, giving her a crushing hug and kiss that might have been heard a block.

"Well, old lady, the boy is champion of the world," shouted the elderly man.

There was a troubled expression on the old lady's face.

"Yes, dear, I know," she said, "but—but are you sure that Jimmy is not hurt?"

Is it necessary to state that the old lady was Jim's mother?

★ ★ ★

Here is gold fever at the very moment of its mounting. In July of 1897, when this story appeared, the gold business in Alaska was still so new that Clondyke hadn't even yet become Klondike and the extent of the strike was still largely unknown in San Francisco.

But new or not, notice *The Chronicle* man's professional poise and restraint in the telling of the sensational news. Even the excitement of a bonanza wasn't enough to keep him from including a bit of "woman's angle" plus an "aw shucks, it was nothing" statement to round out his ending. San Francisco, apparently, has seen its gold rushes come and go.

Gold Rush

July 15, 1897

A story rivaling in intensity of interest that told of the fabulous wealth of Monte Cristo was related by the passengers of the little steamer Excelsior, which arrived from St. Michaels, Alaska, yesterday.

Millions upon millions of virgin gold, according to the story, await the fortunate miner who has the hardihood and courage to penetrate into the unknown depths of the Yukon district. There was tangible evidence in the little steamer of the truth of the story told by the travelers, for in the cabin were scores of sacks filled to the very mouth with "dust" taken from the placers of the far frozen North.

The amount brought in is variously estimated at from $500,000 to $750,000, but it is generally thought that the true figure is much nearer the latter mark.

There came in on the Excelsior some 40 people—among them some women—from what is known as the Clondyke district. There were among them men who had been for more than ten years facing the dangers and hardships of the frozen North in the hope of making a rich find, but who signally failed. Yesterday they reached San Francisco with fortunes stowed in their gripsacks and untold millions to be picked up in that country about which so little is known.

The new El Dorado lies just across the Alaskan boundary in British territory. It is of recent discovery, but already there are at least 3000 people on the ground, and more are flocking in that direction as fast as transportation can be secured.

The discovery of the Clondyke regions presents a story that is uniquely interesting. Around Forty Mile on the Yukon is a tribe of Indians known as the Stickers, and with them is a man who years ago was known as George Cormack, but who now is called "Stick George." September last, at the head of a party of Indians, he left his hut near Forty Mile Camp and started in a southerly direction, saying that he intended to find a new gold field before his return.

True to his word, "Stick George" came back two weeks later

and startled the miners with the announcement that 40 miles away in a place known as Throendiuck, which means "fish water," there was gold to be found in plenty. The streams abounded with the yellow metal and all that was needed was for somebody to pick it up.

It is needless to say that there were many who were ready to accept his story. They flocked to the place, and in time the word reached Forty Mile Camp that untold riches really could be found along the bottom of Bonanza Creek and its tributaries.

Yesterday the steamer was met at the wharf by runners from various hotels, but the Excelsior's passengers cared little just at that moment for hotel accommodations. Four of them took possession of the Palace Hotel bus the moment they stepped ashore. One of them stood guard at the door of the carriage, while the other three carried several heavy canvas and buckskin sacks down the gangway and piled them in the bus. Then the four got in with the sacks and ordered the driver to take them to the Selby Smelting Company Works. The driver began to remonstrate at being thus ordered out of his usual course, but he was cut short by one of the hardy Alaskans telling him in plain language to do as he was told. Nearly all the other busses were pre-empted in the same way.

J. L. Lippy was one of the four who captured the bus of the Palace Hotel. He had most of his pile in a large gripsack, and it was about all he could carry down the plank. He set it down when he reached the wharf, and after a short rest a bystander assisted him to get the load on his shoulder and he went staggering under its weight to the bus.

At the Selby Smelting Works a scene of unusual activity prevailed when the gold dust arrived. When each package had been weighed, and the clerks had cut them open, a large crowd of spectators clustered around, craning their necks to behold the sight.

Mrs. Lippy, who accompanied her husband up the Yukon, was the first woman to go to the Forty Mile Camp from Juneau over the trail through the mountains, a distance of about 1000 miles. She is a slender, refined little woman, but very energetic.

"How did I like my trip to the gold mines?" she said last night to a *Chronicle* reporter. "Oh, it was perfectly splendid. Of course, we had some difficulty, but I was strong and I enjoyed it all.

"The men at Dawson City are of the rough, hardy order, but they were uniformly kind to me. There was really no suffering at the camp, though once or twice we ran out of provisions. The camp reminds me of a happy family with everybody willing to help everybody else."

Up to 12 months ago Lippy was secretary of the Young Men's Christian Association of Seattle, but he has given up that position.

★ ★ ★

The headline across the top of page one read:

TWO HUNDRED FIFTY THOUSAND HEAR TETRAZZINI SING IN OPEN AIR BEFORE THE CHRONICLE BUILDING

GREAT ARTIST REVEALS HER VERY SOUL TO THE PEOPLE SHE LOVES

The occasion was the return to San Francisco of Luisa Tetrazzini, the great Italian diva. Madame Tetrazzini had agreed to sing a holiday concert free of charge at a Market street intersection out of gratitude to the city where she had made her American debut.

She sang well. *Chronicle* critic Frederick Wood wrote the next day: "Every intaken breath was a caress; every exhaled sigh was a prayer; each upraised hand was a benediction; every tintinnabulating scale of molten notes was a hallelujah. Tetrazzini has come and gone to win plaudits otherwheres (sic), but every enthusiast of last night has fast locked in his or her heart a memory that will not fade until the bugles call and the crashing guns tell that the sun has set and life is done."

The event itself was described in a lead story by reporter Ralph E. Renaud, who said it was "too big to grasp." It is pertinent to mention that the affair was sponsored as a public service by *The Chronicle*—and that it was Christmas Eve.

Street Singer

December 25, 1910

Just before she went down to sing her heart out for the people she loves, Tetrazzini leaned from a window in the *Chronicle* building and gazed upon the crowd that stretched away below for block on block, a monumental microcosm of humanity itself. Every gem on the diva's gleaming gown quivered and flashed with her quickening heart throbs.

As she turned inward there was an an expression on her face I had never seen there before. She was quite serious. No smile turned the corners of her lips. No flush incarnadined her cheeks. There was a film over her eyes.

A timid soul would have shriveled from fright. In the recorded history of mankind no artist had ever sung before so vast a throng; no singer, with a voice of gold to risk, had ever dared so much; no woman had ever faced a similar occasion.

From the street a faint buzzing only arose. In a multitude so huge this might almost be taken for silence. An imagination that excitement had terrified would have considered it ominous—they would expect too much, they would rush forward and engulf her, so many thousand ears would absorb her voice until it shrilled and faded to an unheard whisper.

Was Tetrazzini frightened?

Ah no! Her eyes were filmed with tears. Clasping her hands upon her breast, she cried:

"Look! Look! My grrreat familee! See Evarybody my brudder! Evarybody my sister!"

And, spreading her arms and stretching her gloved fingers, she spoke once more, with almost a sob in her tones:

"My 'eart eet is so beeg lak dees! Way out to 'ere an' 'ere! Oh, I am so 'appy!"

In a moment she was smiling again with the familiar, dimpled, roguish smile. Her robe—an old rose, like the flower in her first sweet song—was placed about her shoulders, and she passed down stairs and out upon the platform, as ready to bestow her richest love as the opulent magic of her voice. . . .

I have only a confused and emotional recollection of an event that is too big to grasp at once. It is all like a brilliant dream that leaves one a little dazed upon awakening and only comes back bit by flashing bit. I know that I heard a roar that broke into a long-drawn thunder, like the pounding of storm waves upon a pebbled beach, as the spot-lit figure moved to the raised dais from which she sang. I remember listening to the words of a speaker and then feeling a hush clear to the distant edges of the crowd. Then came those spirit-piercing, sweet, sweet tones that fluttered, rose and floated into the enamored night air, carrying peace and good will to the Christmas throng, speeding a message to the whole world, and pumping the love of a great-souled woman through the valves of every heart.

Surely it was "one of God's choristers" I heard.

When the last note died on the darkness the multitude, as I looked across it from the platform, seemed to convulse itself into sudden motion. Heads were flung back, wild arms sprang upward, shaking hats and caps, while a hoarse and deafening shout issued from I'd hate to say how many thousands of throats, repeating itself again and again. It was a crowd "where the best was like the worst," bootblacks rubbed elbows with bankers, and painted creatures with the fat and wholesome mothers of families; but I'll guarantee that but one emotion, indeed but one sensation, moved them all. Curiosity, excitement, criticism, selfish impulses to push forward, irritation at being pushed backward were sunk in a single, binding wave of gratitude. Before the amazing demonstration ended this found definite direction in the hymnal sentiment of "Auld Lang Syne," carried by the orchestra and welling from the concourse, and the intensely Anglo-Saxon function of three rousing cheers.

When the emotional side of our natures is greatly strained by grief, joy, or sudden delight, little inconsequential things stand out with great distinctness in our memories. It was so with me. Looking over the edge of the railing, I saw an obscure Italian listening to his famous countrywoman. His head was bent down and he was making no attempt to see, only listening. As Tetrazzini sang the tears dripped steadily from his eyes and rolled ludicrously into his moustache. Nearby stood a young woman with a boy, both keyed to rapt, ecstatic attention. Yet she was not so forgetful as the diva began "The Last Rose of Summer" that she did not remember to raise her hand and gently remove the lad's cap. . . .

And, naturally enough, every move, every gesture of Tetrazzini herself is engraved upon my memory. Closing my eyes for a moment, I can even bring her back as she bowed and smiled to the crowd, waving her handkerchief and wiggling her extended fingers. As she stretched her throat for a high, aspiring note I see her robe slip from her shoulders, revealing the dazzling white of her gown and the rounded lines of her form against the glowing gloom that surrounded her. . . .

Perhaps the miracle could have happened in no city in the world but San Francisco, but no woman alive, except Tetrazzini, would have performed it. To be sure Providence was kind and gracious, and the night was as soft and clear as one of the last evenings of an Eastern spring. She had declared her wish to sing in the streets for San Francisco, and sing she would. It is the tenderest tribute ever made to the people of a big city.

Must it not be a happy thought to her that of all the Christmas gifts that are passed in all the Christian lands of the world today, she had the loveliest to give, and gave it where she loved the most.

★   ★   ★

News item, 1917. Statistical reports always make good copy.

Ladies' Choice

January 31, 1917

The women of the Y.W.C.A., the Associated Charities and the San Francisco Center of the California Civic League, who worked so hard to relieve the distress of women thrown out of employment when the Barbary Coast was cleaned up in 1913, probably will not go into relief work in the present cleanup campaign.

The results in 1913 were discouraging, even though Mrs. Genevieve Allen, executive secretary of the Civil League Center says her organization spent about $600 in the campaign.

There were about 500 women on the Barbary Coast at that time, and of this number Mrs. Allen says only 10 accepted help from the women who were making it their business to help them.

Although almost every big business house in the city stood ready to give employment to women who were competent to fill positions, Mrs. Allen says she knows of but one woman who went to work. She took a place as a demonstrator.

The women of the Barbary Coast said they could make more money down there, even when selling soft drinks, than they could in employment offered by the Civic League and kindred organizations and they refused to give up the life they were leading.

One investigator visited 40 women of the Barbary Coast to see if they would go to work at this time. Of the 40, 3 said they were willing to get married; 23 announced they would stay in the old line of business; 8 were going to join relatives; 3 were willing to work at honest employment; and 3 were undecided.

★   ★   ★

For a number of years Robert O'Brien wrote a regular feature for *The Chronicle* called "Riptides." It was an attempt to re-create on a daily basis the great adventure of the Old West.

O'Brien's assignment was to cover his rich beat as a reporter rather than as historian. This report of John Muir's perilous night on Mt. Shasta is typical of the detail and vitality he was able to develop from his research. It was a splendid news story, written eighty years after the event.

Muir's Night on Mt. Shasta

December 19, 1954

On April 28, 1874, John Muir, the naturalist, led a party of surveyors to the summit of Mt. Shasta, 14,140 feet above the level of the sea.

When they had completed their observations, they dropped back to their timberline camp. This camp was located amid the dwarf pines at about the 10,000-foot elevation. Muir and Jerome Fay, a mountaineer, remained there. The surveyors proceeded down through the fir stands and chaparral meadows to Sisson's Hotel, in Strawberry Valley west of the mountain.

But there were still more observations to be made. On April 30, Muir and Fay were to take barometrical readings on the summit at 9 A.M., 12 noon and 3 P.M. Simultaneous readings were to be made in Strawberry Valley. The two sets of figures would make possible an important and significant comparison.

At the timberline camp on the 29th, Muir and Fay turned in relatively late. The stars blazed like cold white fires. The signs indicated clear weather for the morrow.

The adventurers woke at 2 A.M. on the last morning of April, after several hours of shallow sleep. They drank steaming coffee and broiled some frozen venison and ate it. Then they started for the summit. Muir carried a small box of instruments strapped to his back.

It was an arduous but relatively simple ascent. Up they toiled across the snow slope, to the most exacting part of the climb—a mile-and-a-half long ridge, or spine, of rock, flanked on one side by the precipitous ice sheet of the Whitney glacier and on the other by sheer cliffs that dropped hundreds of feet to jagged and jumbled rock heaps below. Sure-footed in the windless air, they clambered up the ridge without incident, and gained the mile-wide plateau of rock ruins and crumbling peaks that forms the mountain summit.

In all the world of wilderness, sky and space that they surveyed, only two things moved: The sprays and steaming vapors that bubbled from hot springs across a quarter-acre of lava crust near the highest stony pinnacle—and, far to the southeast toward Lassen's Butte, a vast expanse of soft white cloud, seething lazily in the rays of the morning sun.

Muir and Fay rested. The temperature rose from 34 degrees at 9 A.M. to 50 degrees at noon. At 1 P.M. a bumble bee diverted them briefly. At least a mile above the springtime blooms of the chaparral meadows, it buzzed about their heads in a casual and friendly way, then sailed off and disappeared.

Meanwhile, as the mountaineers waited for their 3 P.M. instrument check, cloud formations gathered below and to the north, over Shasta Valley.

On the summit, the wind began to blow softly. The temperature fell a little. It was about 2 P.M. Fay gazed west. The vaporous sea boiled closer to the summit.

"I don't like the looks of this, John," he said.

Muir wanted his 3 P.M. readings. "Maybe it'll hold off."

Fay shook his head. "If we don't get out of here in a hurry, we may not get out at all."

"A pair of old mountain men like us?" Muir smiled. "We ought to be able to handle ourselves in any storm that can break this late in the year."

Fay glanced uneasily at his watch. "Sometimes they're holy terrors."

On the dot of 3 Muir took his readings. He jotted them down and hastily boxed his instruments. Now he and Fay and the entire summit were enveloped in the mist, which, banking above them, obscured the sun.

It grew dark. As Muir and Fay ran from the summit, past the hissing springs and toward the descending ridge, it suddenly began to hail. Sheets of hail fell all about them. It struck the summit rocks and cliffs with the crash of a hundred waterfalls. Fascinated, Muir picked up some of the hail stones. Each was perfectly regular, a six-sided pyramid with a heavy, rounded base.

They pushed on a few yards toward the ridge. The wind screamed past the desolate crags. The temperature plummeted to zero. Then it began to snow. Lightning flooded the wild scene with a pale flickering glow. Thunder cracked about them as if the great mountain itself were splitting apart.

Muir huddled in the lee of a lava block. Fay fought his way to Muir's side. Above the howling wind he shouted, "We can't go on."

"We can make it. I can lead us down the ridge."

"If we'd left when I wanted to, we'd be safe by now."

"We can still make it."

"I'm staying," Fay said. He spun away from the lava block. Staggering and struggling against the wind, like a man fording a swift river, Fay made his way back to the hot springs.

Muir crouched in his shelter for nearly 30 minutes, hoping for a let-up in the storm. When none came, he followed Fay to the steaming fumaroles. The mountaineer had made himself as comfortable as possible in the warm sludge. "We'll be safe from the frost, anyway," he said.

Muir unstrapped his instrument box and lay down on his back in the steaming mud. Fay also lay on his back. Thus they presented as little surface as possible to the wind and driving snow. But the snow sifted into their clothing, and packed around them, then froze into a stiff, crusty heap.

The heavy smothering snow thickened the air and the darkness. From time to time the heat from escaping steam became unbearable along their backs, while the upper portion of their bodies froze beneath the snow. The lava crust beneath them gave way, and new steam vents opened. They tried to fill them with mud and snow, or shoved themselves with their heels into new positions. Blistered on one side and benumbed on the other, neither one dared stand in the face of the gale.

In addition to exposure, still another peril haunted Muir. There was carbonic acid gas in the steam of the springs. When he saw Fay dozing at his side, he reached out and shook him.

"Don't forget yourself for a single moment. If the wind subsides, these fumes could asphyxiate us."

The nightmare hours dragged on. Fighting exhaustion, Muir called out Fay's name and Fay called out Muir's, to make sure the other was still conscious. Once, Muir momentarily fell into a dreamy stupor, and fancied that he saw dry pine logs stacked for a campfire.

At about 10 P.M. when two feet of snow had fallen on the summit, the storm suddenly ceased. The wind died. The clouds disappeared, and left the night sky bright with glittering stars.

"Are you suffering?" Fay asked.

"I'm frozen and burned and famished," answered Muir. "I seem all dead—all dead except for my eyes."

He shifted painfully. "But never mind, Jerome," Muir added. "The night will wear away at last. Tomorrow is the first of May, and we'll go a-Maying. What campfires we'll make! What sunbaths!"

When the air grew warmer, they shattered the crusted snow that blanketed them and struggled to their feet. Muir's right arm, benumbed, hung powerless. Their feet were frozen.

Drawing on their last reserves—"a kind of second life," Muir called it, "available only in emergencies like this"—they lurched through the snow toward the ridge. Their trousers were frozen stiff. It was all they could do to bend them at the knee.

But the wind had swept the ridge clear of snow, and they descended it quickly. When they came to the long slopes of loose snow, they slid, shuffled and pitched headlong down the mountainside. Three thousand feet below the summit, they felt the sun warm upon their backs and shoulders. It was a little after 10 A.M. when they reached the timberline.

Half an hour later, they heard someone calling among the snow-laden firs. It was J. H. Sisson, the hotelkeeper of Strawberry Valley.

Eagerly they downed cup after cup of the hot coffee Sisson had brought. For several hours they sat with their frozen feet buried in soft snow. When their feet had thawed, they wrapped them in sacking, and resumed their journey down the mountain.

At the 9000-foot elevation, 3 inches of light snow had fallen during the night. In Strawberry Valley, their mountain blizzard had been an April shower.

They reached the hotel that afternoon and went directly to bed.

The laughter and running footsteps of Sisson's children awoke Muir the next morning. Warm sunshine flooded his bedroom. Out the window, to the east and high above the green meadows, loomed the serene white cone of Mt. Shasta. For a moment, Muir wondered if it had all been a fantasy.

Then the bedroom door flew open and into the room burst the happy children. They brought bouquets of May flowers and scattered them, bright and sweet-smelling, across Muir's bed.

CHARACTERS

The characters San Francisco has always loved best are those it invented. Once born of the popular imagination they were savored and exaggerated. In death they burrowed even deeper into the folklore of the city.

The prototype for all such San Francisco characters was Norton I, an eccentric who assumed the role of Emperor of the United States, Protector of Mexico and a number of lesser honors. He was accepted with great toleration.

Currently, impersonators of Emperor Norton still appear at civic functions. A downtown tavern employs its version of the Emperor as a greeter. And in recent years Norton's grandiose proclamations have appeared in *The Chronicle*, heralding springtime with a hunt for treasure he has caused to be buried within his capital city.

In the case of Norton, San Francisco has kept its tongue in cheek for nearly a century. This report demonstrates some of the legend's original flavor. The headline stated simply:

Le Roi
Est Mort

January 11, 1880

Imperial Norton is dead and turned to clay.

His funeral took place yesterday afternoon from the undertaking establishment at No. 16 O'Farrell street. All the afternoon the remains lay in state in the rear room of the Morgue. Thousands flocked thither for a last look at the man whose peculiarities of mind, garb and person had rendered him familiar to all.

The man of imaginary majesty, Emperor of the United States, Protector of Mexico and prospective consort of the Queen of Great Britain and Ireland and Empress of India, narrowly escaped burial in a plain redwood box. Some people, noting the odd manner of life of the old man, have unkindly surmised that his hallucination was simulated, and that he had adopted his strange life as a cover for a miserly hoard of unaccountably-acquired wealth. When his effects were searched it was found, as his best friends knew, that he had no means.

On his person was found five or six dollars in small change, which was all his store. He had no personal effects of any value, and but for the kindly remembrance of people of means who knew Norton and had business relations with him many years ago when he was a citizen of substance and standing, he would have had a pauper's funeral at the city's expense. A subscription paper to procure a funeral fund was drawn up and taken to the Pacific Club where the sponsors soon had all the money they deemed necessary. The subscription list still lies on the table of the clubroom.

After the autopsy Friday the body was prepared for burial. It was clothed in a black robe with a white shirt and black tie, and placed in a neat rosewood casket, trimmed handsomely but without elaboration. The general interest felt in the deceased was soon manifest. Early in the afternoon of Friday people who remembered the singular old man kindly, many of them gratefully and affectionately, began to call and ask to be allowed a last glance at the familiar face. Among them were several ladies whose dress betokened prosperity. Some of them brought bouquets to be placed on the coffin. One, the daughter of a former well-known citizen and officer of the city government, in addition to her bouquet brought a delicate boutonniere, consisting of a tuberose and sprig of maiden's hair, and pinned it to the lapel of the burial robe.

This lady appeared in deep mourning and betrayed the deepest feeling of any who gathered about the bier. She stated that she had known the deceased from her childhood and when he was prosperous had received many and great kindnesses at his hands. When she was a little girl he used daily to present her with flowers, which at that time were very costly.

Early yesterday morning the stream of visitors to the bier began. By 7 o'clock quite a number had dropped in, some of them laborers who had got off the car on their way to the shops, to take a last look at the remains of one whom none remembered save with kindly feelings; others were business men who stopped on their way downtown for a similar purpose. Soon the number began to increase and there was a steady stream of people pressing through the office to the little back room where the remains lay in state taking a last glance at the features and filing out at the side exit to make room for the constantly-increasing throng of visitors. By noon there were hundreds of people gathered on the sidewalk waiting their turn. Policemen were called in to regulate the entrance.

The visitors included all classes from capitalists to the pauper, the clergyman to the pickpocket, well-dressed ladies and those whose garb and bearing hinted of the social outcast, the bowed with age and the prattling child. Among the throng, however, the garb of the laboring man predominated.

The coffin lid was partially removed, exposing the features in view. They were placid and composed as in life, bearing no sign of suffering in the supreme moment. It was remarked by some of the visitors that the outline of features and habitual trimming of the beard, which were observed in dressing for the grave, presented a remarkable likeness to the last Emperor of the French, whereupon the reporter of a morning contemporary pricked up his ears and made a note of it, and went off to enlarge upon the details of the resemblance with much display of learning, concluding with the statement that the dead man claimed to be an illegitimate son of Louis Napoleon, and going on to show that probably the name on the coffin plate was wrong, which, of course, is highly absurd.

The coffin plate, following the best information obtainable, states that Norton was 65 years old. Louis Napoleon, who was born at the palace of the Tuilleries April 20, 1808, if still living would be his senior by only six years. Norton never claimed to be his son.

The floral tributes, wreaths and bouquets were so numerous as to completely cover the coffin lid, the only exception being the silver plate, which bore this inscription neatly engraved:

Joshua A. Norton
Died January 8, 1880
Aged About 65.

★　★　★

In Benny Bufano San Francisco found itself a character who could almost qualify as beloved—if only he would stop making so much trouble. Yet while the city was so often in controversy with the sculptor it was always somehow a little bit delighted that the controversy existed.

Kevin Wallace, who wrote this profile of Bufano in 1952, had talents in common with his subject. In addition to being a sensitive and highly literate writer, Wallace spent the moments between assignments sketching sharply on paper towels torn from the *Chronicle*'s men's room, or chipping away at hunks of soft stone until they assumed the shape of short, happy caricatures of people and animals.

St. Francis in North Beach

I

August 28, 1952

Beniamino Benvenuto (Benny) Bufano, 54, five-foot-two, shaggy, affable, a resident of a reconverted bookie establishment at 811 Greenwich street (adjacent to the new Columbus Meat Market, where phone messages may be left), is the man who made French Sculptor Aristide Maillol "glad for America that she has given us one great sculptor."

Roger Fry, the severe English critic, defined little Benny as "the outstanding innovator of his time among sculptors" and said "Bufano's huge black granite statue of St. Francis of Assisi is the most significant piece of sculpture done within five hundred years."

Five hundred years—let's see, that would be before Michelangelo (1475-1564), back around Donatello's day (1386-1466), when the Medicis and their set were picking up the tab for the local monument chiselers, and so liberating the great creative spirit of the Renaissance from the red tape of making a living.

Arranging for this kind of liberation has always been one of the nastiest technical problems facing any creative spirit (or anybody else), and Benny Bufano, who thrives on technical problems, has this one licked.

Benny's one-man renaissance of Renaissance economics involves a latter-day Lorenzo the Magnificent by the name of David Moar, president of Fosters Luncheon Service, Inc. Moar has provided Benny with a life-time meal ticket at the plush Powell street cafeteria bearing Moar's name, and pays the rent for Benny's Greenwich street address, a 60-by-25 foot studio plus a kind of large rear closet occupied by Benny's bed.

Moar's idea of art was and is any saleable, tasteful arrangement of meat and vegetables on a lunch plate. However, his chain's art director, Ted Wetteland—who was frightened during his formative years by being thrown out of a class Benny once taught at the California School of Fine Arts—instructed Moar to give Benny what eventually amounted to $20,000 to make a mosaic for Moar's Cafeteria.

Benny went to Italy to quarry three tons of mosaic quartz, melting the 7000 brilliant color shades of the Ravenna spectrum into it, chopping it up into 400,000 pieces, and cementing these into three 17-by-13 foot stainless steel frames, each eventually weighing five tons, bearing designs that symbolize some aspect of peace on earth, good will to men and children and St. Francis.

Benny lived frugally while he was in Europe on this job. His entire luggage on leaving here consisted of one paper shopping bag. (Unlike his friend, Dr. Leo Eloesser, whose globe-trotting luggage is often limited solely to his violin, Benny left his own violin here.)

However, he shot the whole $20,000 on the mosaics before they were installed (two years ago) on Powell street. So the rent-and-board guarantee was made by Moar as a kind of tip, and Benny is pleased by the arrangement except for one detail—he wishes Moar would take down the mosaics and give them to the United Nations building in New York.

This furiously unbusinesslike wish of Benny's is in line with his theory of himself, which he states off-hand this way:

"Every talent we have was given to us to give back to humanity. I'm not interested in selling stuff to individuals. The work of the artist should go back to humanity, where it belongs."

However, as Moar patiently reminds the artist, the cafeteria caters to nobody if not humanity in large numbers.

Meanwhile Benny is not unbusy on other projects in his North Beach studio. Among the works in progress there are:

Two 18-foot crucifixion figures, each hewn out of a complete oak tree; several large sugar pine sections, already halfway sculptured, which Benny chopped down with his own little hatchet in Federal forests (with the ranger's permission) near Lake Tahoe:

A 15-foot wooden giraffe, which will presently be sheathed in hammered lead with mosaic insets;

A beaver to match;

Animals sketched out in several tons of hard palfrey stones Benny quarried in Egypt;

Heads sketched in Big Sur granite boulders, which Benny hauled by hand over miles of beach and underbrush;

An enormous copper head for one of the 150-odd figures of St. Francis that Benny has made (the 26-foot body will be hewn from a tree Benny lately felled at Tahoe, as soon as he finds someone to cart it down here for him);

Portions of an 18-guage stainless steel eagle, a model for two huge eagles he has in mind, that Benny has been hammering into shape for four months now (he is originator and sole going exponent of the fine fantastic art of hammering stainless steel and other hard metals into round sculpture, directly);

A 14-foot harp, made by assembling uncarved bits of sugar pine and eucalyptus, the horn of a water buffalo and a lot of wire— which plays;

Cow horns, buffalo horns, elephant tusks, deer antlers, in process of conversion into likenesses of eagles and other objects;

No end of heavy steel "dollies" (backstop shapers for hammered metal) and heavy hammers that Benny himself shapes in an old hand-forge he got from an earlier restauranteur-patron.

Big or small, grave or whimsical, these projects are none of them commissioned projects, with buyers signed up and parks and pedestals waiting. Benny is just doing them, that's all, to be available when the parks come around.

The studio is also inhabited by a completed bronze St. Francis, a model for Benny's long-projected 186-foot St. Francis, for which six acres atop Twin Peaks are still held by a sponsoring committee; the famous 16-foot stainless steel and stonewear statue of Bach, whose since-replaced Germanic head was stolen by vandals at Carmel the day after Pearl Harbor; proofs of a book of reproductions of Benny's drawings, being published by an art lovers' committee in Florence, Italy; and some interesting photographs on the wall, including one of Yosemite's El Capitan, retouched to show diminutive Benny's most undiminutive project of all—another Saint Francis, 2000 feet tall, engraved on the cliff.

In a nearby yard reposes another finished product too big to fit into the studio—a granite penguin that Benny and some of his friends kidnaped a year ago from Aquatic Park to save it from vandals there.

The Bach and penguin are in crates, like so much of Bufano's major works. "Peace," the 34-foot black granite statue that the 1939's World's Fair commissioned and then rejected, is still crated in a warehouse that charges $7.50 a month for its keep.

However, Benny's urge to give his works to reluctant humanity has been better honored in the past few years by the San Francisco Housing Authority, which has taken over a number of Bufano granites the city inherited from the WPA—Horse and Rider at the West Side Project, Bear and Cubs at the Sunnydale Project, and, at Valencia Gardens, Cat and Mouse, Big Cat, Mouse, Rabbit, Crab and Butterfly, and Sea Lion.

He is represented at Aquatic Park, the WPA project that still infuriates Benny whenever he thinks about it. There is, of course, his famous stainless steel and granite Sun Yat Sen in St. Mary's Square. There is his Louis Pasteur, in the same materials, at San Rafael, and Franklin Roosevelt at Vallejo.

There is the Engelhart collection of Bufanoana at the San Francisco Museum of Art, and the Leon Liebes collection that has been bequeathed to Stanford University.

"And," Benny says, "there are about 250 of the 500-odd sculptures that I've done in private hands in San Francisco—most of them bought from the creditors who attached them when I was in Europe in the Twenties, but some of them acquired from a distinguished admirer of my work who took a shovel and dug them up from the ground where I'd buried them for safekeeping. I didn't sell any of them."

Benny becomes wistful at the thought that his works are held captive by individuals—incommunicado, solitarily confined—instead of being at large in public parks, where humanity can claim them as its collective own.

II
August 29, 1952

For the time being, Bufano will not accept public museums on the same terms as public parks, because he thinks museums should pay something to the artists they exist for, same as they pay their janitors and elevator operators and curators.

Benny's notion that museums should pay artists was typical of the propositions he offered to his shocked fellow city officials during his wartime term as a San Francisco Art Commissioner—a "wartime term" in more ways than one, Benny being an extremely militant champion of the artistic and gentle way of life.

Critics whose phlegm Benny excites have denounced him as a fake (though just how anybody can manage to be a fake, in such an undefinable line as art work, is a question no system of careful logic can answer).

But if he is a fake, he is a whole-souled, dedicated, devoted, life-long and 14-karat incorruptible fake—a genuine article. Take, for instance, the time he lost the forefinger of his right hand:

"As a kid I was very much against war," he recalls. "My grandfather, who had been Governor of Rome, was a Garibaldine, and escaped to this country. My family—I was next to youngest, with 10 boys and 5 girls in the family—came over to New York in 1901, when I was 3. The family hated war very much.

"We thought Wilson would keep us out of war, and I worked for him in his campaigns. I was also playing violin in the Peoples' Symphony, and I was sculpturing then—I began when I was 7 or 8, and I got myself apprenticed in woodworking before I won scholarships to the Art Students' League and the Academy of Design.

(It was in this phase that Benny worked with a number of eminent sculptors, including James Fraser, who designed the Indian head for the old buffalo nickel, and, according to Benny, let Benny design the famous buffalo on the other side.)

"Well, when we entered the war I was very disappointed, being very much against war, so I took my mother's cleaver and cut off my finger and sent it to President Wilson. . . .

"He didn't answer, but I had a nice talk with him just before he died, and what he said was I was a damned fool."

The incident was not taken well in New York at the time, Benny says, and Mrs. Harry Payne Whitney, who had seen young Bufano's works, financed his departure from town. He presently adjourned to China; joined some mendicant Buddhist priests, became a vegetarian and chummed with Sun Yet-sen.

He wound up in San Francisco, and was teaching at the California School of Fine Arts in 1923 when he became overpowered by distaste for the classroom's plethora of squishy clay for copying plaster reproductions of the classics.

"Soft materials make us soft," was and is his theory. "Hard materials challenge us and constantly remind us to keep a vigil on our powers entrusted to us."

So—shunning, as always, administrative red tape—he somewhat boyishly gave all the school's clay and paster casts to the garbage collector one night, replacing them with 80 tons of alert-making red sandstone he acquired cheap, from a wrecker.

"They got rid of me right away for that," he recalls, "but the stone was harder to get rid of. As a matter of fact, they're still using it up there—and using my theory, now, too."

So Benny went gradually around the world, living in a sacred city of Japan, dressing up as a coolie on the docks of Canton, chinning with the Polynesians in Polynesia and the Gold Coasters in West Africa, and similarly talking in Hawaii, Korea, Bali, Java, Siam, India and, finally, his native Italy.

It was evidently his exposure at that time to the colossal and stylized sculptures of the Far East that bent Benny's talents away from the traditional European forms of sculpture and toward the kind of sculptured shape that was described by that eminent critic of sporting events, Westbrook Pegler (who lost a bet that he was a better sculptor than Benny), as "round, rigid as a concrete pipe, and innocent of fold or human line."

Sam Fusco, an attorney, seeing what Pegler saw, described it this way: "Since simplicity leads to revelation, we find truth only when confusion is dispersed. Bufano points toward simplicity . . . by using simple curves, lines and planes, he reduces his forms to a point which manifests his specific idea."

Bufano, pounding away to make what both Pegler and Fusco saw, prefers to talk about "an inner life expressing itself through every particle of the surface, making toward the esthetic revolution of inward simplicity."

The ethical and political counterpart of this esthetic "inner simplicity" he mentioned is St. Francis, whose name it was that presumably led Benny to return to make his home in San Francisco, the city named for Benny's primary and non-paying patron who was also a very poor economist from other people's angles.

Benny's identification with the mendicant tamer of wolf and bird has undoubtedly helped him bear up under a number of incidents that worldly citizens would find vexing, including the vandalizing and burglarizing and burning of various studios he has had here, and the stretches in between, when he has contentedly taken up residence on park benches.

When a Bufano bear was stolen by University of California pranksters, he was able to remark with genuine delight: "Art in action!"

His St. Francis-fixation has also made it more logical for him to accept largesse where he has found it, most famously from the WPA, which provided materials for his biggest works to date, and the San Francisco Press Club which has sporadically sponsored him with free accommodations.

During the war, Benny was President Roosevelt's "only dollar-a-year man without a dollar." He was assigned as an art-talent scout at Army camps. "My $6 per diem wasn't enough for a hotel room in Washington, so I had to stay at the White House," Benny recalls. Presently—right forefinger or no right forefinger—he was drafted, along with his old friend, William Saroyan. He went right on doing his dollar-a-year job, but in uniform, and with pay.

All things considered, Beniamino Benvenuto (Benny) Bufano is at this point a happy man. He would be happier, however, if he could lay hands on some machine tools he wants in his work.

"Or better yet," he says, "if I could have the machine shop at Naval Air Station Alameda for my studio. With the stuff they have there, you can make an airplane!"

★   ★   ★

Not long ago, the Blackhawk, a San Francisco night spot specializing in good jazz music, faced up to a mighty dilemma. The problem was how to get around the law that bars minors in grog shops, when those same minors stood ready to spend a good proportion of the jazz dollar. The Blackhawk people found a way. They put the kids in cages—where only milk and soda pop were served.

Ralph Gleason's 1956 report on the Blackhawk management

hints at the clear-thinking that eventually produced such a Solomon-like decision.

All That Jazz

July 26, 1956

The other night I stopped by the Blackhawk for a chat with Mr. Guido Cacianti, one of the proprietors and my main pipeline into the dim world of San Francisco night life.

"What's shakin'?" I asked Mr. Cacianti, who speaks a language of his own.

"Well," he said, "with all these clubs going the whole town is huckley-bucking. We had Andy Previn in here and he did good. You know that Previn. He's a regular Dr. Heckle and Mr. Hyde. He plays that classical music just like he plays jazz. But wait till I give you the coupe de ville. He's going to name a tune after us. 'Bad Night at Blackhawk!' "

"What do you see for the future of jazz?" I asked Mr. Cacianti, who slowly wiped the bar with a cloth. "Well, they had a riot at one of those teen agents dances so it looks like there's gonna be some trouble with that rhythm and blue music. We'll never go back to the old time area with the bands. It's all those small jazz groups now. They got more rappaport with the people. The only way for a joint to make money these days is to solve the solution with jazz."

"You know," he continued, slowly rubbing the aged mahogany of the bar, "that jazz is spreading out all over. We had a jazz fan here the other day who came all the way from Vienna just to hear jazz. You know, a Venetian."

At this point, Helen Noga, wife of Mr. Cacianti's partner and manager of singer Johnny Mathis, came in. "I got another one," she shouted, nudging me with her elbow.

"A parking ticket?" I sympathized.

"No, a girl that sings risque songs in a French brogue. You ought to hear her." Mrs. Noga turned to one of the owners of Fantasy Records and began a deep conversation about the record business.

"That Johnny Mathis is going to make money," Mr. Cacianti said. "You ought to hear him sing 'That Crazy Valentine.' He's got an album of records on Columbia Music and when he leaves town he's going to work in the Blues Angel in New York."

"Do you really think there are enough jazz groups to keep a club going all year?" I asked.

"The way I see it," Mr. Cacianti said, "it's six of one and one and half of the other. You got to book six months out of the year and the rest of the time play it out of your ears. When a good one comes along, grab it. Like we did with those Mulligans. And the Brubecks."

I looked up on the wall where a sign proclaimed "Shelley Mam and His Quartet" were coming. "Do you make your own signs?" I asked.

"It's a gift," Mr. Cacianti admitted modestly. "You have to be born with it. And," he added, "it has to be when you're young."

I crept out, the night club scene much clearer in my mind.

★   ★   ★

Herb doctor Fong Wan was a character known to San Francisco almost solely by self-proclamation—until reporter Dick Hemp told his fantastic story in 1949. Hemp's meticulous profile of the millionaire medicine man appeared in two parts.

Medicine Man

I

June 19, 1949

Fong Wan, a Bay Area multimillionaire, is also variously known as Fong Poy, Mon Poy Fong, Fong Wan Kwong, and "King of the Herbalists in North America."

He roughly translates the Chinese names:

"I am light of the world. Without me you are in dark."

"Big name, huh?" Fong asked yesterday, then pointed to a framed horoscope on the wall of his office at 860 Stockton street. It depicted a pine tree and a horse pulling a wagon load of salt and according to Fong these ancient Chinese symbols, like his name, strikingly illustrate the pattern of his life.

"Pine tree like me," chortled Fong, a rotund 200-pounder who stands 5 feet, 6 inches—and who spikes his conversation with high-pitched chuckles.

"Pine tree has strong spine and only one heart goes upward. Like tree, I tower on top of mountain and endure all hardships world produce. Like rain and storm and snow on tree, I push away hardships and gain power and intelligence from enemies. Like tree gain nourishment from seasons.

"My mind never change like a pine tree always green. Ha, ha. Wonderful, huh?"

Fong indicated the horse and announced: "I fearless like horse who run 1000 miles in one day—carrying cart of salt to keep people from disease. I live just like my horoscope, what I do everyday of my life, going to supply people with herbs. Everything hard but I use my good brain to make money. Ha, ha."

The 66-year-old Chinese has been dispensing his herbs—more than 1000 varieties in 3000 different compounds he claims to know by memory—for nearly 40 years, despite almost constant harassment from the United States Post Office, the Federal Trade Commission and the State Board of Medical Examiners.

In this time Fong says he has prescribed for some 50,000 sufferers and more or less bested various authorities in 20-odd spirited court battles. His legal ammunition has been supplied in the main by a seemingly endless parade on the witness stand of satisfied "customers."

"I won all time because my patients stand by me," exulted Fong. "By one patient I can prove I beat the whole world."

However, after a 1940 Federal Trade Commission hearing in San Francisco—an action which clipped his grandiose "cure-all" advertising methods—Fong began to spend more time on real estate investments and his San Francisco and Oakland restaurant business.

This latter enterprise consists of the Club Shanghai and Chinese Cellar here and the Club Oakland and Nanking Cafe across the Bay. Fong, who has many relatives—including 11 children and five grandchildren—said he went into the night club business "to put my dependents to work." He has a number of them in various capacities in these establishments.

As a further example of his horoscope in action: Fong presently has on file in Superior Court a $50,000 suit against Charlie Low, another astute Chinese night club entrepreneur, for allegedly "stealing" an acrobat away from Fong's Club Shanghai.

"A hardship like snow on pine tree," commented Fong. "I lose face but lawyers more worried than Fong Wan."

He confidently expects to win this suit and again "tower on mountain."

One Fong coup against Low is already legendary in Chinatown and was struck when the herbalist bought a six-story building at 334 Sutter street—across from Low's Forbidden City night club— and erected a huge neon sign directing passersby to Fong's club around the corner on Grant avenue.

Fong denies there was malice in this action, however, and credits it to his acute business sense. "I know valuable building," he declared. "Never think of Charlie Low at all, I bought building for $90,000 and next day am offered $110,000 to get it back. Ha, ha."

The man of acumen was born May 11, 1883, in Ham Ning village (Kwangtung province)—a town to which he has sent $2000 every year since 1925 for the education of its young.

Fong was "No. 2 son" of nine children and after a desultory schooling in Ham Ning went to work for his father at the age of 15, making bamboo shell lanterns. His father's name was Fong Hang Thew, which means, "You take care of your body and do no foolish things"—another precept which Fong claims to have followed through his life.

He says: "My body pure white like paper. Keep 100 per cent sanitary."

The elder Fong eventually sent his teen-age son on a tourist's holiday to Japan where the future herbalist observed growing militarism and predicted in letters home an eventual Sino-Japanese conflict. His father then paid young Fong's passage from Japan to California in order to visit relatives and his home here became permanent.

Fong, at 17, arrived in San Francisco with $10 and a long queue. He soon got rid of the last item but was never to be greatly concerned about the first.

His uncle was a prominent Chinese herbalist and Fong lived with him on Stockton street and studied the art of herb mixing while learning English at the Chinese mission school, Washington grammar school and later at Berkeley High School. While attending this last institution in 1910 he fell off a bicycle, broke his teeth, injured his jaw and has never been able to speak fluently since.

But his speech is persuasive. Shortly after his accident he bought a paper telescope for 75 cents, set it up on Sacramento street and made $3.75 a night by selling views at the moon. His pitch:

"Just as good as $1000 telescope. If you don't believe me pay me a nickel and see for yourself."

While the people peered he sold them razor blades.

By 1912 Fong had absorbed hundreds of ancient volumes of Chinese herbology, ("Uncle beat me if I didn't study") and he opened an herb parlor in Santa Rosa. In 1916 he became an herb doctor, with offices in Oakland, later opened a branch on Stockton street here, and hasn't been slowed up since.

In his San Francisco office the other day, a young white woman walked in, consulted briefly with Fong who thereupon went into a store room piled high with straw sacks of raw herbs and lined with boxes of more herbs, identified by Chinese characters.

These herbs, all from a firm in Hong Kong, represented part of a recent $39,000 shipment of 102 bales weighing 200 pounds each.

While pulling out various boxes of herbs from the shelves— apparently at random—and mixing them into a compound for the woman, Fong said his customer was in her second pregnancy, he had prescribed for her during her first and like so many others she was coming back because of "faith" in him.

Fong shuffled roots and leaves in tin pans and announced he was making a compound for herb tea, which is brewed by adding four cups of water to the mixture and then boiling the whole thing down to one cup. It is strained and drunk at bedtime.

"This tea give young lady blood and air power," said the herbalist, "strengthen to deliver baby so child come out healthy, strong like tree." (He explained "air power" as "good breath circulation.")

"I talk over with people, then give herbs. More power than God can do."

Fong assembled eight herbs to make the tea compound. They generally looked like pieces of tar paper, white corn flakes, balsa wood and plain old bark. Fong named them as Ong Kei ("Makes more blood"), Chun Kung ("Causes blood to circulate"), Steamed Root ("Makes rich blood"), Bacsec ("Equalizes to make new blood"), Ginseng ("To give air to body"), Baki ("To make air powerful") and Pak shoot and Licorice—both "to equalize for power of air."

"All these valuable formula to make air and blood strong," declared Fong.

He divided the heterogeneous compound into seven plain white paper packages—a week's supply—and gave them to the young woman who then gave him a $10 bill and walked out.

"Very small charge," said the herbalist. "I do it for good of people. Sometime I lose money on herbs. Sometime I make 30, 40, 50 per cent."

Fong follows his preaching and says he's never been sick a day in his life, except for an occasional cold. "I have different compound for that," he said. "Have kind of tea to cool blood down. Ha. ha."

In fact, he's in remarkable physical condition for a man of 66. His youngest child is a boy of three, whose mother is Fong's third wife, 42-year-old Hong May Fong—which can mean either "red eyebrow" or "radiance," depending on how you look at it.

His first wife, who died, was named Fung Ling. ("Means she was a flower, like peacock lily.") That marriage was in Canton in 1910 on a trip Fong took back to China. It occurred in a Methodist church though Fong had been raised in the Confucion religion.

He explained: "My mind is fast. Can change in five seconds."

II

June 20, 1949

Fong Wan's troubles with the authorities have produced a sheaf of testimonials from people who agree with him that:

"I can cure nearly all, anything with herbs."

These individuals declared they had visited regularly licensed physicians and surgeons without avail for such ailments as athritis, tuberculosis, stomach ulcers, colitis, diabetes, heart trouble, malignant growths, infected prostrate gland, paralysis, kidney trouble, obesity, neuritis, enlarged liver, intestinal obstruction, dysentery, high blood pressure, hardening of the arteries, rheumatism, eczema, catarrh, influenza, sinus trouble, bronchitis, violent sneezing, boils, piles, yellow jaundice, dropsy, varicose veins, cross eyes, lymphatic leukemia, deafness, poison oak and ringing in the ears.

Before postal inspectors, Federal Grand Juries and in various courts they claimed they received complete success with Fong's herbs. The testimony of their condition before Fong "saved" them ran as follows:

"My heart was in pretty bad shape. It would just beat a little bit and then sort of wait and then beat again. We called the doctor, and the doctor said. . . ."

"I was not able to walk a block. I was short winded. I had the afternoon fever. I had the night sweats. . . ."

"After nine months the cut made by the doctors had not healed. Each month I became weaker, my breath grew short and I could scarcely walk. I thought that I would surely die. . . ."

"Recently I suffered from growth on the navel and the pain became so severe that I was confined to my bed for three weeks. . . ."

"On March 1, 1932, I broke out with a venereal disease known as syphilis or blood disease. My blood test on November 3, 1932, came back '3 plus' and a test on December 1, 1932, came back '4 plus'. . . ."

To treat these many afflictions, Fong Wan leans heavily on the Chinese science of therapeutics based on the deductions of an ancient Emperor of China known as Shin Nong, the "divine farmer."

He believed that all things on earth are included in five natural elements: water, fire, vegetation, mineral and earth. For instance, since the natural color of the fire element is red—and the heart controls the circulation of the blood and blood is red—Shin Nong said the heart belongs to the fire element.

He then classified medicinal plants according to their relations to the five natural elements. So, medicinal plants of a red color were classified under the fire element and were used to aid heart ailments.

The early Chinese also went so far as to base their five principal musical tones (Kok, Ching, Kong, Sheng and Yii) upon the five natural elements. Thus, Fong Wan says he can tell what ailment is bothering a person by listening to him groan.

He cited an Oakland case where a boy was in such pain he couldn't explain the trouble. Fong said he recognized his howlings as belonging to the Ching musical tone—which is connected with the fire element—and immediately diagnosed that the boy's liver had become overheated by the fire element and that his trouble was inflammation of the liver and intestines.

Fong mixed certain herbs for this condition, fed them in tea to the boy and the patient soon recovered, the herbalist said.

Fong illustrated the various musical tones, moaned low and said: "Yii. That's kidneys. Ha, ha."

This sort of thing has irritated more orthodox practitioners for many years and the Government produced a series of expert medical men at the 1940 Federal Trade Commission hearing here to attack the theories of Fong Wan and to bear out the contention the herbalist's advertising was false and misleading.

These gentlemen generally hooted at Fong's methods as based on superstitious folk lore and attributed the testimonials to a feeling by many people that "the strange mysterious East holds things for us we don't know."

The doctors admitted, however, that two valuable drugs used in modern medicine, digitalis and ephedrin, are extracted from ancient Chinese herbs—namely, foxglove and Ma Huang.

Fong Wan's lawyer introduced a parade of witnesses to testify to seemingly miraculous cures obtained from Fong Wan herbs and these persons were execeedingly loyal to the herbalist.

Despite such testimony for Fong, more than a year later the Federal Trade Commission decided Fong's "methods of diagnosis are based upon doctrines which are of historical interest only and which have had no acceptability in the scientific sense for several centuries."

Fong was ordered to "cease misrepresentation in the sale of herbs" and "to cease advertising herbs as cures or of therapeutic value" for a long list of diseases and disorders.

But the herbalist, astute as always, had already obtained untold advertising from the Federal hearing. In April, 1940, he bought pages of space in the Bay Area's major newspapers and inserted therein the verbatim testimony of the hearing—testimony which was predominantly pro-Fong from his followers. In *The Chronicle* alone this record ran 14 full newspaper pages on April 14.

Though he is no longer permitted to call himself a doctor, he is eager to acquaint listeners with his various interpretations of Chinese materia medica. One is the theory that the best time to shave is early in the morning when "blood is cool and skin firm and taut."

Though Fong's main business has been herbs, he does not neglect his real estate and night club holdings.

He pays nightly visits to his Club Shanghai and Club Oakland, chauffeured in either his 1948 Packard or 1949 Buick by Elmo, a young man who said Fong cured him of a serious disease.

In each night club he follows the same routine: Takes cat naps until the master of ceremonies introduces him after every show. Then Fong rises, grins and waves his arms in a Max Baer-type greeting, and resumes his dozing.

The performers in the clubs, most of whom were imported by Fong from China, universally respect and admire him. Lana Wong, a petite entertainer, and Barbara Yung, a willowy "Terry and the Pirates" sort of fan dancer, acclaimed: "The doctor's wonderful!"

Fong accepts praise and recognition as a matter of course. He hit upon as good a reason as any for his phenomenal success by displaying an exceptionally long and rare "intelligence" line on his left hand, running all the way from his wrist to the first line of his middle finger.

He declared: "Means other people can't follow me because I'm smarter. Everything I do—I sure to succeed before I start."

★   ★   ★

This assignment produced several unusual dividends for *The Chronicle.*

First, there was the story itself. Before it was ended *The Chronicle* had made a page one issue out of Virginia City's brush with the Catholic Church and of the strange war among Lucius Beebe, the two ladies from the gem shop, and Father Robert Jelliffe.

Then there was the fearless writer of the story. So fearless and so literate was he, that upon his return from the Comstock he was set to work as a sporting columnist, reporting fearlessly and literately under the title of Charles McCabe, Esq., the Fearless Spectator.

And last of the dividends was the extraordinary Beebe himself. If he could belch so convincingly on vintage port, irritate most of Virginia City and generally make his mark in life out of simple snobbery, then why should not his talents be on display in San Francisco? So it came to pass, not long after, that Beebe, too, was writing a column for *The Chronicle*—a weekly affair called "This Wild West."

The Priest
and the
Plutocrat

Virginia City, Nevada
July 26, 1959

Lucius Beebe sighed contentedly. The publisher, bon vivant, and gentleman anarchist let out a great inelegant after-dinner belch.

"Well, we got rid of that damned priest," he said.

He took a slow appreciative sip of a vintage port his friend Fred William had selected for him.

The publisher of the Territorial Enterprise was taking his ease beside the swimming pool here. It is the sole swimming pool in "the liveliest ghost town in the world. (Pop. 450. Alt. 6205)."

The sun was setting brilliantly behind the high Sierra. (The sun, through a trick of reflection, sets in the east here. Other things are not always what they seem, either.) The dying sun hit the clean white spires of St. Mary of the Mountains Church in the distance.

Beebe had treated his guests to stout, succulent lamb chops, a good sampling of his cellar, and some of the most urbane and witty conversation in the continent.

At 56, Beebe is the very carrot-cheeked image of a Regency buck who has survived four decades of rare roast beef with Yorkshire pudding and Stilton cheese with port.

He shook a copy of his tabloid-size weekly (circulation: 6000) at his guests, and pointed to the banner headline: "Local Priest Charged In Assault On Crippled Woman."

Billboards pasted all over the Nevada landscape allege Beebe's paper "is livelier than when Mark Twain was on it." This is no lie.

The publisher picked up some sheets of pink copy paper and read from an editorial for the next issue.

The priest he referred to is a plump, amiable 32-year-old Cistercian artist—monk named Robert Jelliffe.

Father Robert, as he is called, had been removed as pastor of St. Mary's by the Bishop of Nevada, after a woman polio victim filed an assault and battery complaint against him for pushing her into a chair.

The priest replied that the charges were a frameup arranged by a group which wants a wide open town as in the days when this honky-tonk hamlet was a booming mining camp.

"Father Jelliffe," Beebe intoned, in a sonorous baritone with a strong flavor of Boston's Beacon street, "has done more than merely betray his own parishioners. He has done Virginia City and all Nevada, this newspaper believes, irreparable and conscienceless harm.

". . . The posturings of Father Jelliffe as a holy man crusading against civic vice is so preposterous as to be hilarious. His sources of information have been, by his own admission, inmates of the State Mental Hospital at Sparks and there are those uncharitable enough to suggest that Father Jelliffe might be urged to join them."

It is fair to note that Beebe, and most other citizens here, refer to people they do not like as either "psychopaths" or "ready for the net."

The status seeker here collects enemies. A 14-year-old boys says, "I've got my enemies, too."

Even gentle Florence Edwards, who owns the Silver Dollar Hotel, points across C street at a gaudy saloon sounding out the measures of "Twelfth Street Rag," and says, "The owner of that place is my arch-enemy."

Beebe continued his reading. "Anyone even vaguely familiar with the Comstock's small town character must view his claims to being framed by a vicious element of the Virginia City underworld as either a childish gesture of self-publicization or the product of limitless self-delusion, which is perhaps an essential to his calling.

". . . Father Jelliffe and the church he represents are strictly free loaders, paying no taxes, contributing nothing of any sort to county, state or nation and presuming to abuse and defame the very taxpayers who make their free-loading existence possible.

"It is hard to see, aside from his own appetite for martyrdom, just what excuse there is for Father Jelliffe to figure in the public affairs of the Comstock at all.

"Neither his office nor his Church gain in stature from his insistence on regarding as a mere convenience to his own ends the community on whose economic charity and amused tolerance he stays in business."

Father Robert came here in August, 1957 to head "The Damascus Foundation of Sacred and Liturgical Art"—an outfit with avant-garde ideas about Catholic liturgy and architecture.

At the same time he was named pastor of beautiful St. Mary's. He had instructions from his Bishop, Robert J. Dwyer of Reno, to "restore" St. Mary's along "American and modern lines."

The trouble started with the "restoration" and spread to all areas of public life. It reached the point where both Father Robert and publisher Beebe, for vastly different reasons, were pursuing the same end. Each sought to gain control of the town.

Father Robert and Beebe were the only really dynamic figures to hit Sun Mountain since the days of the Bonanza kings.

Their clash was due partly to a strong larding of melodrama and megalomania in each personality. Fur was bound to fly between them.

The priest brought some of the most forward-looking ideas in the Roman Catholic Church to one of the most backward-looking communities in Christendom.

And Beebe, for the past decade, has been feeding Virginia City and his readers outside a set of ideas that look backward even here. Politically, he's rather to the right of William McKinley.

Virginia City has a way of gobbling up its conquerors, like ancient China, and will survive both the priest and the publisher. But the struggle between them has left a lot of scars. They will remain a long time.

To understand the roots of the controversy, it is needful to know a bit about this place.

Nevada and Virginia City in this year of 1959 are celebrating the 100th anniversary of the discovery of the Comstock lode. In 1859 silver was found here in the lode. One of the richest gold and silver deposits in the world's history opened up. In the next 30 years about $750 million worth of precious metals were taken out of the Comstock. Virginia City, with a population that sometimes reached 30,000, was the biggest city between San Francisco and Chicago.

This is hard to believe today, when one looks at the town's saloon-based economy (there are 21), its sagging roofs and plank sidewalks with phony bearded Buffalo Bills striding by.

"Comstock gold and silver," says Beebe, "built the city of San Francisco, contributed materially to the winning of the Civil War, elevated Nevada to statehood, financed the great Mackay Cable Co., and enriched noble families still flourishing in Rome and London."

The matter of the publisher and the priest came to a boil when the priest was served with a warrant on July 6. It was signed by Mrs. Marguerite Williams, a 47-year-old polio victim who runs the Tierra Gem Shop on C Street.

Mrs. Williams charged the priest "pushed and shoved her" during an argument in her shop on April 4.

Father Robert says he "set her down firmly" after she had tried to tear off his Roman collar, and says the battery complaint was "framed" by Mrs. Williams, her woman partner and "some men I do not care to name."

On July 14, Bishop Dwyer, just returned from a trip to Europe, issued a laconic statement: "The Chancery Office announces that Fr. Robert Jelliffe is returning to his home community in Wisconsin."

The extreme view of Father Robert expressed by Beebe is shared by but a handful in Virginia City. Father Robert had devoted followers before he was dismissed. His following has swelled since.

Local feeling has turned against both Beebe, for the violence of his attacks, and Bishop Dwyer, for turning his back on the priest whose career he had heartily sponsored.

A devoted adherent of Father Robert is Angela Kinkead, a San Francisco woman who spends her summers here.

The day before Father Robert's dismissal, Mrs. Kinkead got up a "testimonial" to Father Robert. It was addressed to Bishop Dwyer, but the Bishop acted before he received it. The "testimonial" was signed by 80 Virginia City adults. This is a formidable percentage of the town's estimated permanent adult population of 200. The "testimonial" said:

"We people of Virginia City wish to thank you for sending Father Robert to us. Some of us are Catholic, some not. All of us sign our names as a token of respect to you and to the Father. We are grateful to him for what he has done for us. We trust he will continue his work on our Mountain."

Among the signers were: Storey County Sheriff Cecil J. Morrison; Storey County Commissioner William Marks; Storey County Recorder and Auditor, Edna Sames; Chief of Police Emil Engelhard; John Bowie, oldest living resident of the town; and "Garbage Mike," a respected town character who picks up the refuse.

When Father Robert said his final Mass at St. Mary's last week, there were weeping women in the congregation. And not all who wept were Catholics.

The priest left the town, to continue his artistic work at St. Ignatius Church in Sacramento—to most of the people here, a hero and a martyr.

★   ★   ★

It was winter of 1945 and any relief from the grim news of the war was welcome. For several weeks such relief was provided *Chronicle* readers by the unusual case of Francis Van Wie, the Ding Dong Daddy of the D Car Line.

Van Wie was a 58-year-old San Francisco street car conductor and former lion tamer, who ran up an astounding matrimonial record. The running account of his bigamous achievements was taken over from the start by reporter Stanton Delaplane, who wrote it in outrageous fashion, long on the metaphor and short on continuity.

It was Delaplane who dreamed up the Ding Dong Daddy label, which was immediately adopted by the opposition *Examiner* and papers elsewhere around the world. In February the Associated Press reported from Guam that servicemen there had formed a Down with Ding Dong Daddy Club, claiming that it was unpatriotic for him to have that many wives while the other fellows were away at war.

The Delaplane sample that follows here tells of Van Wie's return from Los Angeles. It is typical of the garter-snapping style that went over so big in 1945.

Ding Dong Daddy

January 29, 1945

The airy breezes of the streamlined Southern Pacific Daylight refreshed the previously streamlined memory of Francis Van Wie as he landed in San Francisco last night.

He remembered two more wives.

That made Van Wie a 12-star veteran of the honeymoon trail. But this was no honeymoon trip. The 58-year-old former lion tamer had a burly detective instead of a lovely lady as a companion piece.

The 5-foot-2 conductor rode into town in the midst of a chair-car uproar that included ex-wives (with all expenses paid), high-priced attorneys, low-paid reporters and lithe and lovely ladies.

Attorneys Jim Toney and J. W. (Jake the Master) Ehrlich leaped aboard the train at San Jose. Toner was attorney of record. Ehrlich was the legal flash representing money man Louis Lurie and his group of Van Wie sympathizers from the financial district.

Also boarding the train was George Lewis, society jeweler from Burlingame with three lovely lady friends who said they insisted on coming along just to see the Ding Dong Daddy of the D Car Line. The ladies wouldn't say what attraction the Toonerville heart tripper has that the rest of us haven't got.

There were also the Van Wie wives—tentatively identified as vintage 1944, Myrtle and Josephine. They said their expenses had been paid by the enterprising San Francisco *Examiner*.

Coached by the *Examiner* cameramen, they squeezed into the club car and snarled threats of vengeance at the Muni conductor who married them—among others—because he wanted "a home and peace and contentment."

In the midst of all this, Van Wie recalled for Inspector Jerry Diamond that there were two more wives. There was Adeline whom

he married in Oakland in 1917. And there was Martha Winston—
"she was my common law wife"—whom he married in Milwaukee
in 1920.

Add that to Elizabeth in Wisconsin, 1904; Clara Heise in Chicago in 1912; Mabel in Wisconsin, 1924; Sadie Levin in Nevada,
1941; Ruth Le Clurs in Carson City, also 1941; Julianna in Sacramento, 1942; Myrtle in Reno, 1943; Louise Weller (whom he identified later as Louise Malloy) in Sacramento, 1944; Josephine in
Burlingame, 1944; Evelyn, "the sweetest woman I ever knew," in
December 1944.

The battle-worn warrior of many nuptials sighed as he handed
over the list and said he guessed that was about it. "I was just
looking for a home," he said. "It started out all right, but it didn't
seem to work out after I married them."

From his years of near misses with many a missus, Van Wie yesterday drew his expert picture of the perfect woman:

"She should be small," he said. "Not much bigger than me. She
should be able to cook. But most important she should be con-
genial. I don't like to dance. I like home parties. I like to play
pinochle. That's the woman for me."

And Van Wie, whose woo-woo eyes sputter the dynamite that
flutters the feminine heart, said he actually found "her."

"Evelyn," he said. "That's where I found it at last."

But even Evelyn got all his money. "Just like all the rest," said
home-lover Van Wie. "I always brought my pay check home and
gave it to them."

Van Wie's pay as a Muni conductor was $43.50 a week, on
which he conducted operations that would have put to shame a Wall
street wolf.

Evelyn lives at 1610 Sutter street, and it was there than Van Wie
settled down until the percentages caught up with him. He thereupon left for Los Angeles where the law found him Thursday.

His picture of Evelyn as the eternal soulmate didn't altogether
fit in with a will found in the blue Van Wie barracks bag. In his
newest will he named as beneficiary Mrs. Callie Donna Pearl
Pullen, a 63-year-old Los Angeles lady, who admitted shyly that
she and the dapper gentleman of the car lines had had "several
dates together."

She met him, she said, in romantic old Pershing Square in Los

Angeles where his soft-spoken yearnings for a home were mingled with the cooing of the pigeons.

The Van Wie press notices, already mounting into stacks big enough to swell the heart of a newsprint salesman, launched a crowd into hysterics as Van Wie dismounted in the Southern Pacific station here.

"That's the Ding Dong Daddy," screamed a woman, and the small riot was on.

Van Wie was hustled to a waiting prowl car where police held back the crowd. That was nothing to what is expected at 10 o'clock this morning in the Hall of Justice when the D Line Lothario comes to judgment. Van Wie's courtroom appearance will be before Judge Leo Cunningham to whom he will plead not guilty to several bigamy charges and he will then be bound over to the Superior Court.

But even as the Carbarn Casanova sits sadly in the city clink he can find cheer in a further murmur of affection from Los Angeles. Mrs. Pullen, who apparently just missed being Mrs. Van Wie No. 13, declared: "I hope he looks me up when this matter is straightened out. He's a very fine gentleman."

Mrs. Pullen, it seems, still has hopes.

CRIME AND PUNISHMENT

The lynching of the two killers of Brooke Hart in 1933 set off a nationwide wave of shock and introspection. The furies that were ignited in San Jose were examined in legislative bodies, motion pictures and learned treatises. It was found that the how and why of a lynch mob were not simple to pinpoint.

This is the story of that San Jose lynching, written on the scene and in journalistic haste. Perhaps in its violent confusion it comes closer than any scholarly study in probing the brutal core of a lynch mob. The story won for Royce Brier the Pulitzer Prize for reporting.

Lynching in
San Jose

San Jose
November 26, 1933

Lynch law wrote the last grim chapters in the Brooke Hart kidnaping here tonight.

Twelve hours after the mutilated body of the son of Alex J. Hart, wealthy San Jose merchant, was recovered from San Francisco Bay a mob of 10,000 infuriated men and women stormed the Santa Clara County Jail, dragged John M. Holmes and Thomas H. Thurmond from their cells and hanged them in historic St. James Park.

Swift, and terrible to behold, was the retribution meted out to the confessed kidnapers and slayers. As the pair were drawn up, threshing in the throes of death, a mob of thousands of men and women and children screamed anathemas at them.

The siege of the County Jail, a three-hour whirling, howling drama of lynch law, was accomplished as 35 officers vainly sought to defend the citadel.

The defense of the jail failed because Sheriff Emig and his forces ran out of tear gas bombs. Bombs had kept the determined mob off for several hours. Help from San Francisco and Oakland officers arrived too late to save the Hart slayers.

"Don't string me up, boys. God, don't string me up," was the last cry of Holmes as the noose was put about his neck in the light of flash lamps.

Thurmond was virtually unconscious with terror as the mob

hustled him from the jail, down the alley and across the street to his doom. Great cheers from the crowd of onlookers accompanied the hoisting of the two slayers. Some women fainted, some were shielded from the sight by their escorts, but the gamut of human nature was here in the park. Old women with graying hair and benign faces expressed satisfaction at the quick end of the murderers, and young women with hardened faces broke down and wept.

After Brooke Hart's body was found in the water this morning barricades were put up before the County Jail. The crowd gathered and stayed all day. It was a good natured crowd. It knew the deputies and the police and the state highway patrolmen who stood guard. It bandied words with them.

There had been talk of an organized mob, but as the crowd grew in the evening there was no organization. There was shouting, but good nature still ruled.

"This crowd won't do anything," was the constant reiteration of Sheriff Emig's deputies.

Yet, even as their words of confidence were being spoken, the word was being flashed like a prairie fire through San Jose—11 o'clock! 11 o'clock!

It was shortly before 9 o'clock that the front line at the barricade made its first move of violence. Ten or 15 patrolmen and deputies were against the barricade, which was not 30 feet from the jail door. There was some pushing from behind, and the good natured jeering took on a deeper tone of muttering. Strangely enough, there was little shouting of "lynch them" at this critical stage. It was a growl which was not unlike the throaty shouting in an African film.

Newspapermen stood behind the barriers, a few deputies stood about. Cameramen snapped flashlights.

Suddenly that front line lunged.

The police locked arms to hold them back. There were 15 police and a hundred men exerting pressure against them. They all swayed for a moment, locked in one another's embrace.

The police shouted orders, but they were mere shrill nothings as the mob behind began a deep rumble, dreadful in its menace.

Out of this twinkling of struggle, while the men behind the barriers held their breath, came a blast like that of a gun. The mob was temporarily quelled and uncertain, staggering back. "Shooting! Shooting!" went up the cry.

It was only a tear gas bomb, which had exploded prematurely.

The police gave way, taking one officer who had been burned back into the jail. The mob, after a moment of uncertainty, surged forward but was still a little cautious.

Out of the jail came five or six deputies armed with tear gas sticks. Again the leaders of the mob, those who must bear the brunt, staggered back.

But even as they staggered, they jeered, and the first shouts of "lynch 'em" stabbed through the tumult.

"We'll get 'em now, boys. . . . Bring 'em out. . . . Bring 'em out. . . ." And another dreadful cry went up, a kind of chant which lasted but a minute; "Brooke Hart—Brooke Hart—Brooke Hart— Brooke Hart."

This chant, all of these shouts and screams were choked off in an instant as the first tear gas bombs were fired. The crowd broke and ran. Women and children went screaming out beside the courthouse, handkerchiefs went to eyes everywhere and the jail for a moment stood deserted, a grim, old fortress which seemed in that moment impregnable. Smoke, blue and lazy, drifted in the night air.

"That's the end of it," everyone said, deputies, newspapermen, everyone.

And everyone, unable to plumb the depth of fury which has swayed San Jose for 17 days was wrong. This was about 9 o'clock.

The women and children had run, but there were hardy spirits who stayed. They were the leaders, they were the men who ultimately hanged Holmes and Thurmond.

They couldn't get in close to the jail. The smoke burned their eyes. But they could stand off and throw rocks, and they did. The first rock came soon after the gas started to dissipate.

A new post office building is being built nearby. There was tile aplenty—and bricks. There was also a vantage point from which to throw.

Sixty seconds after the first stone a steady shower was beating down on the stone wall of the jail, clanking against the steel door, making musical tinkles as the missiles struck the bars.

Every rat-a-tat on stone or steel brought cheers from the crowd, and when a window in the jail fell, the cheers were redoubled. The sound of a smashing window seemed to get them all, and they roared at the top of their 200 voices.

The alleyway before the jail door was now wholly untenable. Debris lay everywhere. The scene resembled the front steps of a bombed church during the World War.

Not all of the officers on guard were besiged in the County Jail. Across the alley in Sheriff Emig's office were 10 or 12 San Jose police officers, also armed with tear gas. These officers fired out the side windows and even sent a bomb out the front window of the court house, but the crowd seemed to survive this gas, choking, but still exceedingly interested. The leaders especially stuck, most of them boys between 18 and 23. There were scarcely more than 50 of these determined ones.

After about an hour of this rain of missiles the leaders seemed to realize that they were getting nowhere. You can't knock down a jail with bricks. It was then, about 10 o'clock or shortly afterwards, that the first direct attack was made on the steel door.

From the post office construction job came a 9-inch iron pipe, weighing several hundred pounds, but there were willing hands to lift it. Into the smoke went 15 or 20 men, charging from the crowd across the no-man's land straight for the ancient steel doors of this jail which has stood unbreeched since 1866.

"Boom," went the great pipe against the door. "Yeeoweeeeeeh," went a strange animal cry from the throats of the onlookers.

The tear gas bombs continued to come from the second story of the jail. A rock went through the arc light at the corner of the building and the greatest cheer of all rent the air.

An eerie gloom swam in the courthouse alleys. It was a stage set for the deepest of blue lights, and here was transpiring a drama the like of which has seldom been seen in America.

But at the corner. . . .

A policeman at the corner tooted his whistle. He was directing traffic. If the courthouse had blown up, if the sky had fallen, that policeman would still toot his whistle, directing traffic at the corner of St. James and First streets.

He kept on sending them down First street by the courthouse. Traffic was in a terrible snarl. All about the courthouse, all about St. James Park to the east wandered thousands, youngsters and their girls, women with children in their arms, men and their wives, nice old ladies with their proper daughters.

They milled about, went up as close to the howling front line boys as possible, wandered away, wondering if they would get them or not.

It was a carnival, nothing less, and in all of it you couldn't drum up a straw of sympathy for Jack Holmes and Thomas Thurmond.

But what was going on in the front lines? Darkness wrapped the alleyway and the boxlike old prison. Out of the darkness leaped another sound, the ominous sound of the iron pipe battering against the steel door. Cheers, cheers, cheers, and more blasting of the tear gas bombs, more staggering back by the men who held the ram.

Somebody said help is coming. San Francisco's and Oakland's inexhaustible supply of peace officers were speeding this way in automobiles and on motorcycles.

It must have got about by telepathy, the word traveling to the front lines as surely as it does in an army with phones hooked up to the bomb-proofs.

"Get 'em! Get 'em! The cops are coming!" galvanized the mob and the leaders to more strenuous efforts. Still the bricks beat like an interminable tropic rain on the jail walls and bars and steel door. Still the scene was plunged in darkness, blue darkness in which the slowly drifting smoke of the tear gas seemed to take the reflection from the very sky.

Another ram went into action, a bigger pipe. The leaders leaned as they strained at the great weight and in the darkness lunged at the door again. This time the double door gave way. It gave way with a tremendous crash that stirred an entire block to frenzy.

Into the front corridor went the leaders with their ram. Screaming madly for vengeance they had come at close quarters with the defenders, men they had known all their lives.

Across the corridor is a heavy, barred grating, with a door. This door was open. The ram went through the grating, tearing it from its moorings. On went the ram to the brick wall behind, where it stopped.

In the darkness below, in the no-man's land of a few minutes before, surged the mob, sending up yells in waves, like the ocean surf. It was a steady drum of sound, in which words were indistinguishable. In the second story window at this moment appeared two of the leaders. "We're getting 'em. . . . We're bringing 'em down."

If it was possible the sound from below rose to a greater volume. Those below could not get into the jail. There wasn't room for them in the narrow corridors and cells.

Whatever may be said, the men who occupied the jail stood by valiantly against overwhelming odds. They all knew one another, remember that, the mob and the officers. This was not a masked job.

Howard Buffington, veteran jailer, wept. He knew he was helpless before these men. They ran up the stairways, through the jail. No one could shoot them down. What is the law? No one had been hurt yet. Joe Walsh and Felix Cordray, all of them veterans, were helpless.

The mob knew where the prisoners were, and there was no chance of mistake. The mob leaders knew Thurmond and Holmes personally.

They went to Thurmond's cell on the third floor, the old northeast cell of David Lamson. Buffington went along with the leaders. They took the keys from Buffington. Thurmond, in mortal terror, was clinging to the grating in the toilet of his cell.

Then there occurred a scene probably never enacted before in a lynching in the history of America. The leaders prayed for Thurmond's soul.

They knelt in the jail cell, five or six of them, in the midst of the turmoil and the shouting, and they prayed to God Almighty for the man who was so soon to meet that God.

They arose with the whimpering prisoner, arms grasping him on either side and he stumbled down the stairs, tongue-tied with his last great terror.

The scene in the Holmes cell on the second floor of the prison was a different one. No one prayed for Holmes, believed to be the leader in the Brooke Hart slaying.

Holmes was also concealed in the washroom off his cell, and when the crowd went in he denied he was Holmes. With a last bravado, he shouted: "I'm not Holmes."

But his destroyers laughed at him. Too many of them knew him well. One man struck him in the face. "By God, you are!" shouted the men jammed in his cell. He fell to the floor. Grasping him by the feet they dragged him down the steps and out into the open, where Thurmond had just arrived.

For a moment there was bedlam about the jail. A few on the outskirts of the crowd shouted that one was the wrong man. But those next to the men knew whom they had.

There had been some howling in the jail for Tony Serpa, a youth recently convicted of manslaughter when he had been charged with murder. It was a short-lived cry. The mob leaders were not to be diverted from their purpose.

The snarling mob with their half-unconscious prisoners did not tarry before the jail. They moved with a kind of mindless precision from the alley beside the courthouse to First street, and across that street to St. James Park.

That movement across First street seemed instantaneous. One moment the men were in the jail alley and there was yet a ray of hope for them even though policemen were wandering away in a bewildered manner. The next moment the mob had the prisoners in the park, and their end had come.

A great murmuring went up from the thousands who thus far had taken little part in the actual seizure of Holmes and Thurmond. These spectators, men, women and children, streamed like a mighty tide toward the park. They climbed the statue of William McKinley, and they milled about, gorging the entire west side of the big park.

There was not the remotest doubt where the sympathy of these people lay. "String 'em up!" came from a thousand throats, from women as well as men, from grammar school boys, from business men with spectacles and from working men in rough garb.

There was some delay in getting a rope, some impatience from the crowd. Several men started climbing trees, and every such man was given a cheer. The light was dim in the park, but there were a couple of arc lights and hundreds of flash lights.

After a delay of almost 15 minutes, ropes were produced. Thurmond, who was at the south end of the park, was the first man to be hanged. He was benumbed with fear, and his crazed mutterings were without meaning.

Thurmond was hanged to a low limb. As his body was slowly

hoisted, the crowd broke into frantic cheering. Thurmond thrashed as he hung there, swaying to and fro, seeming to bend his body at the hips in a last spasm of life. For perhaps three minutes he swayed there, his face blackening, his tongue extended, although he was obviously unconscious.

"Brookie Hart—Brookie Hart," cried his executioners to the man who could no longer hear them. The taunts went on as the man's body dangled at the end of the rope, slowly turning, now this way and now that, as though some mocking power were giving all a full view of him.

The crowd ran hither and thither, children scampering to get a better look. Some children in arms were held 25 feet from the dangling man as the mob milled about and gave vent to cries of triumph.

Holmes' execution followed that of Thurmond but a few minutes. In a despairing voice, which was nevertheless clear, he kept denying that he was Holmes. As the rope was let down from a limb, he begged: "Don't string me up, boys. . . . Don't string me up." And finally in a last instant of resignation—for he had been held up by the crowd and must have seen Thurmond's body swinging 50 yards away—he admitted he was Holmes.

"Yes, I'm Holmes," he gasped, and held his head up, and in the next instant the noose dropped over it and with a cheer his body flung into the air.

Holmes did not struggle as long as did Thurmond. It seemed that that last relinquishment of hope had taken the life from him. While Thurmond still dangled, his feet even with the faces of the crowd, Holmes was thrown far into the air. The crowd gasped for a moment as it observed that his body was stark naked.

Now, as the men swung there, both playthings of the wind and the twisted ropes, many who had cried for their execution turned away. Several women fainted in the crowd, but there were thousands who did not faint; there were hundreds who looked on with smiles.

And the burden of all the talk was:

"Well there won't be any kidnaping in this county for a long time."

The dead men swung there. Some of the more violent spirits were for cutting them down and burning them with gasoline. Thurmond's trousers were stripped from him and some of the mob set fire to his coat, which burned for a few minutes.

The bodies hung in the park for almost an hour. Shortly before midnight came squads of San Francisco police officers. The crowd ran. These were the police for whom Sheriff Emig called when he ran out of tear gas about half an hour before his prisoners were seized. They were too late to save anything but the dead clay of the murderers.

★   ★   ★

Barbara Graham died as she had lived—in a tangle of emotional confusion. She was executed on June 3, 1955, in the gas chamber of San Quentin Prison for her participation in the bludgeon murder of a wealthy widow, Mrs. Mabel Monahan, in the Southern California community of Burbank in 1953. Barbara Graham's accomplices in that affair, Jack Santo and Emmett Perkins, died in the gas chamber, too, but as always, it was the prospect of a woman being executed that excited the morbid emotions of the California public. Some two years before the execution, reporter Carolyn Anspacher interviewed Barbara Graham in Los Angeles. Her report is in the great tradition of crime interviews—a blend of toughness, poignancy and insight.

Barbara Graham

Los Angeles
October, 17, 1953

At no time, in the whole of her 30 years, has Barbara Graham wanted more than the appearance of respectability.

"Let's get this straight," she said, "I went into everything with my eyes wide open. I'm not a poor little girl who was led astray. I've done what I wanted to do and I know the difference between right and wrong."

Mrs. Graham thinks it was "wrong" for a jury of nine men and three women to have convicted her of the first-degree murder of Mabel Monahan, a middle-aged Burbank widow. It was "wrong," because she insists she did not pistol whip Mrs. Monahan to death.

"I don't skittle with guns," she said.

Mrs. Graham acknowledges that she has done just about everything else during her lifetime. She was a runaway from her Oakland home at the age of 9. She was classified as "wayward" at 13 and "sexually promiscuous" at 15.

She was married four times. She bore three sons in between arrests for prostitution, perjury, vagrancy, lewd and lascivious conduct and disorderly conduct. She even "messed with the junk" in 1946, she said.

"I don't know why I did it," she said. "But I got high on marijuana and loaded on heroin and then I gave up. I liked myself too much. I didn't want to go that far down. I grant I'm not very up now, but being hooked on the junk is even worse than being hooked on a first-degree murder rap without recommendation for leniency."

Mrs. Graham, herself, feels that nothing she has ever done in the full sweep of her 30 years has been "too bad."

"I didn't hurt other people," she said.

She has no ready explanation for the fact that from her early childhood she was drawn to the lowest element of society. The first man with whom she ran away was a 35-year-old ex-convict. She was 13 at the time.

"I don't remember how I met him," she said. "Somebody must have introduced us."

In conversation with Mrs. Graham very little tenderness ever bubbles to the surface. She remembers the ex-convict with some affection because, she said, he never molested her. Her three sons, she said, are a "touchy subject." And she liked the few months she spent as a child at the convent of St. Mary's of the Palms in Mission San Jose.

"I went over the fence there, too," she recalls. "But it was only to pick fruit in the orchards. With anybody else it would have been just that—picking fruit. With me, it was running away."

Mrs. Graham doesn't remember just when she was at the Convent. It was sometime after her mother had put her in a foster home.

"It was at the home of a woman named Kennedy," she said. "The woman was mean to me. I let the parrot out, I remember, and it messed up a room. She stood me at the corner of the kitchen table, holding a raw onion under my eyes. I stood there for hours. I didn't move, not even to wipe my nose or eyes. The woman laughed.

"Then—it was on Halloween, I think—my mother and the man I always thought was my father came over. Papa brought presents and when he saw what was happening, he moved me out."

She is less definite about the number of times she was arrested for prostitution, lewd and lascivious conduct and vagrancy in San Diego, after her release from the Ventura school.

"I think it was twice," she said.

Told it was five times, the first in 1940, she grinned.

"No kidding?" she asked. "I can't remember. There was once that I pleaded guilty to prostitution because if I hadn't there would have been a Mann Act rap against a fellow I liked and I didn't want this to happen to him. Then there was another time when I was charged with vagrancy—but the five I sure as anything don't remember."

Mrs. Graham said she has had some periods of legitimate employment—most of them when she was on probation in San Francisco.

"I worked as a waitress in cocktail bars," she said. "I worked at a dime store and Western Union, delivering telegrams in the Monadnock Building in San Francisco. I worked for a while as a clerk at a private hospital in San Francisco and in a hospital in Tonopah, Nevada."

But, she said, she ultimately returned to jobs where she made more money quickly.

There was an interlude in San Francisco, she said, when she ran a call house for a friend who was sick and owed her money.

"I never was so bored in all my life—just sitting there answering telephones and sending girls out," she said.

Sex, Mrs. Graham said, has never interested her particularly, even though she has been involved with more men than she can remember. She does have a particular fondness for gambling—if there's enough money in it. She did well, she said, working as a dice girl in Chicago. She did better, she said, working for Emmett Perkins.

(Perkins and Jack Santo were convicted earlier this month with Mrs. Graham of the Monahan murder and sentenced to death. They

also are believed involved in a series of Northern California killings, including the murder of Guard Young, a Chester grocer, and
three small children.)

Mrs. Graham said she met Perkins in 1950, shortly after her
arrival in Los Angeles from San Francisco, where she had become
intimate with an ex-convict and suspected abortionist. Santo, she
said, she met for the first time early this year.

For nearly three years, Mrs. Graham said, she worked for
Perkins, who ran a gambling spot in El Monte, near Los Angeles.

"Poker, low ball and dice," she said. "I'd float out of the Bilt-
more Hotel, the Bel Air, the Roosevelt in Hollywood with fellows
who wanted to gamble and I'd just take them to El Monte. I'd work
in the bars usually—having a couple of drinks and just talking."

The work paid fine, Mrs. Graham said, and she enjoyed it.

"I had nice clothes and met interesting people," she said. "The
clothes I usually bought in San Francisco. I've always been a conservative dresser. I like good, plain clothes and that's why I pre-
ferred to shop in San Francisco. The clothes here in Los Angeles
are too fancy.

"What I did, usually, was to fly to San Francisco for the day. If
my shopping took longer than the one day, I'd stay at a big hotel
where there was an awfully nice old goat who always let me sign
his name to the checks."

Mrs. Graham said she was not particularly worried about staying
in San Francisco, even though a bench warrant was out for her
arrest there for breaking probation. She looked so respectable, she
said, that she was never suspected.

"Most of my friends down here thought I was just a nice married
woman getting a lot of alimony."

"God," she added in a whisper, "I wonder what they think now.
I bet they're dropping in their tracks."

Mrs. Graham says she can find no great difference between the
so-called good people and the bad people; the respectable and the
unrespectable.

"I've seen the best and the worst," she said thoughtfully.
"They're all the same under their clothes. Maybe the respectable
ones are a little worse because they don't get caught."

Mrs. Graham traces her anti-social attitude to inheritance as
well as environment. "How could I have been different with a

mother who was sentenced to Ventura when I was 2 years old?" she asked.

At the moment, Mrs. Graham said, she is in too great a state of shock and too unnerved to do any reading, even though she likes to. She did a lot, she said, during the three weeks she hid out with Santo and Perkins.

"Those two told me nothing," she said. "I was hiding because of two bum check raps here in Los Angeles and the San Francisco warrant. Santo and Perkins kept telling me they would straighten everything out with a lawyer they knew. I guess you'd call being with them guilt by association, but that isn't murder."

Mrs. Graham said she dyed her black hair honey blonde during her weeks with Perkins and Santo. She said she manicured her nails a lot and listened to records. Santo did the cooking, she said.

"I bought a lot of records. I particularly like Mozart and Stravinsky," she said.

She denies almost heatedly that she had an affair with Perkins, even though police said when the three were arrested Mrs. Graham and Perkins were in bed together.

"He looks like a weasel and, believe me, sex doesn't mean that much to me," she said.

"Emmett was always nice to me and I thought he was O.K. I didn't know Santo so well. Neither of them talked to me about any of their capers. Emmett particularly didn't believe in telling women anything.

"I'm glad I don't know any of those Plumas county characters and, as a matter of fact, I never heard Emmett or Jack mention any of them except the women Jack was going with. Harriet Henson and Bernardine Pearney. I had an idea the two men were involved in some activities, but I didn't know what they were. Now I do—and it's too late."

Mrs. Graham said she still can't believe she is in what she describes as "this mess."

"I usually have good control over my mind," she said. "But now I can't concentrate and I can't remember anything, and every night I take a million trips to the gas chamber.

"I don't know how that jury could have convicted me—even with the bum alibi I tried to fix because I was so frightened. I think Mr. Hardy, the lawyer the court appointed for me, did all right. Maybe he could not have done any better, and I wish I could get some money for him."

Mrs. Graham said she finds some solace in religion and goes to church every Sunday. "I'm no fanatic about it," she said. "But basically it helps."

Nothing, Mrs. Graham said, helps her to forget that a 24-hour suicide guard is being maintained over her.

"I'm not the kind to commit suicide," she said. "But if I have to spend the rest of my life in prison—if I have to serve more than seven years—I want it the way it is. I'll take the gas chamber. Maybe that will be better for my kids."

If she ever gets out of what she calls this "Monahan mess," Mrs. Graham said she would like to spend the rest of her life keeping house for her husband and little boy.

But she has very little hope that she'll get out of the "mess."

"The only way I can get any help," she said, "is if I say I did it— killed that old woman—and get my sentence commuted. But I'm not going to do it. I won't cop out. I won't come clean on something I didn't do.

"I'm not afraid of death. That is why I can sit here and tell you that I didn't kill Mabel Monahan. I've been what you'd call a bad girl. I've been that my whole life. But I swear that I never killed.

"Now get out of here before I bawl."

★   ★   ★

This is offered as simple proof that there are mighty and sacred traditions in journalism.

Girl's Own Story
(Love-too-well division)

January 10, 1894

Truly Shattuck, the pretty chorus girl, on account of whom Harry Poole was murdered last Sunday by her mother, consented to tell her story of the crime last evening.

Probably she never looked more beautiful when attired for the glare of the footlights than she did as she sat in the little sitting room of her home at 413 Stevenson street. Tears dimmed her brown eyes at frequent intervals while she was telling her story, and more than once her voice trembled with emotion.

But she had determined to tell all, even if it did bring blushes to her cheeks, and she admitted that she and Poole had loved not wisely, but too well. . . .

★   ★   ★

" 'Hot damn,' he said to himself. . . ."

When reporter Tom Mathews told a story there was hardly a fact left unturned. Not even what the people were saying to themselves.

As re-created by the mind-reading Mathews the piece of journalistic fluff that follows becomes a classic of amusing narrative. The perils of the big city are related, explained and turned into a highly moral fable.

If anyone should argue that the truth is being stretched too thin, let him prove that it wasn't *"Hot damn"* that Mr. Berger said to himself.

A Night with
Loretta

August 10, 1957

Little did Robert Berger know when he went to a swank Nob Hill restaurant that he would run into Loretta Barcroft, a sunny country girl who had proved her way with a sap.

Little did Harvey Holland know as he waited behind his apartment door that he was about to bang a longshoreman, not a big city lush.

And little did any of them know that haute monde restaurants are sometimes inhabited by lowbrow types.

Our characters are Loretta, 18, of 1029 Geary street, a girl with a pretty baby face and a taxi dancer's heart.

Robert Berger, 37, of 150 Haight street, a stevedore with arms big as a side of beef, a naked lady rippling on one and the American Flag waving on the other.

Harvey Holland, 27, of 1139 Geary street, a jobless shipping clerk, who discovered just how tough things can get.

Berger went to the bar of the Nob Hill restaurant to seek a night's diversion. Loretta went there, she said in her childish rhetoric, "to get a guy with a wad." Harvey stayed home, waiting for Loretta to bring home the bankroll.

Berger sat at the bar, waiting for something good and unattached. Loretta marched in, dressed to the nines in a tight, black suit she thought suitable for late evening occasions in such establishments.

Just three weeks ago she received a certain amount of attention for clobbering a middle-aged gentleman with a homemade sap made of a fishing weight, a sock and adhesive tape. She said she had just come from the country and carried the blackjack to protect herself against the very fate proposed by the man. Police piously turned her loose.

At the bar Loretta was refused a drink because she was unescorted. Berger, overhearing, put $5 on the counter and said, "She's with me." He had a week's pay plus overtime in his pocket.

Loretta beamed, and in the subdued light her creamy skin and white teeth seemed to promise the answer to Berger's quest. He sighed happily and bought her a handful of scotch and water at $1 a glass.

"How's about goin' up on Twin Peaks and look at the city and go to the beach," he suggested.

She agreed, but asked if they could stop by her apartment "so I can get into something more comfortable. I can have more fun."

Why, nothing could be better, Berger said, and they squeezed each other's hands as they went outside into the wind.

They drove to Holland's apartment, with Berger growing more euphoric by the minute. "Hot damn," he said to himself.

His uneasiness did not begin until Loretta tried three doors in the apartment house before finding the right one. He stood at the doorway. Puzzled, he saw her go to the far side of the room and fiddle with a lamp switch.

"Come in, come in, it's all right," she said.

"No ma'am," Berger said, being gentlemanly. "I'll keep the door open so you can see where the light is."

"Oh, I can find it. Come in," she said, playfully.

Berger stepped in. "Instead of seeing the lights, I saw stars," he said. "Something warned me and I turned. He hit me right on the top of the head. I went fuzzy."

It was then that Harvey discovered that Berger was not only tough, he was indestructible. He hit him seven times with a chair leg. Berger's knees didn't even buckle.

Berger said, "I told myself, 'Berger don't you fall down or you're done. This guy will kill you. You might even lose your $60.' "

The two fought silently, Harvey growing more panicky. "Help me, help me," he said to Loretta. "He's tough."

Loretta was rather single minded. "Did you get it? Did you get it?" she said, oblivious to the difficulties Harvey was having.

Harvey kept batting away to the accompaniment of Berger's grunts, and finally got him to the floor, one hand on Berger's throat and the other grasping the club. Berger held the club hand and let Harvey choke him. With his free hand he searched for the single-edged blade he habitually takes whenever he steps outside his door.

He once carried a switchblade knife. That became illegal and Berger obediently changed his custom.

His handkerchief was in the way, making it impossible to get at the knife. He held his breath, feigning unconsciousness, then let go Harvey's club hand, rolled over and came up with the blade. Harvey hit him a couple of times in the process, but then things started to go downhill for Harvey. Berger raked him so badly that it took 70 stitches to sew him up.

Berger also broke out a series of windows to attract attention on the street below. Harvey and Loretta decided to disengage. They fled as Berger stumbled to the street. Passersby called an ambulance and he was hospitalized briefly for treatment of extensive bruises, lacerations of the head and a cut finger.

Police followed Harvey's trail of blood to Loretta's apartment a block away. He was taken to Central Emergency Hospital for surgical embroidery.

Both he and Loretta were booked at City Prison for assault and conspiracy to commit assault. Said Harvey simply: "Man, I couldn't get out of there fast enough."

Loretta did not lose her sweet composure. "My goodness," she said, "I didn't even know what was going on."

★   ★   ★

For three days in May of 1946 Alcatraz was in a state of armed rebellion.

From the mainland it seemed that a small-scale war was being waged on the prison island. Gunfire could be heard. Puffs of smoke rose over the buildings. Flotillas of boats gathered in the bay. Units of United States Marines were sent in. The suspense and confusion were multiplied by the lack of official news from the authorities.

On May 4, the uprising was quelled. In an unprecedented action, Warden James A. Johnston permitted newspaper reporters to land on The Rock for a first-hand account of the revolt.

The Chronicle's man was Stanton Delaplane. He listened to the warden, toured the battle scene and then rushed back to the office. There was an hour left before the deadline for the out-of-town morning editions. This is the story that made that deadline.

It was also the first story to bear the Alcatraz dateline since the establishment of the Federal penitentiary there in 1934.

Rebellion on
The Rock

Inside Alcatraz
May 4, 1946

Warden James A. Johnston is telling his own story tonight.

How two-man electrical locks stopped Rufus "Whitey" Franklin, the escape artist.

How a lost key and a bullet-ducking guard stopped a long-planned break.

How Bernard Coy monkey-climbed the gun galleries and spread the bars with a home-made spread—made of brass toilet parts.

It's the first press conference on The Rock. And at the finish Johnston and Prison Director James Bennett led a tour through the cell blocks, nerve-tight with the aftermath of revolt.

"Hey, Saltwater Johnston," yelled the cons. "Tell 'em how you starved us for two days!" Johnston paid no attention.

In his own office, still littered with emergency equipment, white-haired Warden Johnston fought the three-day battle over again.

"About 2:30 Tuesday afternoon I got a ring from the armorer and he said: 'There's some trouble in the cell house. I don't know what it is, but I think it's bad.'

"I said: 'If you think it's bad, kick on the siren.' That means every man on the reservation, on duty or off, arms himself and comes running. Well, I am having lunch, but I grabbed my hat and was over in a jiffy.

"First thing I met was Associate Warden Miller coming out of the cell house. His eyes were watery and his face was black like you'd blacked it with lamp black. He said: 'There's somebody loose with a gun.'

" 'Do you know who it is?' I asked. He said: 'I think it's Coy.

" 'What happened to you?' I asked him.

" 'I heard there was some trouble,' Miller said. 'On the way in I grabbed a gas billy (a gas billy, the warden explained, is a club that you can use to club with or shoot out tear gas). I thought I saw an officer, but it was Coy.

"He said: 'You son of a bitch, I'm going to kill you!'

" 'Then he shot the gas billy back, bursting in my face.' "

Miller told the warden he had given the alarm.

"I can't raise the west gun gallery," said Miller.

"So we figured," Warden Johnston continued, "that Coy must have the gun in that gallery." In the high-ceilinged cement walls of the cell block, Johnston showed what he meant. The cells run three tiers high. There are three sets of tiers in one room. Blocks A, B and C. In another room, narrow and adjoining, is block D. It is cut off by cement walls, lanced by a pair of locked doors.

Block D is for bad boys. Escape artists—solitary. Across the whole building, crossways at the end, runs the gun gallery. The gun gallery is two levels high behind solid steel bars. It is completely away from the cell tiers, a catwalk stuck on the side of the wall.

From this lookout walk, the gun guard—the only man in the room with a gun—commands the long, sweeping corridors between the cell tiers.

"Now when we put a man up there he goes in from the outside," said Johnston. "You can't get in from the inside. You go from outside the building. A lieutenant in charge takes the relief guard through two doors. The first is barred. The second is solid steel with a bullet-proof view slit.

"You can't get in. But Coy did. We found that out tonight."

Here's how Coy did it.

Coy was a floor sweeper—outside the cells.

"He must have been planning this for a long time, he and Cretzer.

"The first thing these men do is case the joint. They case every guard looking for a weak place. They had Burch cased.

"The gun gallery has a door between the big room of A, B and C blocks and D block, too. Burch went through that door on his regular rounds—I want to emphasize that he was doing his regular duty. He went through the door and closed it on the lower level of the gun gallery. He was then in D block.

"Coy was working on the floor in the big cell block room. When no floor guard was looking, Coy just swarmed up those steel bars clear to the roof. You can see up there how the bars curve over, basket-shaped at the top.

"Where those bars were curved they were easiest to bend. They are cross-barred all the way up, you can see that. See?" said Johnston, pointing up to the gun galleries.

"Oh, Saltwater Johnston," sang a con from the cell house above. "Are the street cars still running in Frisco, Johnston?"

Johnston paid no attention. Above the floor guards moved around the catwalks outside the tiers.

"Coy had a home-made spreader made out of rods and screws from a toilet. Nobody knows how long he had it. Maybe months. He had a pair of pliers.

"When he put the ends of the rod between the bars and twisted the nut it forced the ends—and the bars—apart. He managed to spread those bars from five inches to seven inches with an 18-inch cross hatch." (The steel bars are cross-barred.)

"He ran down the ladder to the lower level. When the guard

came back he just slugged him. Coy then seized Burch's rifle and .45. Then he climbed back out the same way.

"Well, we didn't know whether the man on duty up there, Burch, was dead or alive. It was difficult to know what thing you'd do first.

"What had happened was Coy stuck up the floor guards and threw them into a cell. Then with Burch's keys he got into D block and stuck up the floor guards there. He opened the door for Cretzer, who got the .45 pistol. He let 19-year-old Carnes out. He let out Sam Shockley and Hubbard and I don't know how many more were running around loose. There were about 30 men in the big cell room and about the same in D block. All the tough guys in there.

"Coy ran to the kitchen window, sticking up Guard Stucker. Stucker made a break from the kitchen and got into the basement where he locked himself in with 18 cons.

"Coy began firing at the gun towers. You see if they could knock out two towers they had a clear run to the boats through the back door that leads into the yard. The guards ducked."

Meantime, Johnston was radioing San Francisco police and the Coast Guard for help. A hundred and fifty prisoners in laundries and shops were herded into the yard. Cretzer and Coy could see them through the locked back door—through the slit.

Stucker, from the prison basement, reported that Cretzer had the .45. He ran out of the way while Coy was shooting up the gun towers.

"Stucker said he could handle the 18 in the basement all right. Stucker handled himself magnificently. I want to say that.

"We got six prisoners herded that were in the kitchen. Dr. Clark, a relief doctor, and Dr. Farr, the dentist, were holed up with prisoners in the hospital. We couldn't get to them. We told them to stuff the keyhole and sit tight.

"Our gun gallery was out of control. You can see the way it commands everything," said Johnston pointing along the corridors.

"Tell de trut', de whole trut' and nuttin' but de trut', Johnston," said a convict grinning through the bars alongside.

"We sent guards Stites, Cochrane, Oldham, Mahan, Lieutenant Frank and Lieutenant Bergen to fight their way into the gun gallery from the outside entrance," Johnston went on.

Two men were to open the doors of the gun gallery and cover a man who was to enter. In 15 minutes we had to send a stretcher to bring Stites out. We just got him on the floor and before you could tell whether he was dead or alive they brought Cochrane out shot in the shoulder.

"We just got around to ripping the coat off Cochrane when they brought Mr. Maxwell out. His face was covered with blood. He said while he was covering Stites, he tried to shoot through the bullet-proof window slit and a ricochet hit him.

"Oldham, who was covering Stites, got shot himself.

"When Stites opened that door he was silhouetted at 30 feet. They couldn't miss. They were covering the door.

"Burch was lying up in the gun gallery behind the shield that covers the lower half of the lower tier. They had stripped his uniform off him and Coy was wearing the coat.

"Cretzer took two shots at him, saying: 'I'll kill you if you try to reach that phone!'

"They were in control of D block. But they missed the man they wanted—Rufus 'Whitey' Franklin.

"We know one man went with them—Sam Shockley. There were a dozen gas billies up in the gun gallery and they threw those down. Carnes had a knife he got in the kitchen.

"Cretzer knew the electrical system, all right, but he couldn't get somebody to work it with him. In D block the lower tier of cells is controlled so that two men have to pull separate switches to open them.

"When they couldn't get to Franklin, Cretzer said: 'Well, that ———— it all up.'

"Then he tried to find a key to the yard door. Guard Miller had thrown it away when he saw they were in trouble.

"Burch in the gallery heard Cretzer keep saying: 'That———— it up. San Francisco is just as far away as ever.' "

At the first hint of trouble, Johnston said they sent four men on the run. The men were unarmed since guards do not carry arms into the block—only into the gun gallery.

As they rounded the gun tier the convicts simply stuck up the guards and threw them into a cell. They had Burch cornered in the gun gallery, three floor guards in one cell, four rescue guards in another.

The still-blood-spattered cells are side by side at the end of C block, just below the gun gallery.

"By that time they had altogether Coy, Cretzer, Carnes, Tex Thompson, Marvin Hubbard and we don't know how many more running around.

"Cretzer made Sundstrom strip off his clothes in the cell. As he started to take off his pants his wallet fell out. Cretzer picked it up. It had $92 in it. Cretzer took it out and threw the wallet back in the cell.

" 'You can call this highway robbery,' he said.

"Then he stuck the .45 between the bars and said, 'You sons of bitches, we will kill you now,' and started shooting.

"They couldn't get the key away from Miller. That's why they shot him. The rest they shot to get rid of witnesses.

"We could see the door to D block was open and we had to send unarmed men in to close it. We just couldn't take a chance on their getting another gun. Those men had to walk the whole length of the cells through the corridors. They brought out those wounded men."

The cells from which they took them are 15 feet from the open D block where the convicts held the block.

All of the men were conscious when they got out. Sundstrom, who was missed by Cretzer's fire and played dead, walked out. So did Britow. The rest were dragged out. Warden Johnston displayed a scrap of white paper, pencilled by Sundstrom as he lay on the floor of the cell. It read:

"Cretzer killed or shot Joe Simpson in the stomach and chest twice and shot Baker also. He missed me so far." Then Sundstrom signed his name.

"Well," said Warden Johnston, "we learned the story from those men we brought out. We figured the man with the rifle was in D block. But we sent in another officer, Fred Roberts, and he was shot in the back. From the line of fire it could only have come from C block in the big, three-block room.

"We got Roberts out and sent him to the hospital. Maxwell washed the blood off his face and kept going. And the unarmed men who rescued the guards closed the door into D block."

Warden Johnston made no special mention of what it took for the guards who went unarmed in the dim light into those cell blocks.

At this point a flash bulb exploded with a firecracker pop. Everybody jumped and then laughed loudly in relief.

"The Marines asked if we wanted help, and when I said I could use 20 men to guard the prisoners in the yard, they came over zigzagging like it was Iwo Jima or something. They helped a lot.

"This Marine Buckner said he could help us with some stuff. So he got some grenades and he figured out the angles while Miller covered him with a rifle. He had to lob the stuff over one tier and drop it on the next.

"By Friday morning we began dropping stuff down the utility corridors in C block where we figured some of the men were holed up."

Johnston pointed out the geography of the battle. The cons in the upper tier responded with catcalls of "Saltwater, Saltwater."

A cell block consists of three double tiers of cells, facing away from each other. Between them runs a narrow corridor through which run steam and water pipes that feed the cells on either side. The corridor is open all the way up through the tiers.

By hiding at the bottom between walls, the convicts kept out of the line of fire. When the fire slacked off, they climbed the water pipes to outlets on upper tiers. From these tiers they fired on guards and then dropped down again.

"We got the men in from the yard and locked them up," said Johnston. "And we got help from other Federal prisons. Some guards were flown in to relieve our men who were worn out."

We got Thompson and Shockley and Carnes. They lost their nerve and got back in their cells when they saw it was all up. They are in solitary now saying they didn't have anything to do with it.

"We knew Coy and Hubbard and Cretzer were in the C block utility corridor, still able to get up in the tiers and fire. We stationed guards at each end where steel doors close the corridors. One man would jerk the door open and we'd fire a shotgun blast down the corridor. Then we'd slam the door.

"Between times we'd drop fragmentation grenades down in there.

"This morning we started to go in shortly after daylight, one officer pulling the door open and two blasting down the corridor. That was about 7:30."

At 9:45 A.M. officers went crawling in the dark over the pits (the floor of the corridor is simply cross beams, four feet apart with a 30-inch drop between beams. The corridor is about two and a half feet wide).

"At about that time," said Johnston, "we pulled out Coy. He was like this (Johnston put his hands up as though holding a rifle). The rifle was beside him and rigor mortis had set in. He was still wearing the guard's coat.

"A few feet beyond we found Cretzer with the pistol beside him. We think they were both dead last night.

"Hubbard we found by himself. He was the last to die. I suppose he lay there all night waiting for it. He was still limp.

"Coy must have stopped a shotgun blast just as he was getting ready to fire.

"All they had at any time was a rifle with 50 rounds and a pistol with 21 rounds. They threw down gas masks and billies from the gun gallery but they didn't have any more guns.

"Until tonight we thought Coy snaked that gun through the bars of the gallery some way. We just found the spread bars."

Director of Prisons Bennett accompanied the press party through the cells. Most of the convicts lay on their bunks. Bennett said the prison was "Light." "You'd be nervous, too."

The walls are marked with fire and the bloodstained blankets are lying on the bunks where Cretzer shot up the guards. Nobody went into D block. It was still too hot, they said.

"Sometimes they get started throwing stuff between the bars."

Another gun guard walked along the catwalk where Burch was slugged. A few cons crowded the bars to see the flashbulbs go off.

One yelled: "Hey, Saltwater, you gonna get your pitcher in the paper?"

"Let's get out of here," said Bennett.

The first press conference on Alcatraz was over.

★   ★   ★

The road to the White House is not an easy one.

Look, for instance, at this page one headline on the twenty-sixth of January, 1953:

EXCLUSIVE!

BRUTAL, FILTHY
JAILS EXPOSED

CHRONICLE REPORTER DOES
TIME, TELLS INSIDE STORY
OF CRUEL, CROWDED CELLS

Under that headline there was this amplification:

> *Last year more than 600,000 Californians were locked up in city or county jails.*
>
> *One might be a teen-ager in until his parents can raise the money to pay his fine for a traffic violation. Another, a professional killer waiting two months for his trial to begin. Or another, a bookmaker serving a year.*
>
> *Often they serve their time together—in filthy tank cells, ruled by con bosses.*
>
> *A Chronicle staff writer, under an assumed name and unknown to his jailers as a reporter, did time in two of these jails and studied many more up and down California. This is his documented report of a scandalous and dangerous condition too long ignored.*

The Chronicle staff writer's assumed name was Peter Emil Flick. His real name, unknown at that time to his jailers and many other people, was Pierre Salinger.

The Ordeal of Emil Flick

January 26, 1953

I heard a heavy jail door clang behind my back two weeks ago.

A Stockton policeman firmly led me by the arm to a battered desk. An inmate trusty looked at me unsmilingly and said: "Empty your pockets on the desk."

Out came my wallet, a comb, $2.32, a 25-cent mystery thriller, and my watch. The trusty shoved most of the stuff in an envelope, gave me back 32 cents and my comb. I signed a pink booking slip and was shoved into a dimly-lit cell.

Seventeen men were in that cell, lying on a slatted wooden floor with no mattresses, no blankets. The odor of dirty feet, dirty bodies, and stale urine permeated the small, concrete-walled cage. An open toilet sat in the corner of the cell. In another corner, a man slowly moved and retched on the floor. He then turned over and went back to sleep.

In the next seven days which I spent in two of California's county jails, I witnessed brutality, filth and degradation.

I ate inadequate meals. I paid inmate trusties for some decent food or a pack of real cigarettes. I saw men go out of jail and come back the next day because they had no money, no place else to go.

And I got a thorough education in several criminal lines. A check passer on his way to San Quentin told me how to beat the banks on bum checks. A narcotics addict told me the joys of a first marijuana cigarette. A 22-year-old youth told me how to get high on nembutal pills. And a five-time loser told me how to write a writ of habeas corpus and beat the law.

The two jails where I spent my time were picked because they are typical of an antiquated jail system in California—a jail system which annually turns out new criminals to rob our banks, burglarize our homes, rape our daughters, or traffic in narcotics.

As Attorney General Edmund G. Brown said recently: "These county jails are the breeding grounds of crime. They set the feet of petty first offenders on the road to serious offenses against society."

The San Joaquin County Jail at Stockton, where I spent my first four days, was built in 1870 to house 75 men and women. The day I entered there were about 250. It held 512 prisoners last September 29.

By secret arrangement, I was "arrested" on a small side street in Stockton, where I was asleep in an automobile. After being frisked by two police officers I was hustled into a squad car and taken to the jail.

After being booked at the jail as "drunk and hold" I was shoved into Tank 8 to spend my first night.

Most of the 17 men there were asleep. A few sat wordlessly in the semi-darkness. I leaned against the bars for a moment looking around the cell. There were three windows, all heavily barred. The floor was covered with duckboards. I took off my jacket, laid it on the floor and used it for a pillow. . . .

Peter Emil Flick's four days in the San Joaquin Jail continued mean and ugly. Salinger spared no detail as he told of the indignities that befell him. But by the time of his second incarceration in Bakersfield later that same week he was already a good deal more conwise. Thus his report on the Kern County Jail provided less shock and more calm understanding. In many ways it was a more effective piece of exposé reporting.

February 3, 1953

A man, moaning loud outside my cell block, woke me suddenly that Saturday night in the Kern County Jail at Bakersfield.

I glanced at my watch. It was shortly before 3 A.M.

Looking through the bars of our cell block you could see the shining red neon lights of the Hotel El Tejon in downtown Bakersfield and a flashing Coca Cola sign.

Then I heard the moan again, this time accompanied by an unmistakable thud of fist against flesh. The sound of the fist hitting the man continued, each time followed by another sharp moan or sob. It lasted about five minutes.

I never found out exactly what happened. But somewhere in the jail a man was severely beaten that night.

I don't know who did it. Maybe it was some trusties. Or maybe it was prisoners beating another prisoner. Or maybe it was the guards beating another prisoner.

The man's piteous moans awoke practically everyone in our cell block. I heard a man say: "You stupid S.O.B. Now you've marked him up for life."

Saturday had started out as an uneventful day. A sharply ringing bell woke me just after 5 A.M. It had been a sleepless night. You don't sleep much on a thin metal chow table in a fully lighted cell block.

The first morning ritual was the cleaning out of a dozen tin cans and placing them near the cell door. These were for what is passed off as coffee, a weak, brown liquid whose single virtue is that it is hot.

The old time inmates of the cell had this coffee business down to a science. They put out extra tin cans—and these cans were filled with coffee by the trusties for 25 cents each.

Later in the day the prisoners lit fires in their cells and warmed up the coffee. The men in "Left 3", our cell block, were eternally grateful to the church people, who came in three times a week, for at least one thing. They left plenty of religious tracts which made good burning for warming up the coffee.

Three men went out at 7 A.M. Saturday. That's release time. It meant I got a bunk, so I moved in below Jack Allen's bunk. Jack was a Texas-Oklahoma ex-con with a "legal mind." He had a lot of tips about courtroom procedure and habeas corpus and various other practical things like that.

Jack was worried about his girl friend. She had just been released from the women's section of the jail that morning after serving a 30-day sentence for drunkenness. "I know she's having a good time out there, but, man, I hope it's not too good."

The other boys in the cell knew about Jack and his gal. So they phoned up a letter from her and had it brought in by a trusty. Old Jack read the letter over and over. Several hours later, he compared it with a previous letter from the same girl. He decided the handwriting didn't match.

Lunch was the biggest meal of the day. It was served at 11 A.M. We had half of a Spanish-type sausage, potatoes, a few beans and grits. The sausage was very heavily peppered. It took several glasses of water to cool down the inside of my mouth and I was still tasting it some hours later.

One of the men showed me a bag of "goof balls"—a drug—he had gotten from somewhere. "Want to try some?" he asked. I didn't.

Another of the men in the cell block had a medicine bottle filled with muscatel wine. He took a swig every once in a while, but didn't offer any to anyone else.

The highlight of the afternoon was more church services. This time a group accompanied by an accordion. After this, at 4:30, we got the evening bowl of soup.

We were sitting around talking and playing cards when the cell door opened and a well-dressed young man was shoved inside. It turned out he was from the Bay Area, arrested there, and on his way to San Diego to meet charges made by his ex-wife when he was late with his alimony.

He and I found a checker board, used some pink pills, pennies and nickels, and played chess. It was the cause of some comment.

We finally went to sleep about midnight. It was during this night that I was awakened by the loud moans of the man being beaten. Later in the night one of the alcoholics in our tank suffered a severe attack of delirium tremens. He walked around the tank, shaking and muttering. He woke up Contreras, a tough-talking ex-convict. "Get out of here, you bastard, or I'll cut your heart out," Contreras told him. The alcoholic went back to his own corner. He cowered there in the semi-darkness, mumbling to himself through the early dawn hours.

Sunday was the big day for seven of us. We were getting out. For six, our time was up. A seventh had come to me and begged me to buy him out. He needed $6 or he would have to do three more days. He was in for being drunk in an automobile. He had a job in San Bernardino, he said, if he could get there.

I gave him the $6 and he went out. He had said he would pay it back in about an hour. He told me the place where he would meet me. But he never showed up. I didn't much blame him. A man is so happy when he gets out of jail he just wants to get far away.

It was the same way with me. As I walked out of the "Casa Blanca" and down Q street in Bakersfield, I heard one of my old cellmates shout: "Have a good time, kid. Write us about it."

★　　★　　★

What with San Quentin so near at hand, the execution story has long been a staple of San Francisco journalism. The formula once was simple—you recorded every moment of the last day, every morsel of the last meal, every sign as the noose tightened. For dramatic effect it is a formula that can still hardly be faulted.

But the account here—of the untidy end of killer Burton Abbott —followed a more unusual course. The focus was not on the condemned man. Instead reporter Art Hoppe chose to look at the death chamber audience and, somewhat more obliquely, at all of us.

Execution, 1957

March 16, 1957

They came to see Burton Abbott die. There were 53 of them— official witnesses. All were men. Women are not allowed to see a condemned man die.

Fifteen were newsmen, there because they had to be there. The others were college students from San Jose, law enforcement officers, off-duty San Quentin guards, attorneys and just plain curious. Each had a written invitation. The presence of 12 official witnesses at executions is required by law.

They gathered in front of the main gate to San Quentin at 9 A.M. yesterday. No one was late. They stood there, waiting, laughing and joking as men do to hide their nervousness. A chill southwest wind sent rain clouds scudding through the sky and whipped the men's raincoats about their legs.

They lined up and made the long walk from the main gate to the entrance to the prison proper—exchanging quips as they passed the neatly clipped green lawns, the carefully pruned rose bushes and the clumps of Shasta daisies bending in the wind. The whitecaps danced on San Quentin bay.

"Will you deliver this hacksaw to Mr. Abbott for me?" said one man, and everybody laughed a little.

There were fewer jokes as the witnesses neared the squat little building that houses the gas chamber. The word came that a stay had been granted until 11 A.M. The sigh was almost audible.

"Guess maybe he won't need the hacksaw after all," one man said timidly, and there were a few chuckles.

The witnesses were herded into the employees' coffee shop, a small, modernistic structure with floor-to-ceiling windows overlooking the bay, located directly across a wide expanse of pavement from the ugly gas chamber building.

In the warm, steamy atmosphere the tension thawed. The men sipped their coffee, a little quickly at first, and then leaned back, discussing this latest stay.

The hour passed. The witnesses struggled back into their raincoats and were led across the pavement to the guards' recreation room, adjacent to the gas chamber building. Each signed his name in the official log. The witnesses stood in little groups, smoking and chatting, but sudden silences would fall. Around 10:45 most of the men, without being asked, gradually lined up near the exit and talked in lowered voices.

The hands of the big electric clock on the wall crept slowly past 11 A.M. Men asked irritably what the delay was, their brows furrowed, eyes angry.

At 11:08 Lieutenant W. A. Wagoner led the witnesses outside and lined them up between two rows of guards for the march to the gas chamber. "You're out of step," one man said to his partner half-heartedly, but no one grinned. A few drops of rain began to fall.

As the men went through the heavy steel door into the witness room they removed their hats and the few that had anything to say spoke in whispers, as though they were in church. Each man shuffled hurriedly to the rail that surrounds the glass-windowed chamber to get the best spot left.

A short, prematurely bald man leaned over the rail, staring intently at the empty chair, chewing quickly on his gum. A young, curly-haired man with tired-looking eyes glanced once and then gazed at the floor near his feet.

The door to the chamber clanked open and Abbott was led in. The crowd of witnesses stirred as though a wind had blown through. Most craned their necks or stood on tiptoe to catch a glimpse of the condemned man's face.

The door clanked shut. One older man stood, staring intently with his mouth half open and his hand raised, as if he had been frozen in the act of declaiming something. The balding man's jaws stood still, his gum forgotten. The young, curly-haired man looked more intently at his own feet. He swallowed.

There was a faint rattle and clank of machinery as the cyanide pellets dropped into the sulphuric acid.

The condemned man's head slumped and he jerked against his straps. The witnesses in the back rows strained and stretched for a better view. A middle-aged man in front twisted his body slightly from side to side as though to escape the deadly fumes.

The telephone rang.

The only telephone in the building is a small, black wall phone without a dial. It hangs on the other side of the gas chamber where the prison officials stand, where the machinery is. It never rings unless there has been a last-minute stay of execution.

It had never rung too late before.

It only rang once—a short ring, maybe two seconds. The sound echoed faintly through the steel walls out to the witness room. Only a few heard the ring. Only a few knew what it meant. Most of the witnesses did not hear it at all.

The condemned man's head fell forward on his chest and the minutes ticked off.

The witnesses began to shift from foot to foot and whisper to each other. One man cleared his throat. Another coughed. The balding man began chewing his gum again.

There were more whispers. A man with glasses walked around the outside of the crowd to the other side of the witness room for a look from a different angle. Heads turned to watch him pass.

"That's all, gentlemen," said Associate Warden Charles White. "11:18—11:25," he added and the newsmen jotted down the times of the dropping of the pellets and the pronouncement of death.

The witnesses slowly moved to the door, their shoes scraping on the cement floor. The sun had come out and the reflection on the rain-wet pavement outside was brilliant. "Seven minutes," said one. "That's pretty fast."

No one else said anything for a few moments. An older man took off his glasses and wiped them carefully. "It makes you sort of. . . ." But he couldn't think of the words he wanted.

Those who smoked lit their cigarettes, cupping their hands against the breeze. Overhead a few seagulls wheeled and turned.

The invisible cyanide fumes were being flushed out of the chamber by powerful blowers and up through the tall smokestack overhead. As the fumes hit the cold outside air, they turned white— a little white puff that was quickly torn to pieces by the wind.

One of the witnesses saw it. "Well, there goes the last of Abbott," he said.

No one laughed.

★   ★   ★

The script for this story was written in advance. The assignment given reporter George Draper was to cover a murder trial in Downieville—with the accent on Downieville rather than the courtroom.

With the filing of Draper's first story it was clear that he had struck a rich vein. Downieville and its people were a rare slice of Americana.

The portions of Draper's daily stories chosen here offer a fair sample of the tone and direction of his unusual reporting. The trial scenes are omitted and abridged on purpose. If the reader feels he would like to know more about the testimony and such, rest assured that it hardly matters.

Justice
in the
High Sierra

Downieville, Calif.
February 14, 1960

Larry Lord Motherwell, a courtly easterner with an amateur interest in the elderly, is about to go on trial for his life in this dwindling Gold Rush town of 347 souls.

Not since Rose Cooper provided an alternative to the tedium of gold-panning by opening a bordello here in 1851 has this remote Sierra community experienced such a hullabaloo. Two main-drag saloons are laying in extra supplies of grog out of humane consideration for thirsty witnesses, lawyers, jurors and mountaineer spectators. Even the two motels are booked solid for the fashionable Motherwell trial season. And lodgings, as they once were referred to in these parts, are harder to find than a gold nugget.

The click of poker chips in the back rooms of the saloons has been drowned out lately by raised voices psychoanalyzing the prize boarder in the six-cell county jail. What the cracker-barrel philosophers of Downieville are asking one another is this:

Is Larry Lord Motherwell a 43-year-old Lothario who trifled with the affections of Pearl Putney, a wealthy widow, and then killed her on a lonely logging road near here?

Or is Larry Lord Motherwell a clean-cut, Bible-quoting crap shooter, who performed a great favor for the 72-year-old widow by squiring her on a "last fling" of the West?

Motherwell has quietly maintained that whenever he and Mrs. Putney registered at motels as man and wife he was invariably the sole occupant of the bed.

"She liked to sit up in a chair all night and rock herself to sleep," was his gallant reference to their domestic arrangements.

Assistant State Attorney General Lynn Compton, who is here to beef up the prosecution, describes Motherwell as "an inveterate con man."

"He romances people and takes their dough," said Compton. "He hasn't worked for several years, but he's lived pretty good."

Motherwell's murder trial is being held here because Downieville is the county seat of Sierra county.

The only reason Downieville exists at all as a point on the map of a mountain wilderness is because a salmon once coughed up a gold nugget here and the man who hooked the fish struck it rich. That was in 1849, and a sympathy for the bonanza concept has lingered in these parts ever since.

Consequently, Motherwell is held in some respect locally—since the State contends he struck it rich when he staked out a claim on the wealthy widow.

Pearl Putney was the widow of Professor Albert Putney, former dean of the Department of Political Science at American University in Washington, D.C. She was captivated by the charms of the courteous Motherwell, and before long, she introduced him to friends as "my stepson, Dr. Motherwell." Not long after that,

Motherwell and Mrs. Putney were touring the west in a pink and gray car and registering at motels as "Dr. Larry Lord Motherwell and wife."

This, apparently, was only a technicality, because Motherwell's third wife, Josephine, was keeping the home fires burning back in Washington.

On August 14, 1958, Mrs. Putney and Motherwell checked into a motel at Marysville, about 100 miles west of here. They checked out the next morning and Mrs. Putney was never seen again. On her travels she was known to be packing a bag with $50,000 in cash and bonds.

One day after he left Marysville, Motherwell sent a telegram from the San Francisco airport to Mrs. Putney's relatives in Chicago. The telegram mentioned wedding plans, a Caribbean cruise and a Mexican honeymoon and was signed "Pearl."

Early in 1959, Motherwell was seen squandering money at the gaming tables at Las Vegas and police picked him up for questioning. He had a $1700 bankroll.

No, he said, he hadn't seen Mrs. Putney since last August. Police ended up by shipping him to Frederick, Md., where a grand jury was investigating him for a murder back there, a rap that he beat.

Motherwell then dropped out of sight. There were reports that he had joined forces with a 60-year-old snake charmer.

But last August Mrs. Putney's skull was found in Sierra county by a lady out hunting mushrooms, and the FBI promptly picked up Motherwell in Atlanta, Ga. He was living in a boarding house under the impressive name of Craig Dubar Foster. In his pockets were various papers indicating he might have $1 million on deposit in various foreign banks.

Sherriff Dewey Johnson of Sierra County brought the proverb-quoting Motherwell back to Downieville in handcuffs, fed him huge stacks of hot cakes for breakfast and fattened him up for the approaching trial.

Motherwell is optimistic about the quality of mountain justice. "I think I'll come through this thing with flying colors," he said.

Within a stone's throw of his little cell are the old gallows where horse thieves were hanged until 1874. And just down the block is Durgan Flat Bridge, crossing the North Fork of the Yuba River at the heart of town, where Juanita, a Spanish woman, was lynched in 1851 after knifing a miner.

Could there be another Downieville lynching?

"Oh, no, said Sheriff Johnson, "nothing like that."

Downieville, February 29

The "Good Luck" gold mine claim was posted today as grand prize for the winner of the great Downieville trial.

Pub keeper Jim Dick tacked up the deed to the 20-acre diggings on the wall of his Roaring Gold saloon on Main street.

One of these days, perhaps two weeks from now, the "Good Luck" deed will be presented either to Larry Lord Motherwell or the man he's feuding with, District Attorney Gordon I. Smith.

"Maybe it ain't much of a claim—nothing like the 'Cat's Whiskers' or the 'Deadbroke' or the 'Mad George'—but I'll guarantee you there's gold there if a man'll dig for it," said saloon keeper Dick.

Offering of the grand prize highlighted the sporting nature of the mountain mystery unfolding in this Sierra hamlet.

Neither Motherwell nor the district attorney appeared particularly eager to own a gold mine.

"What's Dick trying to do, give me a case of lumbago?" Motherwell asked when told of the award.

The amiable confidence man, locally known as His Lordship, said he could think of better things to do than digging gravel when he gets out of jail.

District Attorney Smith, a non-athletic former bank teller from Marin County, also appeared stunned at the prospect of having to dig up 20 acres of steep mountain land.

Whoever wins the trial and gets the deed from the saloon keeper will have to perform $100 worth of labor a year to keep the property. Those are the rules of the claim.

While the "Good Luck" was being posted as the grand prize, several more prosecution witnesses were called today to build the circumstantial case against Motherwell. . . .

Downieville, March 1

Storm clouds rolled up behind the high Sierra buttes today and the electricity in the air made the old timers kind of edgy.

"Why this feller Motherwell is settin' there in the jail eatin' twice as much as a horse," complained Buckshot Johnson.

Johnson, a mountaineer known for his good humor, was in a grumbling mood because of the weather and the shaky state of Sierra county finances due to Larry Lord Motherwell's murder trial.

The trial has just about drained the local treasury and the Board of Supervisors held an emergency session today to see whether a little more cash could be raised.

"Hell bells," said Buckshot, "why should the county be paying $2.50 a day to feed His Lordship?"

"A man's got to eat," cut in Drifter Malloy, a stocky gold miner with ear muffs.

"Then let him go down to the creek like the rest of us and snipe for nuggets," Johnson replied.

During the depression thousands of unemployed workers from the big cities came to this Sierra hamlet of 347 inhabitants to pan gold. Even today most of the residents do a little "sniping."

The suggestion of the old timers that Motherwell be allowed to earn his daily grubstake by panning in the river behind the courthouse was met with a snort of indignation from Sheriff Dewey Johnson, a crusty mountaineer himself. "We may be simple up here, but we're not stupid," the Sheriff said. He made clear that he meant by this remark that the cost of a deputy to guard Motherwell down at the river would far exceed the $2.50-a-day to feed him.

While these important matters were being thrashed out on Main street, the prosecution continued to weave a web of circumstantial evidence around His Lordship. . . .

Downieville, March 2

A hip-swinging Costa Rican known as "Sweet Anita" Palmer tossed a Cha Cha Cha party last night to celebrate the halfway mark in the Larry Lord Motherwell murder trial.

While the children slept and the old timers curled up in their bedrolls in this mountain hamlet, the casa Anita rocked to the beat of the Merengue, the Rhumba, the Cha Cha Cha and the Guaracha.

The exuberant proprietress of the Motor Inn swiveled and shimmied and shook, while three of her Costa Rican admirers blew their lungs out on the harmonica. "Now we have party every night until the trial's over," said the beaming Anita, whose motel has been jammed with prosecution witnesses for the last two weeks.

In contrast to the excitement of Anita's soiree last night, Motherwell's trial today was a tame affair. His Lordship, as he is referred to by the natives, even appeared bored as a Las Vegas detective read in a droning voice from the transcript of an interview with the defendant. . . .

Downieville, March 7

A gray-eyed gold "sniper" named Ed Reiswig stuck his thumbs in his belt today and delivered a gentle dissertation on the morals and manners of Larry Lord Motherwell.

Reiswig, in his less glamorous role as janitor of the county courthouse, has enjoyed an unrivaled opportunity to converse with and observe the leading man in the big murder trial here.

On his days off, this kindly janitor prospects for gold, rambling over this mountain country that is so steep the old timers say you can see the cows coming home by looking up the chimney.

"One thing I've noticed about His Lordship," Reiswig said, "is that he's a very considerate man.

"Now you take the first day his trial started and the courtroom was packed like a powder tin. There were a lot of cigarette butts and the usual mess.

"So that afternoon when the court is over and I'm getting ready to clean up the place, why Larry comes over to me.

" 'Ed,' he says, 'I'm the cause of all this mess and I know it's making a lot of extra work for you. If the sheriff will let me I'd be glad to help you clean it up each night.' "

Reiswig drew a small bottle of gold nuggets from his pocket and rattled it affectionately.

"He's a likeable man," the gold "sniper" said, "but that's the trouble with those confidence men. You get where you begin to trust them and they give you the business."

. . . Today, a not unattractive spinster of 32 summers told a bizarre story of her motel-hopping with Motherwell only months before he was off and away with the wealthy Mrs. Putney.

Marie Colley, a shapely brunette with a syrupy Southern drawl and a triste look in her dark eyes, said she was a Central Intelligence Agency secretary of "good morals" until she met Motherwell in late 1957.

Although she knew he was married and even knew his wife, she said, she could not resist darting off to Florida with the amiable man on a secret mission. Motherwell told her, she said, that his business was so dangerous and secret he had to be watched around the clock by a bodyguard known as The Dagger.

Their cozy life in a little Miami, Fla., apartment was rudely disrupted, she said, when Motherwell went away and she received a telegram that he was dead.

"It said he had died and his ashes had been spread over the Everglades. And it was signed: The Dagger," she related forlornly.

Miss Colley said she packed her bags and returned to her native Virginia, and then one day Larry suddenly showed up.

"He said the telegram was an error. His twin brother was killed," she said.

Miss Colley was so glad to see the reincarnated confidence man that she left with him again, this time on a long trip to California.

Downieville, March 8

The Sunshine Club bench on Main street was deserted today because all the old timers drifted up to the court house to see Larry Lord Motherwell on the witness stand.

Honorary Mayor Tony Lavazolla led the procession across the rusty Durgan Flat bridge to the courtroom.

Elsewhere in this county seat of 347 people, Motherwell's appearance on the witness stand caused similar flurries of interest.

Guests at the Riverside Motel, for instance, found signs on their doors saying: "Make your own damn beds. We've gone to the trial."

And at the rival Motor Inn, "Sweet Anita" Palmer chucked her duties as proprietress to don her Sunday best and head for the court house.

The forthright Mountain Messenger hit Main street, meanwhile, with a big extra devoted almost entirely to the Motherwell murder mystery.

"This is the biggest story that ever broke in Downieville," said editor Gene Stowe.

In order to read the Messenger's nine solid columns of print on the big trial, Bob Hofsteter, chief of the volunteer fire department, made a hurry-up trip to Marysville for a new pair of glasses. . . .

Downieville, March 10

A clear crisp mountain morning broke over this high Sierra hamlet today.

There was a bit of nip in the air, so the mountaineers rolled out on the double, stoked up the home fires and gallantly served coffee in bed to their women.

"I figure it's a man's job to be first out of the sack," explained a strapping lumber jack as he strode down Main street inhaling the fresh mountain air.

Old timers are divided, and with some degree of passion, on the subject of when the custom of serving coffee in bed to Downieville's damsels began.

Buckshot Johnson, for instance, insists Major William Downie first made the grand gesture way back in 1849.

"Holy smoke," exclaimed Drifter Malloy, his partner, "everybody knows there weren't no women along when the major first came up the creek."

"That's not what I heard tell from the old timers," Buckshot snapped.

"Unless it was a squaw he brewed java for," Drifter replied with a sly wink.

At any rate the argument has been stewing here for nearly a dozen decades, interrupted occasionally by vital questions such as the current one of whether Larry Lord Motherwell's mountaineer jury will hang him on circumstantial evidence.

"Why most places they want to see a murder weapon, a gun or something," said Norm McGreggor, a prospector.

Plenty of other mountain men shy at circumstantial evidence and one buckaroo in the Roaring Gold saloon said he'd lay 50 silver dollars that "His Lordship will walk away free."

At the Downieville post office, meanwhile, postmistress Marie Hinton sorted the mail and found the daily letter Motherwell receives from his wife, Josephine, in Washington, D.C.

Motherwell, an eminent philanderer and fraud, reciprocates by penning a daily note of love to Josephine.

And over at the court house the hotshot prosecutor imported from Los Angeles began his closing argument against Motherwell. Lynn Compton, a former UCLA football hero, stuck his thumbs in his belt and spoke of himself as "a lousy lawyer" who wanted to talk "a little good old common sense" to the jurors.

Defense Attorney Jack Reges yawned, and in other subtle ways attempted to convey obvious ennui over this display of folksy logic. . . .

Downieville, March 12

The mystery of the Alpha Derrer gold mine was being hashed out on the Sunshine Club's bench on Main street today while Larry Lord Motherwell's attorneys unfolded their concluding arguments to the jury.

In a nutshell, the mystery concerns a missing 1700 ounces of gold and the question of whether the Alpha Derrer's caretaker, William Black, was murdered or committed suicide.

George Bachels, one of the last practicing full-time gold miners in California, raised the issue of the Alpha Derrer mystery because it involves circumstantial evidence just as the Motherwell case does.

Bachels met Black and saw part of his gold hoard just before his body was found in 1942.

"I was a young buck then," said the jolly Bachels, "and I was making $4 a day packing meat on snowshoes from Goodyear's Bar up to the Ruby mine.

"The Alpha Derrer was just over the ridge from the Ruby and Sheriff Dewey Johnson asked me to swing over the ridge to Black's cabin and see if the old man was okay.

"Black came to the door hale and hearty, and asked me in. Then he brought out a quart jar that was half full of high grade. He told me the people he worked for owed him about $300 in back wages, so he'd started prospecting on his own and found a rich pocket down the creek."

A few days after that visit, Bachels said, word reached Downieville that old Black was dead.

The death was discovered by the owner of the mine, W. A. Derrer, who paid a visit to his diggings after receiving a letter from Black saying he had 1700 ounces of gold. He found the mustachioed Black in bed, a .38 Winchester by his side, a bullet through the center of his chest and a blanket neatly covering his body.

"There wasn't a trace of that quart jar with that gold," said Bachels.

After a brief inquest conducted by Justice J. W. Robbins, a verdict of suicide was reached.

Then Justice Roberts opened a new area of inquiry. "In this instance," he said, "the story has been circulated that the deceased had considerable gold, and we will now endeavor to clear this up."

Justice Robbins called as witness Tom Bessler of Goodyear's Bar, who wrote the letter for Black that mentioned the 1700 ounces of gold. Bessler explained that he often wrote letters for Black because the old miner was unable to read or write.

When Black asked him to mention the 1700 ounces of gold, Bessler said, he interrupted the old man. "I said to Bill, 'You must have made a mistake. If that is true, you have a fortune.'

"He said, 'Write just like I tell you, 1700 ounces,' and I wrote it just like he told me."

But Justice Roberts observed finally that Black's letter mentioning the gold hoard was "rambling," and he hinted that Bill Black might have been "a little bit off."

"That's what I mean about circumstantial evidence," Bachels said. "You just never know. Like you'll never know whether old Bill Black was murdered or committed suicide."

While Bachels was talking on Main street, defense attorneys Robert Fugazi and Jack Reges were doing some fast talking for Motherwell up at the court house.

"Motherwell may be a liar, an impersonator, a con man and a Romeo," said Fugazi, "but that doesn't mean he's a murderer." . . .

Downieville, March 16

A Gold Rush country jury, deliberating long enough to lunch on baked hash and dine on rib steaks, convicted Larry Lord Motherwell tonight of first degree murder.

The jurors, who received the case at 10:30 A.M., took an intermission for lunch soon afterward. The main dish for everyone was the baked hash prepared by Sheriff Dewey Johnson's wife, Cornelia

—causing one old timer to remark, "This could be grounds for a mistrial."

His theory was that the baked hash, feature of the afternoon menu at the Quartz Cafe, was so excellent that it might prejudice the jury on the Sheriff's behalf.

At dinnertime, however, when the jurors returned to the Quartz Cafe for another free meal on the impoverished county, they had $2.25 rib steaks prepared by somebody else.

Luckiest man in town when the verdict came in at 8:30 P.M. was District Attorney Gordon I. Smith.

Smith was declared the winner of the "Good Luck" gold mine claim, the grand prize for the winning side at the trail. It was put up by Jim Dick, Proprietor of the Roaring Gold saloon.

Motherwell took the verdict quietly. He said, calmly, "It's not what I expected." . . .

NOTE

The unperturbed Motherwell took his case down from the mountains to the legal marts of Sacramento. There, nearly two years later, the State Appellate Court reduced the conviction to second degree murder. The con man received a "from 5-years-to-life" sentence.

LIVELY ARTS

San Francisco, since its earliest Gold Rush period, has been a city of lively arts. In classic tradition, however, the theater was suspect among members of the gentility, as this bit of editorial advice to clean-living womanhood so roundly emphasizes.

The Dirty Drama

May 29, 1869

Miss Olive Logan has done a good and timely thing in attempting to inaugurate a crusade against the wild license that threatens to turn the theater into a mere school of sensuality. On the 14th instant this young lady, who has acquired some distinction as a lecturer, and who has also, if we remember aright, figured with credit upon the stage, delivered an address before the Women's Equal Rights Association, in which she said, among other things:

"I can advise no honorable, self-respecting woman to turn to the stage, with the demoralizing influences which seem to be growing stronger and stronger there every day, where the greatest rewards are won by a set of brazen-faced, clog-dancing creatures, with dyed yellow hair and padded limbs, who have come here from across the ocean. Modest and virtuous women are driven from the stage by the licentious fever for nudity which rages in our theaters."

If women generally will act in accordance with the spirit of Miss Logan's remarks, the "dirty drama" will soon leave the boards of every respectable theater and be compelled to seek refuge where it belongs, in the lower class of melodeons, which self-respecting women never visit. The reform of the disgusting abominations of the leg drama, which outrage morality, decency and good taste, is easy, provided the women will resolutely set their faces against these vulgar exhibitions. A theater that respectable women will not visit cannot possibly enjoy steady prosperity. Woman can reform the stage and purify the drama if she will use her influence to make vulgarity and license *unfashionable*. She can in this way wield a power to which managers will find it not only politic but necessary to succumb.

★　★　★

In 1882 Oscar Wilde made a lecture tour of the United States. The British author and wit had distinguished himself for his scholarship and his eccentricity in dress, taste and manners. His poems had already appeared and he had become so conspicuous an exponent of art for art's sake that he had been satirized in Punch and by Gilbert and Sullivan in their opera "Patience."

It was not for another decade that his drawing room comedies were to make him even more famous and that he was eventually to be imprisoned for "immoral conduct," as it was politely labeled.

On the evening of March 27, 1882, "arrangements having been concluded with his manager, Mr. R. D'Oyly Carte," Wilde delivered a lecture in San Francisco on "The English Renaissance." The audience and the press were somewhat beside themselves with excitement and enthusiasm. But in *The Chronicle*'s report, which begins with an interview aboard Wilde's train, the definitely pro-esthete reporter could apparently not help but apply an occasional western pinprick to the distinguished visitor from Britain.

Lo, The Esthete

March 28, 1882

The eminent esthete stepped through the doorway of the sanctum, and, bowing to the group of admirers, advanced to the middle of the car. The poet was still pale from the effects of the severe shock to his sensibilities, but the sight of the distant hills purpling in the morning sun completely restored him.

"They look nice," remarked a prosy admirer.

"Ah—y-e-s—how utterly lovely—how exquisitely beautiful— observe the softness of the outline so full of the grace and harmony of Nature's handiwork."

Having delivered himself of this rapturous compliment to the wooded peaks of Marin, the poet clasped his hands and gazed out of the window for some moments, lost in the too utterly joyous abstraction of the esthetic. While the poet's eyes were fixed on the environments of the hoary Tamalpais *The Chronicle*'s representative was making a mental sketch of the midday dreamer, and found, when the picture was completed, that it was an odd one for this outlying post of civilization. In an older community the esthete might have passed with slighter attention, but his figure was certainly one calculated to excite the most intense curiosity in California.

He did not look more outlandish than a trapper from the wilds clad in the trophies of the clime, but the outlandishness was of a kind to which Western people have not to the smallest degree been accustomed. Mr. Wilde's hat was of the sombrero pattern, light brown, pliable and of itself would not astonish the Californian. The poet's face was almost boyish, and the closer we examined it the more juvenile it seemed. It was the face of a man of 21 years; a long face made up of a pair of eyes set rather deeply, a large aquiline nose, full lips and a decidedly heavy chin.

The dress of the poet was not less remarkable than his face, and constituted a short velvet coat, rose-colored necktie and dark-brown trousers. The lower garments were cut with utterly sublime disregard of the latest fashion, but the esthete had yielded sufficiently to his shoemaker to allow that worthy artisan to fit him with the newest production of his last. The poet wore the perennial sunflower in his buttonhole, and allowed his brown locks to float over his shoulders and just show enough ambition to curl to prove that they shared the wearer's hatred of the rigidly straight. The amount of ink that has been expended in England and America to prove that Mr. Wilde in the dress of estheticism is a very remarkable person, is the best proof that his figure is sensationally uncommon.

The Chronicle man had expected to meet an odd-looking person and prepared himself against surprise, but, as the poet lounged into the railroad car and leaned out of the window to revel in the picture of blue sky and purple hills, the reporter forgot his resolution, and stared and stared again in mute astonishment. What was particularly mystifying was the fact that this strange being, who looked as if he had no part in the every-day affairs of our prosy life, could not only talk of the matter-of-fact when he pleased like a man of education and refinement, but like a man who was capable of deep thought and vigorous conclusions.

As Marcus Mayer, who has carefully watched the esthete for days, elegantly remarked in forming his estimate of the poet:

"Anyone who picks him up for a fool will get left, and don't you forget it."

"I like your names here so much," said the poet, after he had fed his soul to satiety on the purple of Tamalpais and the blue of the sky over San Rafael. "How delightful it is to hear such names as San Antonio, San Pablo and San Lorenzo, after one's ears have been horribly shocked by such terms as Gringsville."

The poet shuddered as he thought of the presumptuous borough of the East which has proudly taken to itself the title of Gringsville.

Coming to a stretch of green meadow, enriched by wild flowers, the poet exclaimed with the enthusiasm of a woman, and not a very strong type of Western woman, at that.

"How joyous it is to see a spot of green after one has grown so weary of the desolate stretches of the brown and gray! The lack of color in your American landscapes has been to me a source of much regret. In the old countries the landscape is always green and one can at all seasons appreciate to the fullest the beauty and perfection of Nature."

On arriving at the Oakland ferry and during the passage the poet was the observed of all; but though his strange appearance provoked many smiles, he was treated with the courtesy of silence by the curious crowd. The only question he deigned to ask about the city, which he viewed from the upper deck of the steamer, where he stood poised on one leg like the decorative fowl of estheticism, was:

"Have you no old ruins in your city?"

When told that the Mission Dolores boasted of an old church, and a number of adobe shanties the poet's face brightened, but the joy was short-lived. Presently, borne on the wings of the western wind, came the odoriferous offerings of the waterfront, churned into aggressive life by the ferryboat, and the poet turned and fled to the cabin. On arrival at the San Francisco side the poet was adroitly whisked into a carriage and driven to the Palace Hotel.

He will remain some weeks on this coast and meditates a visit to Japan. His fellow passengers speak of him in the kindest manner,

and tell sorrowfully of the reception he got at Corinne where forty
bogus esthetes with big sunflowers and a terrible brass band
serenaded him.

Later that night, the lecture:

                                                  March 28, 1882

Oscar Wilde's lecture on the "English Renaissance" last night
was the means of filling Platt's Hall with the most fashionable audience that any entertainment could attract in this city. The doors of
the hall at 8 o'clock were fairly beseiged by the beauty and wealth
of San Francisco and the face of Manager Locke, as it beamed
from the crowded portals over the slowly moving mass of respectability worth $1 a head, was as utterly joyous as a full blown sun-
flower.

So great was the press of silks and so dazzling the flash of diamonds in the narrow entrance of the hall that it was long past 8
o'clock before the doorkeepers were able to complete their labors.
When the rush had ceased and the audience had been seated, the
hall presented a spectacle that would gladden the heart of the most
ambitious speaker. The gallery boxes were crowded with the aristocracy of Nob Hill, and the glory of Van Ness avenue and the
Western Addition, from Pine to Post street, was spread over the
closely packed chairs on the floor.

At 9:20 o'clock the audience after some futile attempts to attract the poet to the stage by the concussion of kid gloves, deputed
the task to the more vigorous owners of pointed shoes and swell
canes near the door. A few rounds of disapproval from these orna-
ments of fashionable youth caused the doors in the middle of the
set on the stage to open, and the apostle of estheticism stepped
into view. A buzz indicative of feminine surprise and suppressed
comment arose as the poet bowed to the audience and strode down
to the medieval pedestal which Manager Locke had placed for him
near the footlights. The pedestal was of black, and in its niches
were stored several specimens of bric-a-brac.

The poet's attire was even less modern than his traveling costume.
His long hair was brushed back over his ears, and he had just enjoyed the luxury of a barber's chair. His coat was of black velvet,
with lace cuffs. He wore a full lace necktie, which flowed over his

shirt bosom, and left visible just enough of the immaculate linen to serve as the background for some antiquated jewel, which sparkled in the gaslight. His waistcoat was of the orthodox full-dress pattern, but his lower garment was an uncompromising knee-breeches of black velvet, beneath which the not too muscular legs of the poet stood out in all prominence that black silk stockings could give them. The esthete's feet were cased in patent leather shoes with silver buckles. His gloves were white, and as he stood for a moment at the footlights before commencing his lecture, he looked like one of Rubens' portraits. More than one lady expressed her surprise in a stage whisper, and one of these comments, which the poet could not have helped hearing, was:

"Oh, my soul! What a dress!" uttered by a well-known society lady in the second row.

A goblet of water in which some lily or lime juice had been placed stood on the esthete's antique reading desk, and quietly moving the glass aside he addressed himself to his manuscript. His unadulterated English accent, with its cadences so strange and at times so amusing to American ears, made his hearers for some time more observant of his manner than his ideas. He had spoken for several minutes before the audience, having become partially reconciled to his costume and his accent, realized that he was lecturing them on art education with the earnestness of a drawing teacher. He told them of the necessity of the union of the artist and the handicraftsman, which is essential to the creation of admirable models. The power and the beauty of the esthetic movement in England lies in the fact that they have brought the artist and handicraftsman together.

The poet described how, having found the skilled handicraftsman, we must surround him with happy influences and beautiful things. The lecturer painted a gorgeous picture of Pisa in the medieval ages, with the glory of its Gothic architecture. He described the streets where the laborer passing from his daily toil saw so much around him that was beautiful that he must needs treasure some of it in his soul.

The lecturer, who at this stage observed the green necktie which Dr. May brought on the 17th of March to conciliate the Milesian vote in his ward, dealt some terrible blows to the vulgarity of modern dress, and the hideous decoration of the beauties of nature

by patent medicine advertisements. He warned his audience that
without a beautiful natural life all art must die.

He did not desire us to build a new Pisa or bring back the arts
of the 13th century. That would be wrong. The art we want is the
art based on all the inventions of the 19th century, and that are
useful in 19th century life. Estheticism reverences machinery
when it does its proper task; when it relieves men of the labor that
its degrading and soulless, but not when it degenerates. Steam, the
electric light and the telephone are to be judged by the uses to
which we put them.

"The value of the telephone," said the poet, "depends upon
what the two men using it have to say."

★ ★ ★

Pride in its literary accomplishments has sometimes run rampant in San Francisco. But in this case *The Chronicle* took only
quiet cognizance of a local talent four years before he was first
published.

The Boy Socialist

February 16, 1896

Jack London, who is known as the boy socialist of Oakland, is
holding forth nightly to the crowds that throng City Hall Park.
There are other speakers there in plenty, but London always gets
the biggest crowd and the most respectful attention.

London is young, scarcely 20, but he has seen many sides of the
world and has traveled extensively. He was born in San Francisco
in the Centennial year, and went through the California grammar
schools before he started out in the world.

London is a great student, and haunts the Public Library in the
time he has to himself. He is a High School boy, and supports himself as a janitor in the institution. At present he is fitting himself
for a course at the University of California, where he will make a
specialty of social questions.

The young man is a pleasant speaker, more earnest than eloquent, and while he is a broad socialist in every way, he is not an anarchist. He says on the subject when asked for his definition of socialism, "It is an all-embracing term—communists, nationalists, collectionists, idealists, utopians, altrurians, are all socialists, but it cannot be said that socialism is any of these—it is all."

Any man, in the opinion of London, is a socialist who strives for a better form of government than the one he is living under.

★   ★   ★

This could be the best way to write an interview story. Just let the subject write for himself. It works to greatest advantage, obviously, in the case of a literate subject.

From time to time *The Chronicle*'s book department has practiced this theory, providing reports on themselves by writers it felt the readers should know. An outstanding example is this article by Sausalito short story writer and novelist Calvin Kentfield.

Writer at Sea

March 17, 1957

Chances are if a young man with a restless spirit and a creative compulsion goes to sea he'll end up being a writer (or, at least, writing about the sea) if he ends up being anything at all. Very few seamen become painters or musicians but the number of writers who are spawned by the waves and who rise—if you'll go along with an infelicitious image—like Venus, from the foam, is remarkable.

I, myself, decided at the age of eight or nine that I would become an artist (now properly called painter) and I started out to college (not, however, at the age of nine) with that idea in mind. I even painted a few pictures, but very shortly my restless spirit sent me off to sea ("I am sick of these terra-firma toils and cares; sick of the dust and reek of towns. Let me hear the clatter of hailstones on icebergs, and not the dull tramp of these plodders, plodding their dull way from their cradles to their graves," says White Jacket.)

Well, it was the sea that changed me. I very seldom paint pictures anymore, but I write constantly. I think I changed because there's so much time at sea. I used to sail on deck, and these days, once the ship leaves port and is secured for sea, a sailor works four hours on and eight hours off round the clock day after day. Something has to fill the time.

Some seamen (usually officers) have television, which is marvelous as long as you're running the coast, but once you get out into deep water you lose your picture. Some seamen have radios and some tie knots and make little ships in bottles or carve things or do other kinds of busy work and, of course, they do a great deal of laundering, but by and large, they read. Seamen read and read and read. They read anything. I had a watchmate once who ran out of material and asked me to lend him a book so I handed him the first volume of "Remembrance of Things Past." He read about twenty pages into that unfortunate child's insomnia and said to me, "This is a screwy book," but he read it, all the way through.

Once I was on a tanker shuttling from Liverpool to the Persian Gulf which is a long way and on one visit to Liverpool a friend of mine and I stormed into Charles Wilson, Ltd., Booksellers, Church Alley, and bought one copy of every available Penguin book and one copy of every available title in Everyman's Library. And there's nothing more likely to make a writer out of a private citizen any faster than a good book, or even a bad book, but good books make the best writers.

All but one of the stories in "The Angel and The Sailor" arise from personal experience either at home or at sea. I come from Keokuk, Iowa, which is a small town on the Mississippi River. But all of these experiences—either of observation or participation— are, of course, fictionalized and the narrator of a story in the first person is not necessarily the author. In fact, the identity of the author in any story, should he appear, is none of anybody's business.

The title story, the novella, is pure fabrication through and through and has several meanings on several levels but as this is not a critical essay, I needn't explore those meanings now. Writing from outside physical experience, that is, strictly through inventive imagination, is new to me, and I'm happy to discover that I can do it with some success because to rely entirely upon personal adventure for material is a very risky business, particularly as fresh personal adventure these days is hard to come by.

There persists in American literature a cult of direct experience which most everybody blames on poor old Ernest Hemingway, and a lot of it really is his fault, but everybody does not have to shoot lions in Africa in order to write valuable fiction, nor do they need to climb mountains or go to sea, for Art comes out of Life not out of Adventure (a little further on in this piece when my language becomes more poetical, I will call Life *Nature,* but I thought I'd mention it so you'd know, when we get there, I'm not mixed up).

Writing (the creation of fiction or poetry) is, after all, a religious experience, part faith and part ritual, and like most religious experiences, particularly the dark pagan ones, it is not necessarily spiritual. But its aim is the Truth about Life, and in Art the symbol of Truth is that 19th-Century lady, blindfolded and wantonly clad, who used to hang as favorite companion to Hope on the wainscoted stairways of the fairly well-to-do. She is also a very popular figure in public sculpture and usually holds a druggist's scale to weigh Man's guilt against his dram of innocence. In such cases she is usually called Justice but you can tell by the way she's dressed she's the same woman.

Any piece of fiction that's worth turning off the television to read, or worth relinquishing love and sanity to write, is involved in laying Truth bare; but her simple gown is tough as leather and conceals infinite layers of undergarments and every writer knows he can never hope to get more than a peep at the flesh beneath, yet on he goes tearing away with hopeful enthusiasm and a lustful eye, and this is how he makes his living. Surely, it's a lunatic's job, and, in fact, many more writers than one have landed in the bin, and many, many more in the bar. "Thus," says Melville, alias Ishmael, bringing us back to religion, "Man's insanity is Heaven's sense. . . ."

Another vivid image of the writer busily engaged in the pursuit of his livelihood is very like that in the old tale about the little moron who is sitting alongside the road catching raindrops and tying them into various kinds of knots. After a while he is joined by a friend who asks him what he is doing, and with a big sweet smile the first one says, "I'm tying the raindrops into various kinds of knots." "Oh," says the second, "I see." After a long silence, the first one—having knotted several drops of rain—looks up to his friend and says, "You know, I'd be lost without my work."

Because there are *rewards,* that's why he does it. The mystery of creation is as deep as the sea, as compellingly attractive and as terrifying as the sea, and while performing its ritual the fortunate writer may, in the words of Melville alias White Jacket, hear life and death "as he who stands upon the Corinthian shore hears both the Ionian and the Aegean waves." This, of course, is a desirable experience.

And there is the enormous satisfaction of capturing Nature and putting it into order so that the immanent Truth concealed by natural chaos is at last revealed. This can be called tying raindrops into knots, for rain is chaos and a good sailor's knot is a marvel of form and order. And, surely, a well-knotted raindrop is a wondrous and valuable thing.

There are other rewards, of course, such as Fame, Riches, and Publisher's Luncheons, but, naturally, these are transitory.

★ ★ ★

The Beatnik and his problems did not always call for the heavy sociology bit. For instance, when war broke out in 1959 between the Police Department and the poets Bimgo and Bomkauf, *The Chronicle* took a somewhat less than grim view of the conflict. Stories like this one, by reporter Art Hoppe, helped eventually send the various combatants about their business, biding their time for bigger, sturdier issues.

The Poet's Revenge

August 14, 1959

The free spirits who inhabit North Beach were risen in righteous wrath yesterday after a police officer confiscated two poems just because they called him and his fellow lawmen among other things:

Hitlers, anti-Christs, butchers, Torquemadas, S.S. Fuehrers and "numbered blue visages (who) mock the muse (and) trample on her flowers."

The flowers they feel got trampled on the most are the authors of the two poems—sandaled and goateed poets Bob Kaufman, who signs his works "Bomkauf," and Bill Margolis, known in local poetry circles as "Bimgo."

Bomkauf and Bimgo contend they were only exercising their rights to free speech, or, more accurately, free verse. The censuring officer, William C. Bigarani, contends he is only human.

Bigarani, a member of the police department's Beatnik Patrol for the past year, started the current battle by stomping into the Coexistence Bagel Shop on upper Grant avenue about 2 A.M. Wednesday and ripping down the two poems. They were pasted on the window.

Bomkauf and Bimgo were incensed. Bigarani, they said, had long been persecuting them, but now he was censoring them.

"What do you think a police officer is, a robot?" inquired Bigarani, a highly articulate young man himself. "After all, I do have feelings."

It didn't seem surprising that Bigarani was a bit offended. Bomkauf's epic, the more politely worded of the two, ran:

"One day Adolph Hitler had nothing to do.

"All the Jews were burned, the artists all destroyed.

"Adolph Hitler was very bored, even with Eva,

"So he moved to San Francisco, became an ordinary

"Policeman, devoted himself to stamping out Beatniks."

Bimgo's was entitled "Ode for Bob Kaufman, Ancestor of the Beat" and to understand Officer Bigarani's feelings when he read it, one should know that Bigarani wears Badge No. 67.

This ode spoke not so mystically about the police with—

". . . their numbered hypocrisies huge and sixty seven

on their faces

marks of the beast."

It likened such policemen to the Torquemadas and whatnot and wound up with the cheerful toast:

"May their eyes bulge

from their paperbag heads

may their rotting souls

disintegrate among their

rancid foetid nightstick bones"

From all this Officer Bigarani got the idea that "these poems— if you would call them that—vilified not only me but the entire police department and that's why I confiscated them."

That did it.

While no one in particular was defending the poetry yesterday, a whole batch of people were defending the poets. These included, spiritually, the Rev. Pierre Delattre of the Bread and Wine Mission, and, legally, Lawrence Speiser, the well-known civil rights attorney.

Also on hand at a hastily summoned battle conference Wednesday afternoon was Al Bendich of the American Civil Liberties Union. "This looks like a clear violation of freedom of speech," said Bendich.

Speiser fearlessly advised the free spirits to go out and paste their poetry all over North Beach.

As night fell the sweat-shirted troops fanned out through the area, defiantly tacking up the banned poems in The Bagel Shop, the City Lights Bookshop and the other bastions of poetic license. At Cassandra's, which features Zen soup at 20 cents a cup, they met resistance.

"I know I'm brainwashed," apologized proprietor Monty Pike, "but you must put me down as an enthusiastic supporter of peaceful coexistence and I'm trying to get a beer license."

Bomkauf stalked out, irate: "Okay but he better hadn't go around anymore calling himself a poet."

With the lines thus clearly drawn, Bomkauf and Bimgo searched up and down Grant avenue for Officer Bigarani hoping to become jailed martyrs. Unfortunately, Bigarani was nowhere to be found and the two poets finally decided to give up and go cut stencils for their poetry magazine.

"Isn't that the way?" complained Bomkauf. "You never can find a policeman when you want one."

It was close to midnight when Bigarani arrived on the scene. He viewed the new copies of the poems somewhat glumly and said he wasn't going to take any further action without instructions from his superior, Captain Charles Borland of Central Station.

Captain Borland, copies of the poems at hand, backed Bigarani to the hilt. "A police officer has a duty to confiscate material offensive to the public," said Captain Borland, explaining that he felt an attack on the police unquestionably fit into this category.

Attorney Speiser was unconvinced. "If nothing is done about Officer Bigarani," he said ominously, "we will take legal action."

Captain Borland was equally unconvinced. "If nothing is done (about those poems in the window of The Bagel Shop)," he said ominously, "we will take legal action ourselves."

The next step looks legal.

★   ★   ★

After a half dozen years in the cultural capitals of the East, Paul Whiteman returned home to San Francisco in February of 1925 bearing the unchallenged title of the King of Jazz.

As such he rated an interview on the Southern Pacific ferry by a throng of reporters who, with the carefree incisiveness of their trade, asked the maestro what he had to say in defense of his musical kingdom.

"Say, I know a lot about jazz," *The Chronicle* quoted Whiteman as answering. "I used to look down from where I directed the orchestra in the New York cafes and watch the flappers dividing a quart of liquor with their parents. It used to be awful in my dad's time for a girl to divide a pint of beer. Now they smoke and drink in front of their own parents and the parents don't care. There's where the blame lies—on the mothers and fathers. Jazz has nothing to do with it. Music and dancing is cleaner now than it used to be. Do you remember the 'rag' of 1910? Then don't talk about jazz being naughty."

Not much there about music, and who was talking about jazz being naughty? Nobody pressed Paul further in either direction. Or maybe the ferry docked in San Francisco.

The real answer didn't come till later that night when Whiteman's orchestra appeared in concert. *Chronicle* critic Ray C. B. Brown listened carefully. What he had to say holds up as a remarkably modern appraisal of the concert jazz sound of the Twenties.

The Primacy
of Paul

February 28, 1925

Paul Whiteman, who floated away from us six years ago bent upon tonal adventures, returned to us yesterday on the crest of the jazz wave.

Wherever he is, there is jazz at the apex of its instrumental virtuosity and its rhythmic spuming. That was evident last evening when he directed his orchestra in Scottish Rite Hall, whether the listener was an adherent to classical music or a confirmed fox-trotter. It was an audience that epitomized all varieties of musical taste, from

the symphony patron to those who prefer a syncopated tune to all
the symphonies ever written. And all seemed agreed as to the
primacy of Paul.

We may have thought that we knew all that a jazz orchestra
could do, but that was before the arrival of this expert band . . . it
is now the model of its kind. . . .

To a contemporary of Mozart, the list of instruments would
sound like a bad dream—a few violins, a banjo, two pianos, a cim-
balom, a celesta, saxophones, horns, trumpets, trombones, tuba,
clarinet, bass-clarinet, an accordion, drums and traps. . . .

For such an orchestra, ready and capable for feats of color and
dexterity, there should be better literature than Whiteman has yet
been able to discover. With the exception of George Gershwin's
"Rhapsody in Blue," Victor Herbert's "Suite of Serenades," and
Eastwood Lane's "Sea Burial," the program seldom left the mono-
tonous two-four rhythm in which the fox will eventually trot itself
to death. The melodies, when they were not being shaken into
fragments, sang in the sweetly sentimental vein.

The thing that relates jazz to the jungle is the steady unvarying
maddening beat of its rhythm. The thing that relates it to civilization is the variety of its note patterns, the complexity of the metres
that play fantastically above the persistent accent of the time beat.
The composer's fancy has freedom only in these shifting designs.
Give him a tune, and he will present it to you in a weird shape. In
this respect, jazz is like a convex or concave mirror that reflects a
tune grotesquely elongated or absurdly widened.

Gershwin's rhapsody points the way to a new use of jazz idiom.
It is a piano concerto in free fantasia form. While I cannot agree
with Carl van Vechten that it is the best concerto since the Tchaikov-
sky B flat minor, I do find it comparable to the "Burleske" of Richard Strauss in its humor, its effective scoring and its utilization of
the piano's resources. . . .

It has rhythmic boldness and a freedom of movement that
quickens the fancy. Its harmonic background has a pleasing rich-
ness. It's humor has a reckless zest and a carefree spirit.

Gershwin has broken through the formula of jazz and destroyed
its rigidity. Others will aid him in this task. . . .

★   ★   ★

If you have forgotten just how it was in the middle Fifties with a piano, some candelabra and a certain pudgy young man, this will bring it back in all of its indelible truth. The story is reporter Bernard Taper's account of a Liberace concert in the San Francisco Cow Palace. It is hoped here that the opening sentence was an attempt by the writer to get into the spirit of the occasion.

The Solid Rock
of Mother Love

February 23, 1955

Liberace's phenomenal money-making venture at the Cow Palace yesterday was billed as a Pops Concert, but it could more accurately have been described as a Moms Concert.

The mothers of the Bay Region were there in force, along with a scattering of males, to swoon and sigh as for three hours their plump, heart-faced, wavy-haired hero played for them, sang to them, danced for them, confided his every little thought to them and bathed them in his inimitable brand of showmanship.

There were over 14,000 in the Cow Palace and Liberace acted as if he were bound by a silver cord to each and every one of them.

"I love you all, you wunnerful people," he said fervently.

Reclining triumphantly in his white dressing gown on a coral colored sofa after the performance, Liberace praised the Cow Palace. "It's an intimate place," he said in his deep, romantic, nasal voice. "Much more intimate than Madison Square Garden. That's what I love about it. No balconies, no posts. Everybody could see me."

The announced gross for his concert was $42,314.90. Later hundreds of women crowded around his dressing room, a 50-foot trailer parked near the livestock stalls, reluctant to let their hero leave. There were still 300 of them there when he broke away to make a plane to Los Angeles.

San Mateo County Deputy Sheriff Frank Martin said there were eight faintings, two epileptic fits and one convulsion. Not since

Billy Graham was here last November have such crowds been attracted by any public personage.

With sincerity on the grandest scale, Liberace worked every appeal known to showmen during his three-hour performance: religion, patriotism, romance, youthful tribulations ("I'm not ashamed to tell you during the Thirties George and I, we took our coaster down to the County Relief to get food"), danger menacing the hero (his recent illness)—and all these appeals, of course, superimposed on the solid rock of mother love.

He also clowned and ad-libbed gags, and among his sentimental numbers he interspersed sambas and hot boogies, bouncing infectiously on the piano bench as he beat out the rousing numbers.

Everything he did drew a response. The multitude laughed at his most casual attempt at humor and it applauded every time he gave the slightest intimation that applause would be welcome—often. The crowd even clapped at the mention of an Oakland bakery which sponsors Liberace on a local radio station.

"They bake good French bread, too," Liberace said meaningfully into the microphone beside his piano bench. This drew both applause and laughter.

He introduced individually the members of his supporting orchestra, saying of one of them, "I find the people who are very great are usually very modest."

"Frankly," he told the audience, "I've waited a long time for this and I like it up here. I wouldn't trade it for anything in the world."

He warned them all to be sure to come back after the intermission. "Because if I came back and found you gone—God, I'd die!"

Nobody left.

★   ★   ★

At the California State Fair of 1954 a time capsule was buried, to be exhumed 100 years later. On microfilm in that capsule is an essay by *The Chronicle*'s Alfred Frankenstein, who was asked to contribute 1000 words on the current state of music in San Francisco. As it turned out, the 1000 words went somewhat beyond the cultural boundaries of the city. For those who couldn't wait the 100 years, Frankenstein's remarks were also published in *The Chronicle.*

Time Capsule

August 15, 1954

When Rip Van Winkle came back to his native village after sleeping 20 years in the Catskills, he found everything was different and he could recognize very little of what he saw. Old Rip lived in the Eighteenth Century, when things changed fast; a Twentieth Century music critic, bemused on Tamalpais for two decades, could return to his desk and scarcely know he had been away.

Our music year follows well established grooves. Five weeks of Opera in the fall, 22 weeks of symphony concerts in the winter, chamber music and popular concerts of several kinds in the spring and summer—so it has gone within the memory of the oldest musical inhabitant, and so, it seems, it will go on forever. No doubt 2054 really will be different from 1954, but one thing seems fairly certain: on the day this time capsule is dug from the ground, press agents or their descendants will be making the rounds with the casts for the forthcoming "La Boheme."

One of the most distinctive musical phenomena of 1954 is the popular magazine article informing the public that Americans today spend more money for music than they do for baseball, major and minor leagues included. Americans love this statistic, but no one seems to ask if the money is intelligently spent.

A good deal of it is. Our performances, on the whole, are excellent, and a great deal of important musical literature, old and new, is turned over in a year's time. There are few aspects of music which an alert and determined person cannot enjoy in the living presentation during the course of a year's activity. But if that person should want to make some music himself on a strictly amateur basis, he will probably have to do it alone.

Music has become even more of a spectator sport than baseball. It was not so 100 years ago, when to experience music one had, very largely, to produce it. Our public is losing the direct, intimate contact with the art which has always been one of its major delights. It looks as if mechanical progress will lead us further and further away from personal participation, and if so, there may be more loss than gain. To be sure, mechanical invention has very definitely brought us gain in its own way: thanks to it, millions of people know far more about the literature of music than their grandfathers did; but they know less about the pleasures of singing and playing.

In cultural matters Americans place a higher value on what they can buy than on what they can do. This is a national vice which has always existed, but it has always been fought. It is being fought today, especially in the schools.

The schools have taken over a new and crucial role in the musical life of the Twentieth Century. On their lower levels they are infinitely more aware of and more active in music than they were in the century preceding, and on their higher levels, they have exchanged their traditionally conservative role to become the creative spearhead of the era. This is new and very important and one would like to be here 100 years from now to see what will come of it. Conceivably the America of 2054 will have learned to prize its own cultural resources as they should be prized.

One of the commonest of human failings is to dream that all our problems of today will be solved in a dreamable future. They won't be. Neither will they be found insoluble; the optimist and the pessimist are both romantics. The conflict between cultural values and vulgarization will be going on in 2054 just as it is now, although its forms will be quite different. However, one of the most striking lessons of history is that cultural values survive as such and that vulgarities, if they are remembered at all, take on a special kind of cultural status after the passage of sufficient time. The gaudy shows of yesterday are materials of today's historic realism, not untinged with humor.

In fact, a very special reason for wishing one could stay around until 2054 is to see what the youngsters will say about time capsules and the stuff they bury in them.

★   ★   ★

WAR AND PEACE

When war came to San Francisco in December of 1941, everyone was excited except the people. Although the presence of enemy forces in mid-Pacific made an attack upon the American mainland a logical possibility, military and civil authorities found it difficult to impress upon the citizenry a proper state of hysteria.

The following account of San Francisco's first days at war is from the news summary in *The Chronicle*'s "This World" magazine, a regular Sunday supplement.

The First Week

December 14, 1941

Early Monday evening fire sirens shrieked an alert and police cars raced through the city warning residents to black out. Detector apparatus of the 4th Interceptor Command had picked up the drone of "unidentified enemy" squadrons in the air 100 miles due west of San Francisco.

Some citizens laughed, some cried "hoax," some said "practice," some squatted in bathtubs or basements. Many went up on the roof to watch the fun. All radio networks went off the air.

Street lights winked out, but throughout the business districts neon signs continued to blaze. On one midtown building a finance firm's electric sign spelled out an ironic "SAFE". Christmas shoppers bustled in and out of stores, whose brightly lighted windows bespoke business as usual. From Twin Peaks "blacked-out" San Francisco sparkled like New Orleans at Mardi Gras time.

Brigadier General William Ord Ryan of the Interceptor Command reported the enemy planes approached within 20 miles of the Golden Gate, then split ranks, some going north, the others south. The drone faded away. Three naval vessels slipped out of the Gate for a reconnaissance and army planes scouted far over the sea looking for an enemy carrier.

Thrice more that same night air raid warnings forced radio silence and a blackout of street lights. But Tuesday came and San Francisco awoke, a city unscarred. Some were irritated, in the belief the army had faked the raid. Others were enough alarmed to talk of evacuating their children inland. There were some who insisted they had heard the attacking planes overhead. Most just shrugged and concentrated on the meager accounts of the fighting in the Philippines.

In Washington the War Department was besieged by the press for details of the "raid" on San Francisco. The Department bluntly said it had no information of any attack on the city. But here on the coast General Ryan repeated his claim and Major General Jacob E. Fickel, commander of the 4th Air Force, backed him up.

Even firmer words came the same day as Civilian Defense heads met at City Hall to discuss more effective blackout methods. Seeking the cooperation of the military they got both cooperation and a tongue-lashing—the latter administered by short, balding, bespectacled Lieutenant General John L. DeWitt, commander of the 4th Army. His leathery face set in stern lines, the General grated out his words:

"You people do not seem to realize we are at war. So get this: Last night there were planes over this community! They were enemy planes! I mean Japanese planes! You think it was a hoax? It is damned nonsense to assume that the army and navy would practice such a hoax. . . . We will never darken this community unless enemy planes are threatening.

"I have come here because we want action and we want action now. Your blackout was completely ineffective. Why bombs were not dropped, I do not know. It might have been better if some bombs had been dropped to awaken this city. I never saw such apathy. . . . It was criminal, it was shameful.

"Unless definite and stern action is taken to correct last night's deficiencies, a great deal of destruction will come. If I can't knock these facts into your heads with words, I will have to turn you over to the police and let them knock them into you with clubs.

"Bombing is bound to come to San Francisco if the war continues. Don't be jittery. Learn to take it. You've got to take it. And if you can't take it, get to hell out of San Francisco now—before it comes."

While his audience swallowed hard, General DeWitt stalked from the meeting room. Mayor Angelo Rossi called for comment. Walter Haas, president of the Chamber of Commerce, spoke briefly: "Give us our orders and the business community will follow them." That night all neon signs were off. Major merchants agreed to close their stores at 4:45 P.M. The city's next blackout, early Wednesday morning, was nearly 100 percent effective.

But even so, civilian defense was not yet rolling at high enough speed to suit Fiorello La Guardia. The barrel-shaped director of the Office of Civilian Defense burst into town, en route from Los Angeles to Seattle. In the four hours he was there he needled officials into a spasm of activity.

Mayor Rossi met the "Little Flower" at the train. "I've a meeting scheduled at City Hall with all the leaders—", Rossi began. With an impatient gesture, La Guardia barked: "I don't want any damned mass meeting! Get me the Fire and Police Chiefs from every city in your Bay Area. Get 'em all—they're the men I want to see. Nobody else. See 'em at 11 o'clock."

While fire and police officials of seven counties were being hurriedly corraled, the little New Yorker shaved and changed clothes. At 11 sharp he bounded into the Mayor's office. For 40 minutes he mowed down the assembled officials with clipped phrases and sharp commands, then called the press.

"Just had a most satisfactory conference," he snapped. "Stressed necessity for training, more training—training every day. Train fire fighters, train air raid wardens, train messengers and first aid workers and rescue squads. Train 'em. Train 'em!"

Next day La Guardia was followed into town by his chief assistant, Mrs. Franklin D. Roosevelt. The First Lady arrived ready for work, but found city officials unprepared for her visit. When Mayor Rossi finally assembled local leaders in the Supervisors' chambers, hours had been lost.

The Mayor began: "Mrs. Roosevelt is here to give you an important message." The city's guest promptly rasped: "I am not here to give you any message. I am here to get down to work." She explained that La Guardia was handling the protective side of defense and she was concerned with the health, welfare and human needs of civilians under war conditions.

When Mrs. Roosevelt called for questions, Fire Chief Charles Brennan asked: "How can we train people to fight fires when we haven't got equipment?"

Civilians, answered Mrs. Roosevelt, could be trained to put out incendiary bombs with no more than a bucket of sand. Even London's children knew how.

"But how can I train them without equipment?" Brennan repeated.

Patiently, Mrs. Roosevelt explained again. Equipment was not necessary for training. The idea was to use whatever was available.

"I haven't any equipment," said Brennan, and sat down.

Sheriff Daniel Murphy spoke up: "We should be thankful each day for our daily bread." he sat down.

San Francisco's Civilian Defense Director, Eric Cullenward, was too busy to attend the meeting, but issued a statement to the people:

"Don't pull into a shell. It's bad for morale. Go on living as always."

He then assured the populace that night baseball games will be held as usual next summer.

★   ★   ★

Five months after Pearl Harbor San Francisco was still trying to untangle its civil defenses and to make ready for whatever blow might fall.

This report on a day of crisis was spread eight columns across page one of the *Chronicle*.

Eventually the word "snafu" came into the language. Still later the United States won the war.

Air Raid Alert

May 13, 1942

The Bay Area—except San Francisco—underwent a 25-minute air raid alert yesterday morning.

San Francisco got in on only the last eight minutes of the alarm, while Alameda, San Mateo and Marin Counties received the signal immediately after 11:20 A.M.

Police and Civilian Defense officials charged they did not receive the warning until 11:37 A.M., exactly 17 minutes after the 4th Interceptor Command ordered the alert for this area.

Bombs did not fall. The "unidentified aircraft" that caused the alert were identified as "friendly."

But if bombs had fallen they would scarcely have been noticed, so great was San Francisco's confusion.

The warning was so short here that school and defense officials were still being notified when the all clear came at 11:45 A.M. The all clear was mistaken for the red "imminent danger" signal at the central fire alarm station where city electricians touched off the air raid sirens after all danger had passed.

The sirens, in turn, didn't exactly work out as they were supposed to. At least one, the one at Clay and Jones, didn't sound at all. And those that did work caused trouble—

* Lights were shut off at the main post office. Elevators stopped.

* A mounted policeman rode into the center of the intersection at Seventh and Mission streets, commanding traffic to halt and ordering motorists to shelters.

* Hundreds of school children, released just before the all clear, ran towards their homes as the sirens shrieked.

* Others, in six junior high schools that were never notified of the alert, were still at their desks and scampered for shelter.

Chief of Police Dullea said the first word he had of the alert was from a newspaper reporter, who informed him an alert was on in Oakland. "I checked Oakland police and they confirmed they had received the alert from the 4th Interceptor Command," Dullea said.

Dullea then ran to the Bureau of Communications, which receives the signals direct from the Interceptor Command. "Sergeant Joseph Perry said no alert had been ordered," Dullea reported.

Perry called the Interceptor Command.

"Heavens, yes," they said, "you're supposed to be on alert right now!"

That was 11:37, and the signal then was given over police radio and fire alarm systems.

Army spokesmen for the 4th Interceptor Command declared

San Francisco police had been notified immediately at 11:20, and that police confirmed receipt of the signal both visually and audibly. It was officially entered in the 4th Interceptor log book that San Francisco had been notified.

Dullea ordered Lieutenant Frank Winters, director of the Bureau of Communications to take statements from all men who had been in the communications center between 11:20 and 11:37.

Five police officers had been in the room. None had seen or heard any signal, Lieutenant Winters reported to Dullea.

Civilian Defense Director Jack Helms demanded an audience with Interceptor officials and implied it was not the first time the signal system had failed here. "There are previous wrinkles I want to iron out, too," he said.

City electricians explained the mixup that set off the sirens on the all clear in this way:

"When we received the alert, our men took their stations, waiting for developments. We keep the siren circuits open until an alert sounds, so there is no danger of a short circuit sounding a false alarm.

"On the alert, we closed the circuits, so one button would operate them all. When the white light at the end of our signal board lighted up signalling the all clear, it shone through the next-to-the-last light, the red one which means bombs are imminent.

"The man at the siren station mistook it for the red signal and set off the sirens.

"We noticed the mistake a minute later, and did the best thing we could. We changed the sirens to a steady blast, which is the all clear signal."

★   ★   ★

Jack Foisie at war was the perfect mating of reporter and story. Covering the waterfront and military beats in San Francisco, reporter Foisie was ever direct, uncomplicated and unflustered. Under the stress of war he remained direct, uncomplicated and unflustered.

The result was exciting. Foisie's natural calm and understatement only intensified the drama of Americans on the field of battle.

This report from Sicily was filed by Staff Sergeant Foisie both to *Stars and Stripes*, to which he was assigned, and to *The Chronicle*, from which he was on military leave.

A Walk to
San Stefano

With American Forces in North Sicily
July 31, 1943

It is not a pleasant walk, these last four miles to San Stefano.

You are with the "point" of Company G of an infantry battalion advancing up the road. You are about two hours behind the retreating Germans. You think another company has come down from the hills and beat you into town, but you're not quite sure.

You march in extended order and you keep looking for snipers in the hills and mines under your feet. Your eyes soon get tired from looking, first at the hills and then at your road.

You come to a blown-out bridge with combat engineers already at work carving out a bypass. There is a sign that reads: "Mines cleared four feet on side." You stay exactly along the middle. After passing the curve you hear a muffled explosion behind you. You run back and find that the rear end of a bulldozer has run off the four-foot safety limit. It was a pressure-type S-mine, designed upon contact to hop up out of the ground and explode at about three feet, throwing out a can full of silver-ball shrapnel. The bulldozer pretty well pinned down the shrapnel, but one ball did go through an engineer's leg.

A jeep passes you by. It is the first vehicle through the bypass and you think he is going to get into town before you. You curse the mobility of some of the army.

Then comes the second blown-out bridge. Combat engineers are here, too, but they have only been able to clear a footpath. The jeep driver is a daring fellow and he seems determined to beat us into San Stefano; he is retracing his way to where he can reach the railroad tracks that parallel the road. He does and speeds up the tracks. You again curse his mobility.

The jeep enters a tunnel and there is a dull explosion. The medics start to rush down to the tunnel and someone says, "Hey, you'd better let me go first." An engineer with a mine detector begins sweeping a path for them. You are suddenly glad you are a walking infantryman, but only for a minute.

The sun is hot, the straps of the light field pack are cutting through the sweat-soaked wool shirt, and the blue Mediterranean down from the curving highway is tantalizing. You ask for a dry match, since everything in your pockets is wet with sweat. In return, you pass the cigarettes, and they clean out your last pack. On the bend in the road are what look like small shell craters in the asphalt surface. You wonder who did the nice shooting, and then a sergeant says, "Watch out for those soft spots, they're anti-tank mines." An engineer comes along and probes with a bayonet, and it strikes metal.

"Take it easy, Joe," says the guy who is working with him, "those things are touchy." The two get down on their knees around the mine, and from a few yards off it looks like they're shooting craps. If you're a damn fool you come closer, and, looking over their shoulders, you see them digging out the dirt around the mine to see if it's boobied—that is, if it will explode when lifted up. Satisfied, the engineer called Joe lifts out the German Teller mine, and the other guy unscrews the cap and defuses it. "Now it's completely harmless," says Joe, and he lays it down very carefully away off the road. There is soon a pile of these Teller mines; each one looks just like an oversize discus.

You've been walking for over an hour now, and white lines of salt begin to appear in your sweat-soaked shirt. Your canteen is still half full, but the water is warmer than luke-warm. There is a spout of cool mountain water emptying into a cement basin in the shade of a grove of big-leaved trees. "How about a 40-minute break?" O.K., but you'd better jump from the asphalt to the bank, those road shoulders are always mined.

So you leap over the soft shoulder and land on the bank, lean back and relax. The weight of the pack leaves your shoulder. The grass is cool and soft. You stretch out flat—and that saves your life. The guy who had been walking in front of you, the fellow carrying the Browning automatic rifle, had been the first to refill his canteen from that spout of cold water, and the first to find that the Germans had put a ring of S-mines around the foot of the basin.

Someone else shoulders the Browning automatic rifle, a medic is left with the wounded man, and a guard is placed near the fountain, and you hike on toward San Stefano. You are still thirsty.

The town has been in sight for some time, but when you get around the last bend there is still a long elbow with the bridge across the river San Stefano at its joint. The bridge, of course, is blown. One complete section in the middle is just a mass of crumbled bricks in the river bed. It's like a freckled-faced boy with a missing front tooth.

You are tempted to take to the railroad tracks that go straight across into town, but then you remember the jeep in the tunnel. This is good country for snipers and you look for them. The commander of the "point" talks in his walkie-talkie to the company commander who is perhaps a half mile behind with the main body of men. It is decided to reconnoiter the road block at the entrance to the bridge. Two men are selected and you are not one of them. A halt is called while they go ahead. They walk on opposite sides of the road, one 25 yards in front of the other. They disappear around the bend. Two minutes of silence will mean that the roadblock is undefended.

There is a sputtering crackle and then several more in rapid succession. The command, "Disperse left and right!" is given. The rifles are no longer on the shoulder; you hear the click of the safety on the rifle of the man next to you. There are several more crackles. Your steel helmet no longer feels heavy; you feel like ducking behind a tree but the others are only dispersed, looking with their eyes and ears. There is another crackle; it seems to come from the direction of the bridge. One of the scouts comes running back.

"Mines. All around the bridge. A patrol from another company coming down from the hills ran into them. Got quite a few. They need a doctor."

"Doctor up front! Pass the word back," orders the point commander. The word is passed back: "Doctor up front!" There is more talk on the walkie-talkie; it is decided to try and get the doc through; the engineers will be up shortly, but there is no time.

It is decided that the doctor and a platoon will attempt to make their way around the roadblock, through the barbed wire entanglements, cut across the river bed 100 yards up from the bridge, scale the opposite bank and then work back around to the bridge.

"Mortar platoon up forward! Pass the word back," orders the point commander. The mortar platoon files past with solemn faces, eyes alert for mines and snipers. The doctor is put in the center and they space out 25 feet between each man. They climb the hill and enter a mushroom growth of pillboxes. They pass a sign which when translated reads: "This is a military zone."

You are the last man in that file and this is one time when you are not anxious to pass anyone. The file is stopped by the first of the barbwire. Where there is barbwire there are often mines. "A guy only lives once," smiles the leader, and steps forward with the wirecutters. The wires part and the file moves forward. Now you are descending into the river bed and now you are stepping from rock to rock, carefully avoiding soft sand for that is a good place to hide mines.

You reach the other bank and there on the ledge above you is an old Italian civilian, all smiles and a weird mixture of languages. He is wearing sandals made out of rubber tires. Naturally, he announces right off that he lived 23 years in Brooklyn.

Okay, Joe, tell us about that later. What we want to know, can you lead us around the minefield. Yes, he says, he knows all about the minefield. He saw the Germans plant them. Yes, he will show us the way, only he would prefer that someone went in front of him. There is a few minutes of debate on who is going to lead and the old Italian man finally consents for a pack of cigarettes.

He leads you along the bank until you come onto the wounded and the dead about 50 yards in front of you. You were taking the same path that these men had taken.

"For God's sake, get back," screams one of the wounded men. He is lying on the ground in his shorts. They are red with blood. His back is toward you. It has been raked with shrapnel.

There is another man, unwounded, attempting to make the wounded man comfortable. The unwounded man dare not move for fear of setting off another mine. "Get out of here," he shouts, "don't make it any worse than it is." There are other men lying where they fell.

The file backs up. This time the Italian who once lived in Brooklyn is ordered to take us up over the ridge and then swing around to the road. The old man explains that he is very old and cannot make the hill. There is nothing to do but go on without a guide. Shoot the old man, you say? No, remember that he was in the lead and would have been the first to go. Blame it on an old man's mind.

You climb the terraced ridge and then turn toward the road. Your eyes are glued on that soil. You follow in the exact footsteps of the man in front of you. The man in the lead—perhaps he follows in the footsteps of God. Every snap of a twig, each rattle of a pebble makes you twitch and shudder. If you think at all, it is about what you said in your last letter home.

The leader reaches the bank overlooking the road. He jumps and lands on the firm asphalt surface. He is safe. The next one jumps. He is safe. Each one jumps and is safe. You jump and you are safe.

The doctor walks in the middle of the road down to the bridge. There is a cart at the end of the bridge. It was the touching of this cart that set off the first of the mines. The doctor goes to work.

The mortar platoon starts up the last hill into town. You stay in the middle of the road. There is a dead German lying on the side of the road. Perhaps, you say to yourself, he was killed by one of his own mines.

You enter San Stefano. The townspeople, pathetically friendly, come out to greet you. You ask in your best Brooklynese Italian if there are any snipers in town. The people say there are not. You ask if there are any booby traps. The people say there are none.

You pass the back side of your sweaty wrist across your eyes. You no longer look at where you are about to step.

★　★　★

This is a story written in the midst of hysteria. It is nervous and excited and perhaps exaggerated. In the telling it casts aside all remnants of professional poise. But by these very qualities it was able to paint vividly and accurately the mood of that riotous night when San Francisco celebrated the victory over Japan.

This was no studied approach. Reporter Stanton Delaplane returned from the chaotic streets pale and frightened, worried about the fate in store for the good people of the city.

Victory Riot

Market Street, 8 P.M.

August 16, 1945

A looting, smashing crowd is tearing up Market street tonight.

Windows are crashing from Sixth to Third streets. The police and shore patrol are unable to and not trying to stop it. There is barely five minutes without the clatter of plate glass punctuating a steady roar of voices and the explosions of firecrackers.

The authorities may not admit it, but the crowd tonight is out of hand. You couldn't stop it if you tried. Not short of tear gas and fire hoses.

Most of the mob is made up of sailors—sailors without hats, or in civilian hats, or officers' hats. Many of them are drunk. A good fourth of them are staggering drunk. Every few moments a bottle sails through the air and crashes in the streets.

There must be a lot of casualties. A few minutes ago I noticed that both my hands had blood on them and I don't know where it came from.

This is not the crowd of last night. That was a surging mob with a large sprinkling of people who had to show off in various ways— from the sailor who swung a dead rat on a string to the girl whose picture we have on the city desk, the lower half bare and the upper half in an unbuttoned pea jacket. She is standing in the crowd at the base of one of Market street's monuments to American culture.

The crowd tonight is an ugly crowd. The ringleaders—the ones who are breaking windows—are mainly sailors and hoodlums who are taking advantage of the day of celebration to smash and break and loot.

These were some of the things I saw a few minutes ago:

Four sailors kicked out the window of a leather goods shop at Fifth and Market and threw the contents into the crowd. Someone tossed a pail at the other window. It shattered over the throng.

Three sailors grabbed a girl out of the crowd and held her while another, staggering with liquor, stripped off her shorts. They ran away into the crowd waving them in the air.

A sailor kicked out the window of a dress shop and was grabbed by the Shore Patrol as he rolled around on the ground with a window dummy. The mob surged around yelling, "Let 'm go! Let 'm go!" They let him go and the dummy lay on the ground in a puddle of shattered glass.

There were two types of crowds. The participants and the watchers. The participants were mainly sailors, laced with hard-looking young women and a great number of teenagers of the bobby-sox type.

There was a line of demarcation. If you stayed on the north side of Market or the middle of the street, you were a participant, a window breaker, subject to the hazards of thrown bottles, stripped clothing, firecrackers or a friendly slap on the jaw.

If you stayed on the curb on the south side, you were a watcher and few of the participants crossed that invisible line to bother you.

On that non-participating south side there were a lot of people who ordinarily frown on vandalism and riot and rape. But last night they watched with a tolerant eye and a certain sympathetic satisfaction as the windows shattered. They did not, however, go over to lend a hand or to take things from the windows.

There were a lot of women and a lot of children. Quite a number of San Franciscans kept the youngsters there to see the experts take the town apart.

The breaking mob was well backed by its own women, the majority of them in the high school brackets, all strangely alike with scarves on their heads. Where sailors didn't have girls they seemed to have little trouble pulling the kids off the sidewalks. Most of the girls were operating in pairs and would be picked up together.

Even last night we knew that much of this sort of thing was going on. Much of it was held out of stories in view of the victory celebration. One of our truck drivers saw a girl being held down and raped by a small crowd of sailors in a Mason street doorway just off Market. A few minutes ago three sailors grabbed two passing girls and pulled them up a Fifth street alley. The girls were protesting, but they were not yelling very loud. The cop on the corner made no move—if he saw it.

Reporter Delaplane's fears were never realized. What he saw was the worst of it. At 11 P.M. he went back to the scene of battle and the authorities, having let the mob spend its furious happiness, began to move in. Delaplane wrote this anticlimactic, but reassuring, postscript:

Market Street, 11 P.M.

Navy shore patrol, military police and city police are moving down Market street, sweeping sailors, soldiers and civilians before them without discrimination.

It is a careful, tactful and firm operation that still could blow up into a mass battle. But police are giving the crowd no time to make up a mass mind to resist. They move in heavy bodies down the sidewalks while police cars move six abreast and three deep down the middle of the street. A few more windows are being smashed during the march, but there is no other violence. I just saw one sailor break for the open but he is going down under a mass of shore patrolmen. Well-dressed women headed home from last shows at the theater are being herded along with the rest.

The center of Market and Powell streets is headquarters. Under flaring lights Chief of Police Dullea and military police officers are grouped around a radio patrol car.

Everybody is headed off Market street, and now police are even beginning to sweep up Powell street, clearing the sidewalks and the bars. The people who can't walk or who stagger too much are being loaded into patrol wagons. No one is immune. High ranking brass is being picked up right alongside the seaman with a bottle in his fist and a woman's hat on his head.

The massed crowd passes slowly, leaving an empty street still filled with wreckage under the night lights. The dummy is still lying in shattered glass. She is in one piece but someone has stolen her wig.

As the crowd disappears down the side streets you can still hear its muffled roar, punctuated by shrill cries of exuberance, an occasional clink of falling glass. It gets fainter and fainter until Market street is altogether silent.

On the corner of Fifth and Market, the worst spot of all just half an hour ago, a lone MP swings his club in rhythmic circles.

★   ★   ★

The first men to return to the United States in the Korean war prisoner exchange were the badly wounded. The arrival of the first five prisoners at Travis Air Force Base near San Francisco was covered with all the fanfare of the big national story.

Reporter Ruth Newhall, on the assignment for *The Chronicle*, came back to the office appalled and angered at the soldiers' reception. Her story was a powerful indictment of the communication media in its coldly competitive pursuit of news. *The Chronicle* printed reporter Newhall's story across the top of page one.

Return of
the Heroes

Travis Air Force Base
April 30, 1953

The five American prisoners of war who returned here today agreed reluctantly to give interviews.

They had refused to talk to newsmen when they departed from their plane, but were persuaded to change their minds at the base hospital here.

They were thrust into an incredible bedlam.

The interviews were held in the hospital auditorium. Three hundred reporters, photographers, radio, television and newsreel men attended. The big room was ablaze with flood lights, noisy with the shouts of camera and radio technicians, and cluttered with cables, wires, microphones and cameras.

The litter patients were carried in and placed on beds; one bed had seven microphones attached to it. The walking wounded sat nearby.

Questions were shouted at the men, and the weary soldiers replied as best they could.

Airman Second Class Robert L. Weinbrandt of El Cajon, a litter patient, cou'd hardly go through with the job.

The blond young airman lay on the bed under floodlights, with a battery of a dozen motion-picture cameras focused down on him. News photographers, crawling on the ground between the big cameras, popped flashlights.

Every newsreel cameraman shouted at him at once.

"Just lean into the mikes and say it's great to be back."

"Tell us how it feels to be back home."

"Just talk about the Communists and brutality."

They all continued to shout, until one cameraman, louder than the others, attracted the bewildered boy's attention.

"Bob, now Bob. Just say slowly and loudly into the mike: 'All I had to eat was rice.' Can do?"

Bob stared at him and shook his head. "No can do," he said clearly.

Reporters leaned over him and asked about his outfit, and how he lost his legs. He answered them briefly, telling them about the frostbite he suffered after he bailed out, and he saw no other Americans in his four months in a hospital.

Then the newsreel men began shouting again.

"Take a drag on a cigarette," said one.

"Tell about rice, lean into the mikes!" shouted another.

Weinbrandt looked around desperately, and an officer pushed up and leaned over him.

"Major, when can I go? These fool questions. . . ." Weinbrandt fell back on the pillow.

The major said, "Tell them you're glad to be back, and we'll get you out of here."

The boy leaned toward the mike, and said, as if with his last strength, I'm—I'm awful glad to be home."

The other litter patient, lying on the bed separated from Weinbrandt by a night stand decorated with roses, was Marine Private First Class Alberto Baez Pizarro, of Rio Pedras, Puerto Rico.

Someone stepped up with a microphone.

"Tell us, Private Pizarro," he said, "who amputated your legs?"

Pizarro had one leg amputated above the ankle and the other one above the knee.

Pizarro answered, "A Chinese doctor."

The man with the microphone pulled it back to his own face. "Did he do it for torture or punishment?" He moved the mike back.

"He did it to save my life," Pizarro answered simply.

★　　★　　★

In the summer of 1960 *The Chronicle* sent a reporter and photographer to the remote spot in Kings Canyon National Park where that day rangers had announced spotting the wreckage of a wartime B-24 bomber.

Photographer Barney Peterson and Reporter James Benet flew over the mountains that night, and at dawn, with the help of a guide, started on horseback over Bishop Pass into the canyons of the middle fork of the Kings river. There, on the next day, they climbed a 2400-foot canyon wall and came to the lake where the plane was found.

Benet's report was as much a picture of the primitive and lonely Sierra country as it was an account of the solving of a wartime mystery.

The Lake of
the B-24

August 1, 1960

We have climbed to a grim corner of the High Sierra that has just given up its secret—a secret of six men lying dead amid the wreckage of their B-24 bomber for 17 years.

It was a veteran mountain man who asked the question that was in all our minds as we looked down on the little granite-locked lake that is their tomb.

"I wonder how many more there are in these mountains that we'll never find."

For this is a lake like hundreds of others, little blue flecks scattered over the great Sierra. Many of them are unvisited because they have no fish, there is no easy trail through their basin, their rocky shores provide no grass for stock and no comfort for the campers.

This is a lake like these others—but in this one as I looked into the cold, transparent water I could see the shattered wreckage of the bomber. It is so smashed and twisted that there is no shape to it, no smooth curve of fuselage or sweep of wing, but a shadowy mass below, its outline fading into the blue depths.

On the rocky northeast shore of the lake are hundreds of fragments. They lie as if strewn by a careless giant—bits of sheet metal, twisted instruments, a propeller blade. The force of the impact snapped the heavy aluminum castings to which a seatbelt was fastened. The force tossed half the seatbelt and half the casting, still bolted together, a hundred feet up the granite slope.

The bits of plane are clean and new-looking, the aluminum shiny, the dials readable, the switches and mechanisms workable. All appears just as it might have been when the snow first melted after the crash. But it was 17 years ago.

That is how long the mountain kept its secret. After all the years the story of that stormy Sunday night is perfectly readable to one who stands by the lakeside.

Across the lake is a ridge, rising to separate it from two other lakes. Here lies a big wing fragment. Beyond is a great spur of the mountains that are called the Black Divide.

A line from where we stand amidst the lakeside fragments, through the wing fragment, points straight to one of the peaks. It towers to about 12,500 feet. Our lake is at 11,246.

We know the B-24 radioed its base at Fresno as it returned from a training flight to Tucson, Ariz., that it was caught in one of the Sierra's terrible winter storms.

It strayed too low. The peak that caught its wing and dashed it down more than a thousand feet into the lake—then frozen and piled high with midwinter snows—stands among much higher ones. Many are over 13,000 feet. North Palisade, a few miles east, rises to 14,246.

Once below 13,000 feet, the bomber didn't have a chance. When it struck, it burst into fragments, many of which were sprayed for hundreds of feet. But then, when the snow and ice melted, most of the wreckage slid down into the diamond-clear depths of the lake. There it lies.

Glimmering below the surface are the white tombstones of the airmen—parachutes burst open by the impact and still moving and flickering in the water after all the years.

One of the men who first found the wreck saw a boot in the water and fished it out, only to make the horrible discovery that it contained a foot. The flesh had been preserved by the cold.

Under the water, then, the torn bodies lie as carefully preserved by nature as Egyptian pharaohs. And even better, for the pyramids have been despoiled by men for centuries. No men come here.

For there are such places, improbable as it may seem in the modern world.

"I just couldn't say how many lakes there are in this country that hardly anyone visits," said Dudley Boothe, the packer who climbed with us to the lake. He runs the Rainbow Pack station, operating over Bishop pass, the nearest entry to the area.

"I've been in these mountains all my life, and I've had the station for 11 years, but there are plenty I've never seen."

The little lake of the B-24 might have been unvisited for much, much longer if a pair of geologists, scanning a rugged wall of LeConte canyon through field glasses from their camp high in Dusy basin on the opposite wall, had not become interested in the rock.

Jim Moore, a Geological Survey scientist, and Frank Dodge, a Stanford graduate student who is his assistant, planned a mapping and ore-sampling climb.

Leroy Brock, the ranger stationed in the canyon—the region is so remote that this is only the second year the ranger station has been in existence—accompanied them on his day off to improve his knowledge of a bit of country he knew was almost never seen.

All three are hardened mountaineers, but even they needed several hours to climb from the ranger station, on the middle fork of the Kings river at 8800 feet, over treeless, granite slopes to the lake basin.

By the outlet of the lake into a little creek that plunges down forbidding cliffs Leroy Brock saw a splash of yellow color. Looking closer, he identified it as an aircraft oxygen bottle. The B-24, missing since that Sunday night of December 5, 1943 had finally been found.

Strangely enough, the day after the B-24 vanished, another from Fresno's Hammer Field was lost about 70 miles west and a little south. Two men parachuted from that plane, and they said it came down near Huntington lake, due west of here. Their bomber was sought, but it couldn't be found—until 1955 when Huntington lake was drained. There it was.

The cases of the two B-24's are not unique. Federal aviation officials say there are hundreds of aircraft still missing in the California vastness.

At our little lake (like many a mountain lake it has no name and needs none, for nobody wants to go to it or even know of it) the fragments were so small that flying over it we could see nothing. The secret was safe except for the accident of a pair of iron-legged geologists with a curiosity about rocks.

Now come the newspapermen, and eventually an Air Force team to give the bodies a burial more reverent, though no more dignified, than the one the mountain gave.

Then, in a few weeks, the new, man-made scars will be softened by the rippling waters. There will be only a few conies squeaking, a few hummingbirds whirring to break the absolute stillness that fills the granite bowl.

★   ★   ★

NEWS IS WHERE YOU FIND IT

This was an unlikely story, and an even more unlikely assignment for a grown man.

A couple of girls wrote in asking, "Dear Editors: How about helping us meet Elvis Presley?" For some reason the editors paid attention, and for some reason the ever-wise editors were able to see it as more than a stunt.

The result was a sequence of eyewitness reports by nursemaid Tom Mathews, who drew the task of shepherding the girls to Hollywood and Presley. In Mathews' hands this cute affair became a marvelously funny sociological study of a national phenomenon of 1957 and of female human beings at age fifteen.

A Journey to
Elvis

I

February 27, 1957

The Misses Donna Dickson and Nancy Laity are well-scrubbed, good-mannered 15-year-olds, sound of wind and limb, clear in the eye, strong in the stride and weak in the heart.

They suffered this latter condition in mid-summer when they were struck by lightning while listening to the radio. The bolt was shot by Elvis Presley, the boy Zeus from Tennessee.

Since then they have poured on all the pressure their weekly allowances would allow to promote the entertainer. This is a dollar a week apiece.

They called station KOBY every day and demanded "Too Much"—or some other stirring rondelay.

They spread their funds around the juke boxes seeking, like a Madison avenue ad executive, to blanket as wide an area as possible.

They have given up two complete sets of boy friends.

They also developed a sense of futility that would have shattered the minds of a dozen adults. For here they were doing more for Elvis than a full armored division could accomplish and he didn't even know they breathed.

Twenty five letters they wrote. No answer. Birthday telegrams.

Christmas cards and valentines. No response. They laid off the publicity campaign long enough to save money for a three-minute call to Memphis. No answer. They tried Hollywood. No answer. Elvis was protected from everybody but his mother.

Miss Dickson and Miss Laity wrote *The Chronicle*.

The guile in the letter would have served a Borgia. "We have a great treat for you," it read. "Why don't you sponsor a trip for two girls, namely us, to go down to Hollywood and interview Elvis Presley.

"We think *The Chronicle* is the best paper in San Francisco, and it wouldn't cost you much to send us. We wouldn't even eat and that would save money. . . ."

Inquiry showed the girls had no problems except that of being 15. "They are above average students and good citizens," said Marie Welch, dean of girls at Lincoln High School.

Two weeks ago, the girls were told they could go. They went to Mass the next day. Miss Dickson lost five pounds in the interim and Miss Laity gained four.

The day before they left, this reporter went out with them to spend their last school day before the trip. Lincoln High throbbed with the story. The student body split pretty evenly on whether they were fortunate or out of their minds. Generally the boys held the latter opinion.

William Witt, their English teacher had to give them a test early. It was on Cyrano de Bergerac.

"Mr. Witt said the other day he didn't like Elvis," said Miss Dickson. "I said, at least you've got his hairdo."

"And I said he's got more than one sport coat," added Miss Laity.

They walked into Mr. Witt's classroom and sat down. He smiled and took up the test questions. Either he was forgiving or he had forgotten. "Whom does Cyrano accuse of making love to a musketeer in a bakery shop?" he asked.

"Mr. Witt, do we have to have the right spelling?" asked Miss Dickson.

"You cannot spell Cyrano E-L-V-I-S," said Mr. Witt with enjoyment, proving that every houn' dog has his day.

After the test the lunch bell rang and they went to the cafeteria. Many girl friends gathered around their table and asked how they had been chosen to go. Some of them were quite snippy.

"I don't know who has a better right," said Miss Dickson. "We saw 'Love Me Tender' (his only picture) three times the first day, once the next and three times the day after that."

She admitted that she and Miss Laity saw the work only occasionally thereafter. "We cried the first three times and the fifth time," she added.

They said they had memorized the dialogue of the film and are fond of quoting such famous lines as "You ain't got no right to do this" or "Shut up, I don't want to hear no more."

A young man with an athletic air came up to the table and asked if it were true they were going to see Elvis "in person." His name was Jim Bender. They said yes.

"I think he's weird," said Jim. "Simple. Beautiful." No word is so contemptuous as "beautiful" at Lincoln High School.

"Shut up, I don't want to hear no more," the young ladies said. It fractured everybody. Jim retired, mystified by the convulsions.

Miss Dickson and Miss Laity said they did not own any Presley jeans, sweaters or T-shirts. "Let's face it," Miss Dickson said, "the clothes are a little cheap."

"But I've got an Elvis Presley bracelet and wallet and lipstick," she added and spilled out her bag to prove it. In addition to the memorabilia it contained the following items:

Two sticks of fingernail whitener, one lipstick brush ("I never use it because it won't work right"), a Muni ticket, an eyebrow pencil, a pair of dice, a champagne cork, perfume, a coral lipstick, a Presley "Tender Pink" lipstick, a Futurama lipstick, two makeup sticks to lighten the lipsticks, an eyelash curler, tweezers, a buck bag to clean shoes;

A set of colored pencils for biology, a roll of Scotch tape, a mirror, one bobby pin, a calendar, mascara, two pens, two fingernail files, a ruler, a key to a diary, an eraser shield, pearl fingernail polish, a comb, an eraser, an address book, a basketball game schedule, a pencil, a fitted manicure set, a handkerchief, a three-inch-thick wallet, a one-inch-thick wallet.

"Mine's about the same," said Miss Laity.

The girls went off to gym where their teacher congratulated them and asked if they needed a chaperone. They said no, their mothers were going.

"Well, tell him I named my car Elvis," said the gym teacher. "I think he's adorable."

"Do you feel kinda nutty about all this attention?" Miss Laity asked Miss Dickson.

II

February 28

It was the first plane flight for Miss Donna Dickson and Miss Nancy Laity. Both were nervous.

But they looked like transatlantic pilots compared to their mothers. Mrs. Robert Dickson and Mrs. Harold Laity were equally new to air travel and they did not possess the transcendental purpose of their daughters.

It was this purpose, a visit to Elvis Presley, that caused them all to get up at 5 A.M. on a stormy morning. Guests of *The Chronicle,* the mothers were to act as chaperones and also as nurses in case their daughters fell apart.

And in case you just came in from an Antarctic cruise and don't know Presley from Pepsodent, you should realize that eight of his records have passed the million mark, that he receives 4000 fan letters a day, that RCA executives are afraid he'll learn how to sing and that he has 40 sport coats and four Cadillacs—a yellow, a pink and black, a white, and an all-black, presumably for funerals.

Many people think Elvis is a pain and some think he is a menace. There are more who believe he is a shrewd entertainer and there are others who think him the sweetest thing to come along since the invention of the strawberry soda. Miss Dickson and Miss Laity must be counted among these.

Except for Mrs. Laity tripping on the front steps and Nancy announcing that she had a stomachache there was calm and thoughtful silence until the party boarded the plane. The TWA stewardess came by, asking for last names and destinations.

"Dickson, Los Angeles."

"Dickson, Los Angeles."

"Laity, Los Angeles."

"Laity, Elvis Presley."

"Are you going all that way just to see him?" asked the stewardess, obviously one of the enemy who rates Presley somewhere between bad manners and marijuana.

"There's always ONE around," said Miss Dickson, looking prim. Both girls consider attacks on Elvis as assaults upon themselves.

"I don't see why so many people are always knocking him," said Miss Laity. "We like him and we aren't juvenile delinquents."

"They don't like the way he wiggles," said Miss Dickson.

"I don't especially like that," said Miss Laity, "but then it's awfully hard to do and you have to give him credit for that."

What the girls called the Presley "wiggle" has caused near riots all the way from New York to Oakland. More than 12,000 teenagers crowded his home town of Tupelo, Miss., when he appeared there. They turned a county fair into a pandemonium. Three thousand youngsters stormed his dressing room in San Antonio and 15,000 showed up to squeal at him in San Diego.

He was the first personality to trounce the Ed Sullivan show. He appeared with Steve Allen one night during the summer and Sullivan's Trendex rating went down so much he signed Elvis for three appearances for a reported $50,000.

So you can't blame Miss Dickson and Miss Laity for some of their enthusiasm.

Over Santa Barbara, Miss Laity became pensive. A fly walked across her window. "That poor, little fly," she said. "It's so far from home. Isn't it funny, they don't even know the difference."

As the plane let down over Los Angeles Mrs. Laity had a moment of panic. She couldn't get one of her new shoes on. The foot had swollen. Grimly she shoved and with the courage of a Marine walked off the ramp to the waiting limousine. On the way to Paramount studios a stop was made to replace the new alligator pumps with something sensible.

Lindsay Durand, publicist for "Loving You," the new Presley movie, greeted the car at the gate. She had arranged for a tour of the studio before going to the Presley set. The girls made the tour in record time, goading all the adults like mahouts.

On the set they met several of the people in the movie, but not Elvis. He was coming later. Shown his dressing room, Miss Laity said, "Look, he's got a football." Miss Dickson was too reverent to speak. They returned to where the cameras were operating and were introduced to Dolores Hart, the feminine lead.

"What does he say about the kids who like him so much?" asked Miss Laity.

"Not much. It embarrasses him," said Miss Hart.

"Oooooooooooo, there he is," said Miss Dickson. Elvis was about 30 feet away and surrounded by the technical crew. He had been primed by Miss Durand.

He pushed out of the circle and walked forward, throwing them a salute with his hand. He clucked a couple of times with his tongue and said, "Hi, babies. Let me take you to lunch."

Hand to mouth they could only stare. Each nodded assent and the stars that come from tears shone in their young clear eyes.

III

March 1

When Elvis Presley asked the Misses Donna Dickson and Nancy Laity to lunch, they said they "almost died."

But seated with their mothers in the special dining room of the Paramount commissary, where Elvis had said he would join them later, they were near recovery. They were half way through their hamburgers, milk shakes and French fries.

"This is the best day of our life," said Miss Dickson.

"My stomach is growling," said Miss Laity. "I hope he doesn't hear it."

"I'm going to ask him when does he go into the Army and about Natalie Wood and what is his favorite color," said Miss Dickson.

"What can we ask him about Natalie Wood without sounding stupid?" asked Miss Laity. Miss Wood had been known to have dates with Mr. Presley.

"Let's ask him if he cares about somebody," said Miss Dickson. "That way he won't know who we mean."

"You see all these real famous people here like Wendell Corey and Lizabeth Scott and they're nothing," said Miss Laity. "Ooh, there's Yul Brynner. Hey, ma, there's Yul Brynner."

The mothers couldn't have been more delighted. They looked with bright interest.

"Look at them look at Yul Brynner," said Miss Dickson.
Then here came Elvis.

"Ah found ma thrill," he sang and sat down. "Ah got a sore throat from singin' too late last night," he said. He was in Apache-brown makeup, a white handkerchief knotted around his open neck to protect his sport coat. Rust gabardines and black loafers completed the uniform.

He is impressively tall and his hair no longer looks like the rear of a duck. It is very long, very sleek and very black. The forelock still hangs in front.

"D' you get out of school today?" he asked.

"Yes," they said. "We saw your picture 11½ times."

"Couldn't you stay through the last time?" Elvis asked.

"We came in during the middle once," Miss Laity explained.

Elvis ordered a glass of milk. His fingers drummed incessantly on the table. He reached over and took a sip of Miss Laity's milk shake. Miss Dickson looked stricken. He took a sip of hers too. The milk shakes vanished immediately.

To questions, he said his favorite song was "Don't Be Cruel," his favorite color was black, and that he had not heard from the Army. "Ah'll go where they put me," he said.

"Do you like Natalie Wood?" asked Miss Laity, forgetting her plans.

"A friend," he said. There was a sigh. "It wasn't love. Ah don't wanta fall in love. Ah'm just not lookin' for somebody."

He took both of them by the hand, and gave a squeeze.

"Would you sign our shoes?" asked Miss Dickson. Both girls put up their new white oxfords and he signed three of them. "Ma, get the other pen," said Miss Laity, in consternation. Elvis finished his signatures.

"Don't believe what you read in those scandal magazines," he said. "They're really choppin' me and it ain't true."

Miss Dickson and Miss Laity looked as if they were about to take up a holy crusade. "I'd like to be your mother," breathed Miss Dickson.

"Babies, Ah got to go," said Elvis. "Ah got to get made up. Ah'll see you on the set."

The lunch had lasted 32 minutes.

At Elvis' place at the table there remained his glass of milk, three quarters full. Both girls had the same thought.

"Do you think he might come back?" asked Miss Laity.

"Let's finish his milk," said Miss Dickson. And they did.

They went back to the set and were saluted by Elvis. This time he was in logger boots and tattered blue jeans. He asked to pose with their mothers.

"Us, too?" they chorused. "Sure," Elvis said. "If there weren't any mothers there wouldn't be any daughters." Everyone was very pleased.

"He isn't stage struck at all," said Miss Dickson.

Presley at this time was going brrrrrrp into the microphone, breeeeeep on a stray clarinet and bingy bangy bingy on his guitar, all to amuse the stage hands. The girls watched the endless rehearsals with untired eyes.

Miss Durand said the limousine was waiting to take them back to the airport. With their heads turned backward, they left, tripping over cables and stumbling into extras. Elvis was singing a soft ballad, "Loving You."

Once into the limousine, Miss Laity broke up. She cried all the way to Pico boulevard. "My dream is ended," she said, and looked at Miss Dickson. "It was too much," said Miss Dickson, and began to cry, too.

Presently, the crying stopped, but not the sadness. "I've got a lump in my throat as big as when I saw 'The Eddy Duchin Story'," said Miss Laity.

"It's horrible when you have so much fun and then it's all over and you feel so bad," said Miss Dickson.

"We sure got a lot of souvenirs though," said Miss Laity.

The young ladies had been as slick as Raffles. They had his milk glass, his water glass, his tray of salted nuts, his spoon and his napkin.

"I'm never washing this hand," said Miss Dickson. "Which one are you going to save?"

"He used this one the most," said Miss Laity. "I'm never going to wash this sweater, either. He put his arm around it."

"I think I'll just rot away in the clothes I'm wearing," said Miss Dickson. Both fell into a catatonic state.

At the airport, Mrs. Dickson and Mrs. Laity ordered turkey dinners and a Manhattan. The girls morosely asked for one Seven Up and Coke. "How could you, mother?" said Miss Laity, as Mrs. Laity began on the entree.

★   ★   ★

The Department of the Interior had announced its intention to build a relocation dam at the Echo Park site in Dinosaur National Monument. Dinosaur lies 275 miles east of Salt Lake City, Utah; the projected dam would flood the canyons of the Green and Yampa rivers which contain many unique and imposing national beauties.

In June, 1954, reporter David Perlman spent six days running the Yampa and Green rivers in that majestic wilderness area. His report, which struck a powerful blow for conservation, was also an exciting lesson in appreciating the primitive land around us.

The Wilderness

Dinosaur National Monument
June 29, 1954

At Big Joe and Tepee Rapids on the Yampa river, and at Moonshine Draw and Sob Rapids on the Green, you hold your breath when the white water breaks.

From a few yards away you can see the water boiling and hear its roar as it plunges over hidden rocks, sending spray high and rushing into whirlpools alive with treachery.

You can look upward at a thousand feet of canyon wall rising sheer above you; you strain at the oars to keep your bouncing rubber boat headed straight into the seething current.

There's no way out of the rapids now—no way to go except straight through. So you hold your breath and make the plunge.

The boat bucks like a live animal. Waves break over your bow and the slick, sharp edges of giant boulders rear up like butcher knives. The boat shoots faster and faster, and suddenly the rapids are behind you. It's been a surging, exhilarating thrill; in a moment you breathe again and look ahead to the challenge of the next white water.

From Lily Park, in Colorado, to the lower reaches of Split Mountain Gorge, in Utah, is little more than 40 miles, and an airplane can fly over the placid, wooded parks in 10 minutes. But along the rivers that have gouged their way through mountain ranges over millions upon millions of years, the distance is nearer 80 miles, and it has just taken me six days to make the canyon trip by boat.

I accompanied a group from California's Sierra Club. There were college kids along, and elderly men and women, and children as young as 4½. I joined them because the two rivers they were going to see, the Yampa and the Green, are the crux of a great controversy now raging in Congress. These two ancient waterways join in the heart of the Dinosaur National Monument; their waters mingle and then flow southward into the Colorado.

The fight in Congress centers at the confluence of the Yampa and the Green. Here the Bureau of Reclamation is seeking authority to launch a vast water project for the Upper Colorado River Basin with a mammoth dam 500 feet high, a dam that would impound the waters of the Yampa and the Green for hydro power and flood control, a dam that would change the living canyon bottoms into a hundred miles of silent reservoir.

Along the Yampa river, not far upstream from the proposed site for Echo Park Dam in Dinosaur National Monument, there is a deep and mysterious stretch of canyon that men call the Grand Overhang.

Its vast sandstone wall reaches upward and outward for hundreds of feet, blotting out even the sky directly overhead. You run your tiny river boat close under this immensity of sandstone, as I did a few days ago, and you find yourself in the most intimate contact with the timeless quality of earth.

It was 200 million years ago that this great overhang was sculptured in the living rock. But its story began far longer ago than that. It began in the dim, pre-Cambrian past when vast seas heaved over the land troughs of the American west.

For age upon countless age the silts and sediments of vanished rivers laid down their deposits in these seas. And the slow cycles of organic birth and death sent a gentle rain of living matter down through the water to cushion the sea bed and add still more immeasurable depths to the rising bottom.

Eventually this watery region became a great flat plain, ringed by volcanic mountains and threaded with sluggish rivers. Here, in the boggy fastness of the river borders, lived the dinosaurs of the mesozoic era, cropping the succulent water plants and preying, at last, on each other.

Then the seas moved in again, burying all this early land life and burying, too, the river sediments. And after still more time the seas receded, new rivers coursed across the land, and there began a great revolution that lasted millions of years. It was a mountain-building epoch, and the land slowly became folded, seamed and uplifted as the earth's crusts responded to deep, internal pressures.

The land rose ponderously, like the back of a brontosaurus heaving itself from a swamp. In a long line, running uniquely from east to west, the Uinta mountains of Colorado and Utah arched higher and higher. The southern flanks of those mountains soared in dizzy escarpments.

But oddy enough the rivers of that ancient time clung to their courses, despite the mountain-building revolution. With each upward thrust of the mountains, the rivers bit ever more deeply into the rising land, and etched the spectacular gorges that are now the heart and magnificence of what is called the Dinosaur National Monument.

Only a few days ago, at fabled Steamboat Rock, I watched the Green river flow down from the north, still carrying in its waters a heavy burden of silt as it continues to wash and expose the red quartzitic cliffs of the Uinta mountain formations that date back a billion years.

On the Yampa, our caravan of boats rowed beneath sheer canyons carved from Morgan sandstones, deep maroon and heavy with fossils, laid down in Pennsylvania times 230-odd million years ago. The rushing current swept us past other cliffs where the red Morgan rocks give way to the brilliant buff-yellow walls of Weber sandstones, a newer formation some 30 million years younger than the Morgan.

These are the canyon walls that would cease to exist with the building of the Echo Park Dam, their panoply of geologic history drowned beneath the fluctuating levels of a reservoir. . . .

The canyon country in Dinosaur National Monument is the backdrop for a pageant of legend and history that stretches back to the dawn of man. There were Indians here ages upon ages ago and only last week we climbed cliffs above the Yampa into caves filled with relics of civilizations long extinct.

At Meeker Cave, flint arrowheads lie in the dry silt where legend tells of the massacre of pioneer women abducted and herded past the promontories of Disappointment Draw and Vale of Tears.

At Mantle's Cave, above Castle Park, stand the undamaged sandstone cists that tell of Indian progress. Preserved through the centuries, these storage bins of the early Basketmaker Indians are rude earthen pits 1700 years old.

Later ones in the same cave demonstrate historic refinements; cists with upright sandstone slabs for walls; beehive shapes where the rough slabs have been improved with red mud mortar. The invention of that mortar must have been a giant step in history.

Then the latest ones, those that date back only 1150 years or so, are the most refined of all, with woven willow reinforcements and basketwork lids.

There is evidence along the Yampa and Green of later incursions, too, that came a thousand years after marauding Apaches and Athabascans had driven the peaceful basketmakers into extinction. There are the tumbled log-and-sod cabins of cattle rustlers and bandits who hid out in this remote, impassable land during the last century. At Anderson Hole, a tiny gem of a box elder grove, there's a cabin tumbling into ruins that still holds a dusty, broken mandolin and the quilt of the lonely man who lived there. On the high canyon rim there are cabins with gunports, built like fortresses.

At four isolated valleys within the 208,000 acres of Dinosaur there are even homes where men live today, cultivating a few acres of crops and grazing stock on the sagebrush-spotted benchlands above the canyons.

One of these ranchers is Charley Mantle, a weatherbeaten, drawling cowman who homesteaded at Castle Park after World

War I. Mantle and his poised, attractive wife have raised five children in this wilderness, 90 miles from the nearest town.

Their log home stands next to an orchard irrigated by a mountain spring; nearby is another log cabin where Mrs. Mantle conducted a school for her own children and those of her nearest neighbors who live 12 miles away.

Only a step from their home is a sheer sandstone cliff, and imprinted in the rock there are a series of mysterious designs—the chiseled petroglyphs of ancient Indians who left an artistic message that no one has been able to decipher.

A hundred miles of this riparian land; these sandy beaches and wooded groves where we camped; these enthralling relics old and new, would be flooded beneath Echo Park reservoir if the dam builders win out in Congress.

Anthropologists have testified in Washington that the Indian artifacts can be removed, and that evidence of the canyon civilization exists elsewhere as well. But this is a National Monument, supposedly to be preserved inviolate against invasion of any sort.

The fight in Washington is to change that principle of inviolability in just this one instance—but in the setting of a precedent it may turn out to be far more than that.

★　★　★

If it is true that the primary function of a newspaper is to inform its readers, this story might well take its place as one of the all-time standards—at least in the yak tail division.

It was reporter Robert de Roos's feeling at the time that the odds were strong against *Chronicle* readers knowing much about such tails. A bit of research effort, a dash of deadpan writing, and yak tails were removed from the realm of the unknown.

Yak Tails

July 11, 1948

Four mystic Tibetans (all Tibetans are mystic) leave San Francisco for Chicago today, bent on peddling yak tails to the merchants of the United States.

They want to sell $2 million worth of the tails. With this money they will buy agricultural machinery.

When they arrived, as members of a Tibetan trade mission, no one seemed to know what yak tails were good for. Even the mystic Tibetan hucksters, Shakabpa, Chamkyimpa, Sey and Pangda, did not know what yak tails were good for. They were sure, however, that yak tails must be good for something because they sell well in the United States.

The shocking ignorance about yaks and yak tails was cleared up somewhat yesterday. This newspaper can now report that there is much to know about yak tails.

Yaks (Bos gruniens) live on the elevated Rupsu Plateau in China and Tibet. They are rarely seen because their long, shaggy hair blends so well with the long, shaggy landscape up on the Rupsu Plateau.

Whenever a Tibetan gets wind of a yak (and a yak is something to get wind of) he runs and catches it. Yaks are used as draft animals and their milk is used to make butter which Tibetans smear in their hair.

There are two species of yak. One is the black yak. The black ones are very unsociable. So are the two-toned ones. In this connection, it is interesting to note that baby yaks have no special name. Little electric eels, for example, are called elvers.

Because the Communists control that part of China where yak tails come from, there has been a great shortage of yak tails in the United States. It has been impossible to get yak tails through the Iron Curtain. There is a steady demand for yak tails because yak tails make the very best wigs and beards for department store Santa Clauses. During the war, after the pre-war yak ones wore out, Santa Clauses had to use inferior beards made of wool or mohair.

Wool beards and mohair beards cannot be combed and they are not as crinkly and attractive as yak tails.

Genghis Khan, the terrible Mongol conqueror, knew about yak tails, too. His household standard and later his imperial standard was made of nine yak tails. Whenever the people Genghis Khan was conquering saw nine yak tails they knew Genghis Khan was around.

Yak tails make excellent chowries, too.

A chowry is a whisk made of yak tails and is used to keep flies off people.

Best wishes for the success of the Tibetan trade mission in the United States, Sey, Shakabpa, Chamkyimpa and Pangda.

★   ★   ★

It must be understood that this story wasn't really there at all. But it was a dandy newspaper idea.

This was the situation: Three of California's most northern counties and one in southern Oregon were in their usual snit over getting the short end of everything from the state lawmakers. Somebody up there said something about seceding and forming a brand new state. That remark got out via a brief and skeptical wire service item.

That's how it stood when Delaplane arrived on the scene for *The Chronicle.* The story remained flimsy, but under the Delaplane touch it developed both folksiness and a veneer of rugged authority. Where it all might have ended, who knows? Because a week later it was December 7, 1941—and who cared?

The following is compiled from the Delaplane dispatches that the Pulitzer Prize committee voted the best reporting of the year.

The Sovereign State
of Jefferson

I

Yreka, Calif.

November 26, 1941

The garage man who "dreened" my car last night in 18 degrees-above-zero weather said he could put this whole matter of seceding border counties in a shotgun shell.

He said folks wanted roads up here and if they didn't get them pretty soon, there was no telling what they might do. They were worn out, he said, with yammering at Sacramento for 30 years with no results.

"It gets so bad here in the winter folks can't hardly get out of the back country," he said. In fairness, he added that there wasn't any place in particular to go when you did get out, but people being what they are, they wanted to get out anyway.

That's the personal side of the story. And probably one of the main reasons that 5000 people in Siskiyou, Modoc and Del Norte counties in California, and Curry county in Oregon, are talking big about forming the 49th, Sovereign State of Jefferson.

There is a solid financial reason, too, which has pulled in the business leaders. This is the time, they think, to develop this area, larger than the New England states and rich in the defense-industry metals of copper, chrome and manganese.

"It's been laying back in those hills for centuries and it'll lay there another century if we don't get it out now," said O. G. Steele, division manager of the California-Oregon Power company and head of the commission to form the new state.

On a large scale map he traced a belt of copper running from over the Oregon border down into Trinity county between the Klamath river and Highway 99. "There's a road in there," he said, "but it's one-way in spots and crossed with 10-ton-limit bridges."

Along the railroad tracks here there are piles of chrome ore, 600 tons of it, carted out in small quantities. Good roads—that is, improvement of the Klamath river highway—would allow many times the current production by means of heavy machinery and trucks that can't cross those light bridges.

Truck drivers coming back from the hair raising road from the copper mining towns of Happy Camp and Orleans tell how to dynamite away part of a hill on a steep curve in order to get around it.

Gun-toting citizens of these rebel counties are thinking partly in fun, but mostly in earnest about this new state. "We'll either get the roads or we'll scare hell out of the Legislatures," one of them told me.

The people up here already have a name for the State—Jefferson. They said Mayor Gilbert Gable of Port Orford, Ore., and California State Senator Randolph Collier of this district, would run for Governor; Steele for Lieutenant Governor; George Milne, mining man from Fort Jones, for United States Senator and Heine Russ, who manages the Yreka Inn, for treasurer. A lanky cattle man named William "Buffalo Bill" Lang has offered to drill a state militia and Homer Burton, mortician, also announced himself candidate for Controller.

All the State of Jefferson needs is the approval of the citizens of California and Oregon and an act of Congress.

Originator of the whole move is Port Orford's Mayor Gable, who was described to me today as a "slick article and a man who could give some of the smart San Francisco politicians a lesson." The wily Mayor probably started out merely to get a little attention to his forgotten county. But his action is defended strongly by George Milne, the mining man, who was born 64 years ago on Scotts Bar when miners were taking $60,000,000 worth of gold out of Yreka, then known as Thompson's Dry Diggings. Explained Milne in regard to Mayor Gable: "Somebody had to bite a dog."

This is still a cold, wild country where strangers at night leap precariously along the street from one hot buttered rum to the next. And the garage man says ominously, "You can't tell what folks up here will do when they get a notion."

Five years ago, outraged citizens lynched a man. Forty years ago they lynched four at a time. The pictures of their pendant bodies are on the wall of the Siskiyou Daily News. Local historians have forgotten the reason, but Burton, the mortician and candidate for Controller, said it was just a civic cleanup job.

"The people here got tired of paying the sheriff so much to feed those four in his jail," he said.

II

Yreka (State of Jefferson)
November 27

Rough-shirted miners with pistols buckled on their belts, barricaded the main highway north and south tonight, declared for "patriotic independence" for their 49th State and defied Governor Olson to collect the penny sales tax.

If California wants copper, they wired the California chief executive, "they can come up here and dig for it. We have plenty."

Bonfires blazed between the white-frosted hills along the highway as the temperatures stayed in the twenties and the sky threatened to pour snow on the towering Siskiyous. Motorists were stopped by huge signs reading: "STOP—STATE OF JEFFER-SON."

Booted mining men of Yreka passed out handfuls of yellow proclamations of independence. "Patriotic Jeffersonians intend to secede each Thursday until further notice," the proclamations read. "For the next 100 miles as you drive along Highway 99, you are parallel to the greatest copper belt in the Far West, 75 miles west of here. The United States Government needs this vital mineral, but gross neglect by California and Oregon deprives us of necessary roads to bring out the copper ore.

"If you don't believe this, drive down the Klamath river highway and see for yourself. Take your chains, shovel and dynamite."

The highway signs bore the new State Seal—a double cross on a mining pan.

Motorists were asked to distribute the Thursday rebellion proclamations along the road. Drivers took the highway blockade with good humor and took hundreds of the independence notices north and south.

The defiance of Governor Olson was carried along by Homer Burton, local mortician and candidate for Controller of the new state, who announced today that merchants will be asked to put State of Jefferson "good roads buckets" on their cash registers and put the sales tax into it, to be seized by Jefferson if California and Oregon fail to see the light.

The 49th State drive gained a new convert today; Lassen County offered to join forces with the rebels of Del Norte, Siskiyou and Modoc counties of California and Curry county of Oregon. "We offer to bring in the only active volcano in the continental United States, Mount Lassen," they wired the citizens' committee here. The committee itself was signing its pronouncements: "State of Jefferson Citizens' Committee, Temporary State Capital, Yreka."

III

Happy Camp (Secession Counties)
November 28

Like the copper belt of the Siskiyous, I am stranded between highways.

There is a road from this mining camp, halfway between Yreka and the Coast, that leads to Grants Pass Highway. But Ed Thurgelow, a miner and humanist, said he wouldn't advise the 32-mile trip over the snowy tops of the mountains. He said cheerfully they would probably find my bones by spring all right and give them a decent burial. That is, if I didn't wander from the car during my final agonies and run afoul of a mountain lion.

The Klamath River Highway is one of the most scenic in the West. It wanders in a brown sand ribbon through the tall, piney mountains alongside the Klamath river rushing in white water toward the sea. It runs through people's back yards and dives into canyons. It crosses weather beaten bridges of 10-ton limit. And, of course, it is the reason for the secession to form the 49th State of Jefferson.

I was headed this morning to see Mayor Gilbert Gable of Port Orford, Oregon, the instigator of the secession movement. But the same thing that stops copper production around here is delaying me tonight.

IV

Hard Scrabble Creek,
November 29

In San Francisco they said: "Look for the publicity man behind this secession movement."

I found him today on the rim of the continent. He is the mayor of a logging town of less than 1000 persons.

Mayor Gilbert Gable is not by any means the man he describes himself to be—"the hick mayor of the westernmost city of the United States." Gable is the sparkplug that is setting this secession world on fire.

To get to Mayor Gable and to get his story out I am on a 200-mile trip skirting the secession counties—from Yreka to Medford, to Grant's Pass, and eventually down to a telegraph office at Crescent City.

Hard Scrabble Creek is the last of the rushing little mountain streams that I crossed, and it is a good dateline for the story. Up Hard Scrabble Creek is one way to the rich copper, manganese, chrome and quicksilver country. But with no roads it might as well be in the heart of Tibet.

Returning to Mayor Gable. He first hit page one when he threatened to secede Curry County and join it to California.

Like its neighboring counties, Curry has unlimited deposits of chrome, a vital defense mineral, according to Gable. He charges that bit chrome interests with deposits in Rhodesia and New Caledonia are lobbying in Washington to stop the development of chrome in this area.

"Chrome used to be $20 a ton," Gable explained, "and the big chrome users could lay it down in New York and Seattle from overseas and make a profit on it. We can lay it down for $35. It wasn't worth mining before. But now the going price is $48 a ton. Figure it out. Why should the companies who can do it for $20 and take the new, big profit—why should they let us cut their prices?"

"There is only 90 days supply of chromite ore in the country," he continued. "Those big boys can demand battleships if necessary to go over to Caledonia or Rhodesia and bring it out. I don't know what you call it, but I call it thievery."

While mining men move deliberately and wrote long letters to the Legislature, Gable moved for secession. As a result of the publicity, he says, he has already received 21 letters and telegrams from capitalists asking about developing the chrome and quicksilver deposits in Curry county. A few more stories and Gable won't need the OPM money he has demanded of Washington.

As you come over the mountain passes with the wet sky scraping the top of your car and the narrow, straight pine trees out of sight in the clouds, there is a temptation to write this story as a travelogue.

No country in the United States is more beautiful. Nor is any more inaccessible. The men who cross it trudge with their ore-laden mule trains. They want truck roads that lead to the sea and they want starter-money so they can dig out the chrome and put it on flat cars for the markets.

This is a new "gold rush," and these secession counties are determined they are not going to be left behind in this bonanza. That, in short, is the story of secession on the Oregon-California border.

★   ★   ★

A few years of Vance Bourjaily's misspent youth were mis-spent at the *San Francisco Chronicle*. Here his apprenticeship for the avant-garde novel included such old-garde assignments as the convention of the Western Nudist Conference at Los Gatos, California. In keeping with journalistic practice, the re-porter, of course, also got to take his clothes off. This is Vance Bourjaily's report on his nudist day, with a low curtsy toward Samuel Pepys and *The New Yorker* magazine.

Pepys Among the Nudists

July 31, 1949

Descended from bus at Los Gatos. Adjusted mind by replacing uneasy speculations with proper reporter's attitude of impersonal alertness. Speculations regained upper hand immediately. Hailed cab.

Cleared throat before telling driver destination was Hillside Lodge. Driver asked if I meant nudist camp. Asked who he thought would win National League pennant. Driver no baseball fan.

Reached private road, and driver pointed out the no longer used outer gate, where guard was formerly stationed at telephone. Drove on to inner gate, at which two or three men waited to inspect cre-dentials. Produced credentials and inspected men. Men had no clothes on.

Saw two fully dressed men on horseback; learned they were mounted patrol provided by Sheriff to discourage curiosity.

Was told that 150 families had signed in, not including members of lodge. Guests were from California and Nevada; cars parked all over, many with trailers or with awnings strung from their sides. People lolling on cots, eating sandwiches, reading comic books, polishing cars. People had no clothes on.

Felt conspicuous in gray flannels, cord jacket, bow tie—usual costume for blending with background. Was shown to quarters, told to leave gear. Communed with self for several minutes; decided to blend. Patted gray flannels loving good-by. Had no clothes on.

Found man named John who had invited me; was introduced to

everyone in sight. Began acknowledging introductions with "How do you do?," but all were so healthy that phrase seemed silly. Switched to "Nice to see you;" abandoned it quickly. Developed cordial grunt for acknowledging introductions.

Ages ranged from 6 months to 75 years old. Old fellow was father of operator of lodge. Most members own cabins on grounds, spend weekends and vacations. Camp 15 years old, in better financial shape now than ever before.

Everyone bursting with health. Even adolescents had fine complexions. Still felt conspicuous: stomach too pale.

Was shown about. Cabins, lodge buildings ramshackle, but serve well. Two swimming pools, plus wading pool for children, volleyball and badminton courts. Nudists gregarious and hearty, hence like volleyball.

Attended convention meeting. Counted 104 noses. Had been told effort is made to balance number of men and women in groups, but found 76 men to 28 women at meeting. Reflected that meetings are men's work.

Became impatient with fine points of constitutional interpretation, and read literature. One pamphlet was open letter directed to California Legislature in which had been introduced a bill forbidding children in camps, on grounds nudism encouraged juvenile delinquency. Never saw less delinquent-looking children anywhere; never saw more aggressively moral atmosphere. Was not suprised to learn bill never got through committee hearings.

Second pamphlet discussed nudism as religion. Learned the number who viewed movement that way has dwindled. Most simply sun and health enthusiasts.

Other matters discussed at meetings: Standards for membership (very strict). Provisions for isolated nudists to become members (very vague). Situation regarding certain magazines that purport to endorse nudism but actually exist to publish salacious pictures (very bad). Synonyms for "nudist" which would not connote "crackpot" to the public mind (very tentative). "Sunbathers" won't do, since a good many people sunbathe without stripping altogether. Favorite suggestion "epidermist."

Motion to adjourn heartily applauded. Apparent tattoos on many members; found them to be identification patterns made with pen and ink. Device representing an individual's lodge would include his or her first name. Others wore caps with names embroidered on them. These in lieu of the lapel cards used at ordinary conventions.

People streamed up hill to volleyball court where round-robin began. Temperature over 100. Withdrew into shade to watch. Man named Fred who is YMCA athletic director in week-day life officiated, giving hearty instruction and encouragement, reminding me painfully of pallid boyhood.

Went for swim, and read Hillside Lodge rules as posted. No alcoholic beverages permitted.

Call for dinner sounded; dined on roast beef. Paper napkin felt peculiar on nude lap. Was told chef works at leading S.F. hotel. Like most nudists, chef lives double life, telling only most trusted friends and neighbors how week ends are spent.

Nudists assumed clothing as evening cooled; most started with shirts or sweaters, adding bottoms later. Got into flannel shirt, and volunteered to help with dishes. Fellow-volunteer wore nothing but apron.

Adolescents gave brief play about man who begs doctor to cure dumb wife; noted slight evidence of delinquency in plagiarizing a plot from Anatole France.

Perked up when floors cleared for dancing, feeling reputation for competence might be established—not having caught qualifying word "folk." Decorum of Virginia Reels and square dances quickly abandoned for frenetic Polish, Dutch and Russian numbers. Began to understand secret of physical conditioning of Red Army. Folk dancing lasted till 1:30. Reporter didn't.

Called out of bed at 6:30 next morning. Too bewildered to do anything but grab pants and start out. Remembered and returned pants to hanger.

Swam and got ready to catch morning bus home. While waiting for ride to town fell into conversation with sweet old nudist couple. They were dressing for church.

★   ★   ★

The executive editor of *The Chronicle* in 1936 was a red-haired twenty-seven-year-old named Paul Clifford Smith. The precocious Smith had taken editorial charge the year before, with the paper at a low ebb of depression listlessness. Smith was out-spoken, maverick and always dynamic—an adjective he favored strongly. *Chronicle* listlessness was banished forever.

The times in 1936 were angry, and so was the editor. The lettuce capital of Salinas, 100 miles to the south of San Francisco, was locked in a nasty labor struggle. *Chronicle* reporters at the front were being threatened. The motives of the newspaper were being questioned and its fair name stood in peril. Pen in hand, Executive Editor Smith rode to the rescue. Truth was his weapon —the whole truth as told in a series of articles that bear undeni-able evidence of the power and excitement of personal journalism.

It Happened
in Salinas

I

September 23, 1936

American common sense at last is mobilizing its real forces in Salinas. At least such was the indication in the growing public sup-port for the 800 citizens who Tuesday night protested the high-handed actions of the so-called forces of "law and order."

For 15 days Salinas has lived under a ruthless dictatorship of the exact sort described in Sinclair Lewis' sensational novel, "It Can't Happen Here." It did happen in Salinas, and it is high time some-one spoke out on the facts. This story has nothing to do with the merits of the strike, nothing to do with the merits of the employers' cause.

For a full fortnight, the "constituted authorities" of Salinas have been but the helpless pawns of sinister fascist forces which have operated from a barricaded hotel floor in the center of town. Under this dictatorship, minor children, boys under 21, have been depu-tized and armed; high school students have been pressed into serv-ice for the manufacture of clubs; nauseating and dysentery gasses have been shot along crowded streets by high-powered bomb projectors; news photographers have been beaten, their plates destroyed and cameras disabled; reporters from the conservative press have been menaced by police officers and denied protection by State highway police when threatened with "lynching" by power-mad deputies, some of whom were, in addition, glazed by the glow of a too-free indulgence in alcohol.

Other instances of the stupidity which has reigned supreme for two weeks in this normally peaceful California salad bowl are too numerous to enumerate just now, but will be related before these stories are brought to a close.

To justify this mad scene, there has been concocted a series of the most preposterous red scares that has yet been foisted upon any community of Americans. Even the Governor of the State of California swallowed, hook, line and sinker, many of the more ridiculous concoctions of the professional red-baiters. By now all America knows the story of how Governor Merriam fell for the one about the communists planting red flags in the "battle area," and how plaintive were the complaints of his own Highway Commission the next day after the State Highway Patrol had uprooted the hundreds of flags with which the commission had carefully marked details of certain highway work to be performed.

Behind these terrorizing concoctions about the "communist menace" are the minds of one or two conscious fascists; the cooperation of agencies of law and order which, subservient to the commands of persons they believe to be sincere and honest 100 per cent Americans, have been the helpless pawns of the forces unleashed by the masterminds; a local press which dare not gainsay the masters of the village and a chain press which long has advocated just such a break with American tradition on the ground that thus is American tradition preserved.

The fact that there have been communists in Salinas during the past two or three weeks does not affect these conclusions. Such a scene invites communists. Nor do such conclusions establish any sentiment remotely related to sympathy for the cause of the strikers. The strike itself has not been the issue in Salinas for more than a week.

Beginning tomorrow *Chronicle* subscribers will be taken behind the scenes in this amazing story of Salinas. . . . This account will reveal a sad chapter in current history—a sad chapter that must not be repeated in California.

II

September 24, 1936

The current Salinas crisis first came to the attention of the metropolitan press on September 4, when 3200 members of the Fruit and Vegetable Union, an American Federation of Labor affiliate, walked out on strike after a break with growers and shippers over a "preferential employment" clause in a proposed contract.

On Thursday, September 10, members of the Growers-Shippers Association began erecting barricades around selected packing sheds in Salinas and Watsonville, making it apparent that it was a physical showdown that was approaching. Friday *The Chronicle* dispatched two of its crack men, Stanley Bailey, reporter, and Barney Peterson, photographer, to the scene of the potential hostilities.

Already the barricaded areas had taken on the appearance of military zones. State highway patrolmen arrived in increasing numbers, announcing that their only interest in the anticipated affair was "to keep the highways open."

On Saturday, Ignatius H. McCarty, private detective, arrived in Watsonville to demonstrate a brand of gas bombs. *The Chronicle* newsmen watched the demonstration in a field near the barricades. McCarty's products were tossed into the grass. Caterpillars writhed and died as Peterson snapped pictures. He previously had been ordered off the highway by a State highway patrolman. Later he was permitted to take photos from the State highway nearby.

The forces of law and order were further mobilized over the weekend. *The Chronicle* enlarged its field staff, adding three reporters and another photographer.

On Monday, the strikebreakers arrived at the barricaded sheds.

Tuesday brought the first movement of lettuce from the fields to the sheds. At break of day hundreds of cutters went to the fields under heavy guard. Then, sharply at 6 o'clock 18 lettuce trucks rolled out of the stockades with the president of the Associated Farmers at the wheel of the first truck. Masses of pickets milled silently along the course taken by the caravan toward the fields.

At midmorning, Salinas Police Chief George Griffin gave the pickets five minutes to disperse. The order produced no results. Police, highway patrolmen and deputies advanced on the crowd, laying down a gas barrage as they marched.

Reporter Bailey was standing, watching, near a scattered group of strikers. The officers directed a barrage of gas at him. Handkerchief to his face, Bailey ducked around the corner of a house, trying to hold his breath. Stifling, he called out, *"Chronicle,"* to the advancing officers. The officers halted in their rush toward him, clubs upraised, only when Photographer Peterson appeared, armed with his news camera, and "identified" Bailey.

The pickets were dispersed.

On Wednesday loaded lettuce trucks began to move down Gabilan street. Again pickets gathered, this time to be forced from Gabilan to Main street, near the central business section of Salinas. With this, a second caravan rumbled down Main street, ordinarily closed to truck traffic.

A beer truck, halted by traffic lights, impeded movement of the lettuce caravan. It came to a halt. A picket yelled to the beer truck driver to stay where he was. The driver obeyed. Men jumped from the picket line and pulled crates from the loaded lettuce trucks. The fight was on. The crowd was dispersed. Sheriff Abbott issued a call for citizens to be deputized. Several hundred responded at once. Later in the afternoon the streets of Salinas swarmed with armed deputies. Streets and alleys were cleared of strikers and bystanders.

Photographer Peterson was arrested on the Mayor's direct order, and held incommunicado in the lobby of the Jeffery Hotel, headquarters of the shippers, growers, citizens' committee and law enforcement officers. The Mayor later explained that he thought Peterson was a communist. He said that in the excitement it was necessary to investigate every suspicious character, and that there were a lot of communists carrying cameras around the place. Peterson's news camera was a $200 Graflex.

A few minutes later the Jeffrey Hotel room used for *The Chronicle* field staff headquarters was visited by Sheriff Abbott. The Sheriff was told at the door who occupied the room. Stating that he "didn't give a damn whose room it was," the Sheriff made an entrance, an "inspection" and departed.

That evening deputized citizens, seeking to disperse a crowd near the Labor Temple, threw gas bombs onto the temple property. Five members of *The Chronicle* staff witnessed the bombardment. Gas shells landed in the yard and burst against the side of the building. The place was saturated with tear and nauseating gas. County Supervisor Earl McHarry was struck by a gas bomb fragment.

Police Chief Griffin was on the top floor of the Jeffrey Hotel at the time of the raid on the Labor Temple property, several blocks away. Chief Griffin denied that the Labor Temple was bombed. *The Chronicle* printed his denial. The denial was misinterpreted as a "retraction" on the part of *The Chronicle*.

One of Chief Griffin's officers, named Adcock, later encountered Reporter Bailey in the hotel corridor. He informed Bailey that if he ever caught him outside he would "kick hell" out of him. "Remember it and let it be a warning to you," said heavily armed Officer Adcock. Officials later disclaimed responsibility for Officer Adcock's action. Mayor Leach said Mr. Adcock was "just a hotheaded Irishman."

Again *The Chronicle* field staff reported, in detail, what it had seen. Again *The Chronicle* editors printed what its field men had seen, plus what various officials had to say about the situation. Then came an amazing series of protests to *The Chronicle* from a half dozen "spokesmen for the forces of law and order."

Chester Rowell (editorial page columnist) and I took an airplane to the scene and at once went into a meeting with Mayor E. J. Leach and a number of Salinas citizens. Sincerely and honestly many of them told their stories to us. They were alarmed. The communists were in their midst, they said, and they feared what the morrow would bring. Rumor was on the rampage. We checked a number of these rumors during our meeting and found them baseless, with the single exception of a report our newspapermen had picked up to the effect that strike headquarters was about to be raided by a party of deputies in a search for arms. The raid was made, and no arms found.

During the meeting one of the citizens whispered to me, "Mr.

Smith, you stand back of your reporters in this affair. They are right, but I can't say so."

Our meeting ended with what appeared to be a full understanding of each other's problems and purposes. Mr. Rowell and I believed we understood the members of the citizens' committee and the Mayor, and we believed they understood that we were going to continue to print the news as it was.

After dinner Mr. Rowell repaired to the Santa Lucia Inn, on the outskirts of town. After further study of the picture at hand, I followed suit about half past one in the morning.

A call from reporter Harry Lerner at about 2 o'clock informed me that a number of deputized citizens and police officers, patronizing a local bar, had just resolved to "get Bailey and beat hell out of him." There were other suggestions that Bailey be lynched. A check and double check revealed that the latter suggestion was being adopted as the more reasonable idea.

Bailey, quartered in the center of town at the Hotel Jeffery, was ordered out to the Santa Lucia Inn. Another check was made on the situation, and it was decided to remove Bailey from the uninviting scene being arranged by the so-called representatives of law and order.

Requesting a highway patrol escort to the airport, we were refused because "there are no cars available and it's a little out of our jurisdiction anyway."

Our plane warmed up. Reporter Bailey was lifted off a dark field at half past two in the morning and returned to San Francisco —much against his will.

★　★　★

Here is proof of something that telegraph editors have always known. Give them a typewriter, a telephone and a little time and they can report a war as well as the next guy.

Telegraph editor Robert McCary, already equipped with telephone and typewriter, muttered loudly enough one evening in 1959 and he got the time—almost two hours of it. This was enough to produce a piece of research and reporting that told

San Francisco newspaper readers more about this peculiar African conflict than they had ever been told before.

Watutsis vs.
Banana Beer

November 15, 1959

A curious war has broken out in Africa—a war that pitted seven-foot rulers, aided by pygmies and airplanes, against the serfs who have humbly tended the giants' cattle for centuries.

It is a war among people whom almost nobody knows anything about, fought in a place almost nobody ever heard of.

Here, gleaned from interviews with anthropologists, world travelers and other experts, and from various reference works, is the background of the weird Watutsi War:

Three hundred years ago, the Watutsi tribe of giants marched into the hills of Central Africa. They came from Egypt or Ethiopia —no one knows for sure—and they were impressive warriors.

Seven feet tall, carrying spears longer than themselves, they marched into the area called Ruanda and Urundi. Before them walked drummers, beating war drums decorated with souvenirs of previous battles. Behind them came herders, leading the lyre-horned cattle that were, and are, the base of the Watutsi economy.

The tribes living in Ruanda and Urundi had never seen anything like the Watutsi before. The tribes were the Batwa, four-foot pygmies who were the original natives of the area, and the Bahutu, a five-foot sevenish tribe who had conquered the Batwa 200 years earlier.

The Batwa and the Bahutu took one look up at the Watutsi and surrendered. The Watutsi had conquered the area without lifting a spear. It is important to remember this.

In the three centuries that have followed, the Watutsi have developed a sophisticated feudal society that is far from the primitive way of life that the average American usually associates with African tribes.

One expert describes the level of development in Ruanda-Urundi as "similar in civilization to Europe between Charlemagne and

Louis XIV." That is a span of 850 years. Another expert narrowed it down "to the way people live in some parts of Texas."

Supposedly he was speaking of the rolling grassland, dotted with the igloo-shaped huts of the Bahutu herders and supporting the cattle of the Watutsi.

Generally speaking it is a stable, if complex, society and the Watutsi kings have ruled it with a firm grip.

The giant warriors, about 10 per cent of the population, are the aristocracy. The ordinary-sized Bahutu, an overwhelming 85 per cent, are the workers. And the pygmies, who make up most of the remaining fraction, are something like pariahs.

As in any feudal society, the barriers break down from time to time. Poverty-stricken Watutsi have been known to work for better-off Bahutu. Under some circumstances, pygmy Batwa may wed Watutsi women, thus rising in caste tremendously.

At least a third of the population is Roman Catholic. Only a Catholic can become king.

But Catholicism has not dispelled all the ancient taboos, and this has been a problem for the Watutsi. The taboos are elaborate, but basically it calls for a person's diet being in inverse ratio to his social status. The higher he is, the fewer things he can eat.

Watutsi may find themselves restricted to beef, cereals and a strong beer made from bananas, Bahutu get a more varied diet, and Batwa may eat anything they can catch.

This, among other things, has left the Watutsi a softer people than they were when they marched in 300 years ago. The Bahutu, on the other hand, have worked hard and multiplied and now outnumber the Watutsi 8 to 1, besides being in better shape.

There is a tribal tradition that says: "The year of the death of a king is a year of trouble." King Rudahigwa died in July, the first king to die without leaving a son. He was succeeded by his younger brother, Kigeri V.

Shortly afterward, grumbling began in Ruanda, for it was about then that the Bahutu got wind of a plan to give the territories independence. Early in this century the Germans took over the area. After World War I the League of Nations had control, and since 1946 Belgium has ruled Ruanda and Urundi under a United Nations trusteeship.

On November 1, a group of Watutsi got into a fight with a

Bahutu chieftain and killed him. This was the incident that pro-voked war. Soon Bahutu fighters were raiding the Watutsi areas, killing and burning. The Watutsi called in the Batwa pygmies, expert archers and dart blowers who, for some reason, hate the Bahutu more than they hate the Watutsi.

Belgium, in the hope of restoring peace, has sent in airplanes and 2000 troops. The fighting continues.

One thing is clear in the confusion: Despite the airplanes and the pygmies, the humble Bahutu are walloping the tar out of their seven-foot masters in every encounter. No matter how the strange war ends the Bahutu have already chalked up a moral victory.

And the legend of the invincible Watutsi, who never had to fight a war before, will be dead, drowned in 300 years of soft living and banana beer.

★   ★   ★

Words to live by, especially recommended for the writers of short editorials:

A leg for the underdog . . . It's how you play the game . . . Look for the silver lining. . . .

It would be difficult to find any purer application of the maxims than this Pollyanna editorial written in the dawn of 1929. The subject was Roy Riegels, whose run in the wrong direction had merely cost California the Rose Bowl game by a score of 8 to 7.

Sunny Side Up

January 3, 1929

It was almost worth the pain and disappointment over the strange outcome of the California-Georgia Tech game to have so fine an example of sportsmanship as that shown by Roy Riegels since his bewildering 75-yard run to his own goal line.

There is vastly more regret over the chagrin of this splendid young athlete than there is over the loss of the game. This senti-ment has been heightened by the manliness with which he has faced full responsibility for his bewilderment.

In that crucial play he had been in collision with at least two of the hard and powerful Georgians. He had emerged from the scramble spinning like a top. Had Riegels had the least taint of weakness of spirit he would have seized the circumstances as a full and satisfactory explanation of what followed.

But Riegels offered nothing except his splendid and manly assumption of full responsibility.

In his behavior under the trying circumstances he has scored as great a victory as if he had carried the ball the other way and over the Georgians' goal line.

★   ★   ★

A newspaper, it says everywhere, should detect and record history as it is being made. This is such a record. The year was 1958. The month, September. The writer, Art Hoppe.

Hoops

September 8, 1958

The name of the independent researcher who first placed a large hoop around his middle and gyrated has unfortunately been lost in the subsequent confusion. But wherever he gyrates now, he gyrates with the heartfelt blessing of the Nation's toy industry.

In the past 60 days anywhere from 5 to 20 million Americans have plunked out somewhere between $8 million and $30 million for hoops—depending upon whose estimate you accept.

Whatever the figures, factories across the country are working frantically around the clock turning out hoops of wood, aluminum, rubber and plastic to load into the trucks waiting at their doors.

And on each street corner stands a little girl, staring vacantly into space as a hoop orbits lazily around her waist.

"This," said one local wholesaler, with awe in his voice, "is the biggest thing since Scrabble."

The unnamed genius who originated modern hooping was probably an Australian. Hooping, *The Chronicle* learned from reliable Australian sources, has been the rage among children down under for more than a year.

In this country most of the credit—along with a goodly share of the cash—is going to Arthur (Spud) Melin, 33-year-old co-owner of the Wham-O Manufacturing Co. of San Gabriel and his attractive wife, Suzy.

A friend in Australia sent the Melins one of the Australian-model bamboo hoops with the thought that they might do something with it. On the sunny morning of April 5—Mrs. Melin remembers the historic date well—the Melins and their eldest daughter, Linda, 9, took the thing out in the backyard. The family mastered the art of hooping in 15 minutes and Melin decided to run off a few test models in his toy factory.

The first models, wooden ones, were well received by children in the neighborhood. Melin and his partner, Richard Knerr, also 33, decided to gamble on production of plastic ones. The name, they figured, should suggest the modern uses of the hoop, so they settled on "Hula Hoop" and hoped to sell a few thousand of the things.

Wham-O!

Today, more than 2 million Hula Hoops later, Wham-O has expanded its San Gabriel plant in Los Angeles County to cover a city block and has opened new Hula Hoop factories in Newark, N. J., and Chicago. All are working three shifts in an unsuccessful effort to meet the demand.

Unfortunately for the Melins, a hoop isn't patentable and a score of alert firms have jumped into the market to help Wham-O fill the needs of a hooping public. Today the prospective hoop buyer can choose not only a Hula Hoop, but a Hoop-Zing, a Hooper-Dooper, a Spin-a-Hoop, a Hoop-La, or a Hoop-Dee-Doo.

Prices range from 79 cents retail to $1.98, with the top-priced ones—like Hula Hoop—made of high density polyethylene. None of the manufacturers is saying what it costs to produce a hoop, but one toy expert puts the figure at about 25 cents.

Typical of the firms that have leaped into the breach is the Moore Manufacturing Co. at 18th and Potrero streets, a firm that generally makes garden hose, plastic pipe, conveyor belts and other mundane products.

Six week ago President J. Max Moore cautiously decided to turn over one-sixth of his production to hoops. As of now, Moore has turned out a quarter of a million of the things; his factory is working three shifts producing 9000 a day; and his customers' trucks are lined up at the shipping room door carting off the hoops as fast as they emerge from the assembly line.

"I have never heard of such a thing," says Moore.

The manufacturing process looks simple. The plastic pipe runs out of an electronically-run machine in a continuous stream. One man saws off nine-foot sections while anothers bends these around in a circle and staples a wooden dowel in the joint.

Presto, a hoop!

Actually, Moore says, the process is more involved than it looks. The specifications for the pipe and the recipe for the Styrene and Polyethylene mix, and the temperatures of the air, gas, and water are all crucial. These details and recipes, Moore says, are a trade secret.

The secret, however, that the Nation's toymakers would gladly give a zillion dollars for is the secret of what has made hooping the craze that it is.

As everybody knows, hoops as toys predate Buster Brown. The main thing new about the modern hoop is what is being done with it. In that earlier, more leisurely age, hoops were rolled down the street with sticks. This is about the last thing a hep hoopster of today would think of doing with his.

The basic skill these days is to put the hoop around one's waist and get it in orbit. This requires gyrations that would bring a blush to the cheeks of Buster Brown and applause from a customer at Minsky's. In fact the name Hula Hoop is somewhat misleading. The primary motion is more akin to Tempest Storm's than Hilo Hattie's.

From this movement today's hoopster proceeds to twirl the hoop with other portions of his anatomy, from his neck to his knees and from his biceps to his fingertips. They also serve, juvenile experts say, for skipping rope, both front and sideways, salt and pepper.

More sedentary types may play "giant horseshoes" with the things, according to Wham-O's brochures, sailing the hoops 30 feet in the hope of ringing any convenient target.

Part of the lure of the toy is obvious to the toymakers. The hoop is a "skill toy" and the basic skill is easy for children to acquire. Hoops are brightly colored and they move rapidly. They are also a competitive toy. But unhappily and mysteriously, a lot of other items with all these same attributes are now gathering dust on toy shop shelves.

Here are some of the more subtle reasons for hooping's success as advanced by the experts.

"They have a nostalgia value," said Norman Altfield, owner of the California Notion and Toy Co. "Dad remembers playing with the hoops when he was a boy and wants his children to have the same fun."

"Because of the laws of physics involved," said another toy wholesaler, "they are easier for small children to work than large adults. Any toy that a kid can work better than his parents has a good chance. It helps the kid get a little of his own back from the grownups."

Also involved for adults is the health angle. There is no question that hooping is a good deal of exercise, especially for the area of the body that a good many adults would like to trim down the most. Indeed, one obstetrician in Southern California has recommended hooping for new mothers.

The all-out promotional campaign has also helped. Pictures have been distributed to the press, magazines and television of hooping football players, hooping dogs and hooping grandmothers. In a unique way the hoops also promote themselves. "About the only thing you can't do with a hoop," says Alan Frankel, owner of Amber's Toy Shop, "is gift wrap it." Thus every departing customer is a display ad.

The Chronicle asked Dr. C. H. Hardin Branch, professor of psychiatry at the University of Utah and secretary-elect of the American Psychiatry Association, if he felt any Freudian implications were involved in the success of hooping.

"The first time I saw a young lady twirling one around her hips I wondered," said the doctor, "but I noticed she spun it up around her neck and enjoyed this just as much.

"The only thing that puzzles me about hoops is how children all over the country seem to break out with the things at exactly the same time. I sometimes wonder if there isn't a highly-organized children's underground with a secret method of communication undreamed of by the adult mind."

The toy makers would like very much to know, as they make out their production schedules, just how long the craze might last.

"We don't see any end to it," said Wham-O's Melin, happily. "It'll taper off, sure, but we think it will be a permanent item, like tops or yo-yos."

Wham-O has already come out with "Hoopees," small 18-inch hoops at 79 cents a pair which one twirls on his hands or feet while spinning the larger Hula Hoop around his middle.

Within a week or so, Wham-O will also bring out an expandable Hula Hoop for bigger people. "We've also got some other types up our sleeves, but I don't want to say anything about them yet," said Melin. "This is a big thing."

The Chronicle asked its reliable Australian source how hooping was going these days down there.

"It was still a big thing last summer," he said. "But come to think of it, when I left a few months ago, I can't remember seeing a single, solitary hoop."

★   ★   ★

Here was proof, in the summer of 1960, that the newspaper-sponsored adventure could still take hold of the popular imagination. The adventure of the Last Man on Earth was in the classic tradition. It set out to find the answer to a momentous question. It built up a dramatic climax, complete with suspense and controversy. Its grasp upon the reading public was so effective that the rival press of San Francisco thought it expedient to take notice and to argue its merits.

The Adventure, as proposed by *The Chronicle*, was a simple one. The suburban Bud Boyd family would go off to a California wilderness to learn whether the "last" family could survive if it had to abandon civilization after the ultimate calamity.

The 41-year-old Bud Boyd was *The Chronicle*'s outdoor writer, an expert fisherman and an experienced woodsman. With him went his wife, Betty, and three children, Susan, fifteen, Sharon, twelve, and Bruce, eight, "vacation campers" at best.

For their test in the wilderness the Boyds chose to limit their equipment to an axe, five pocket knives, a 50-foot length of clothesline, some twine, salt, and the clothes they wore.

For emergency use they did have some extras, a first aid kit, spare eyeglasses for Bud, a flashlight—and a sealed rifle.

To record the adventure the Boyds took along a typewriter, paper and camera equipment in a metal case. To get the story out the Boyds were to drop off copy at a specified time in a milk can cached away from their camp. An outside courier would make the pickup later, after the Boyds had left the drop-off site.

The test started with high hopes for success. There was no exact goal in time. Roughly, the Last Man would have made it if his family had reached such a state of well-being that it could announce itself ready to face the next seasonal change.

On the first day the Boyds reached their campsite. The whole family joined in building a lean-to shelter that proved inadequate to its first test. It held out neither the rain nor the cold of the first night. On the second day the Boyds improved their shelter with only slightly better results.

These excerpts are from Bud Boyd's daily reports. We pick up the Last Man on Earth as he began the third day.

Last Man on Earth

In the Wilderness (3rd day)

The night was bitter cold again. In spite of all the work of yesterday to improve our shelter, we slept miserably. Our fight for survival is against two things: cold and exhaustion.

Strangely enough, although all of us are hungry, we don't seem to mind it as much as the other problems. . . .

Yet we need some kind of food. And it is up to me to find it. This morning I reasoned that our best chance lay with catching trout. I had no fishhooks, line or rod. But makeshift equipment of a sort was at hand. I cut an alder pole. I unraveled a length of twine to separate the three strands, and fashioned a line. I took one of Sharon's rings, broke and twisted it, and fashioned an eye on one end of the bit of metal, and worked the other end into a barbless hook.

While the family slept I walked down to the lake where trout were rising by the hundreds. It looked so easy. It wasn't.

The ring, with its bit of flashing stone worked like a lure all right.

I cast it to the water. I could see trout dart and strike as it touched the surface, but in spite of everything I failed to hook a trout.

I moved around the lake, fishing here, there, everywhere. Finally, where the water shelved off deeply I let the "ring lure" settle to the bottom. When a trout picked it up, I let him hold and fight it, then I set the hook, and I caught him. He was an 8-inch brookie, all red and spotted, and without question, the prettiest trout I'd ever seen.

So I caught six more and went back to camp. The family was still asleep. Today they would have food. . . .

(3rd day, later)

The constant stooping, bending, lifting and crawling on our knees is adding to our sense of failure. After all we are human beings. We have lived our lifetimes on our feet. Now we are living on the ground.

To sleep, we lie down in the dirt. To eat, we squat crosslegged. We must crawl to enter our shelter. We squat before the fireplace to cook. The constant bending and flexing of our muscles has hurt each one of us. Our backs, legs, shoulders and thighs are sore and stiff.

We conclude that getting off the ground was man's first step to progress. He invented a bed, chairs, table, the waist-high cooking stove. They are simple things. But far beyond our wildest dreams at this moment.

(4th day)

We have a mountain meadow near our lake. A host of wild plants grow there, but now for the first time, I realize my knowledge of botany is inadequate. I see and recognize skunk cabbage, which I understand has an edible root. I am not sure yet. I also recognize the spiny stems of our old lawn pest, dandelion. I believe that the young shoots of this weed are edible also.

So today we go grubbing in the dirt. We trekked to the meadow, the children removed their hats, and we began the task of seeking and cutting dandelion stems. They are thistly to the touch. But we cut two handfuls of the choicest stems. We also cut a handful of skunk cabbage tubers. The children carried these back to camp while I tried my hand at fishing. . . .

After catching a few trout, I hurried back to camp where Mother and the children stood disconsolately. "How do we cook the herbs?" Mother asked.

This started our project of the day. And it wasn't easy, because our bellies grumbled and in this case, haste made waste.

Without a cooking pot or kettle, we figured to steam the leaves and stems. We dug a firehole in the earth. At the same time we put a batch of stones inside our campfire and heated them for half an hour. Then we shoveled the hot stones from the fire, put them in the hastily dug pit, and put a few skunk cabbage leaves on top of them.

Then we added the dandelions. We put on another layer of skunk cabbage leaves. We quickly covered the leaves with earth and then I bored a small hole through everything and ran to the lake for water. I scooped up a cupful in my hat, ran back, and poured this down the fire pit. Instantly a thread of steam came up. We figured we had it made. We sat around the steam pit, counting the minutes till it cooked.

"How long will it take?" Sharon asked.

"About twenty minutes," I answered.

We waited the long, agonizing time. At last we carefully removed the layer of dirt and ashes. We lifted the top skunk cabbage leaves, and there was our dandelion dinner—bathed in mud created when I poured the water down the hole.

We threw the whole filthy mess away and cooked our fish. That was all we had to eat tonight.

(5th day)

We had a terrifying experience last night. After a sunny day we went to sleep. The customary night-time wind failed to materialize, and we slept the deep, death-like sleep of sheer exhaustion.

Suddenly I heard a noise. Something was pulling and tugging at the brush wall of our lean-to. Betty heard it, too. She sat up quickly, so did I, and in that instant of becoming awake I saw the fire was out. It was black as pitch.

In sheer, frantic panic I groped for the flashlight which I kept next to the sealed rifle. I couldn't find the switch. My thumb slid wildly, and then the brush wall parted and we could see the bear.

He was a great, black hulk of darkness framed against the star-glow sky.

I found the light. The beam hit him full in the muzzle and he reared in fright, seemed to tumble over in his haste and was gone. We could hear him crashing through the fir and manzanita thickets as he ran. For the first time I knew the meaning of true fear. . . .

I couldn't sleep through the two, terribly cold hours which preceded the dawn, so when the first dim glow of daylight touched the sky, I took the fishing rod and went down to the lake. My first awkward cast touched the water and a trout hit. I missed him. Another cast, and another strike. This time I managed to set the hook made from Sharon's ring, and caught the fish.

I moved down the lake, made another cast and hooked a larger trout. As he splashed and cartwheeled on the surface I tried to ease him out. Then the line broke.

The loss of that lure and hook was immeasurable. I mark this as the greatest disaster of my lifetime. . . .

The Boyds' sixth day in the wilderness was one of brief success and lucky discovery. Bud partially overcame the fishhook tragedy by whittling a sliver of manzanita into a barb that worked as a fishhook until it softened from immersion. Then son Bruce went frog hunting and the Boyd family ate frog legs for the first time in its history.

But the day's biggest triumph came later, and it, too, belonged to young Bruce. He led the way to the remains of a hunter's cache. In it were: a blackened skillet, an empty coffee can, an aluminum cup, plate and spoon, an empty Wesson Oil jug, a torn piece of canvas.

For the moment, with the help of these treasures of civilization, life appeared to be on the upturn. The next day Bud described the whole family's festering "mass of cuts, scratches, insect bites and blisters," but he also was able to describe the day as "actually pleasant." The main difference seemed to be the skillet and coffee can, which made possible the boiling of water and the cooking of wild vegetables.

The rest of that day was taken up with unsuccessful attempts to set snares for game. So on the eighth day Bud made himslf a bow and arrow. He tested his weapon and practiced with it. He was ready for the hunt.

(9th day)

I planned the perfect hunt today. When I finished the bow and arrow, I began to plan. I lay awake and tried to think like the deer I was going after. I worked out every detail.

The deer was a big, fat buck. I have watched him high above the lake, where he lives on a granite bench. I know his habits intimately. He feeds in the early morning, but he doesn't wander very far. He crops at wild peavine, which is starting to grow now, and then he lifts his heavy neck to strip young manzanita blossoms.

Then he lies down in the sun, chews his cud, and finally when the day grows warm, he moves back off the bench and makes his bed beneath a towering, spire-pointed cliff.

I watched him while I worked around the camp. I knew he drowsed at midmorning and that would be the perfect time to sneak up on the rocks, with the wind in my favor, and then shoot him from the rock. While he lay in his bed. Not over 20 feet away.

I even thought of more than that. I considered the inadequacy of my weapons, and tried to compensate with intelligence. For example, I reasoned that my crude arrow, with its wooden point, would never cut through hide and bone and flesh to find the vitals of a deer. A shot into the chest would just bounce off because of the bone structure. So I figured to aim for the paunch. I planned my shot to hit the belly. I wanted to hit the deer, let him run and stop, then I would stand up straight and tall where he could see me, and I would walk away.

I would let him see me so that he would feel secure, and lie there and get sicker and sicker. Eventually he would be unable to run away. Then I would go back and get him.

This morning I waited for the buck to bed down for the day. I waited until the thermal drafts were rising, and then I took my bow and single arrow, and I began the hunt. I went high around the mountain hideout. My legs ached from the climb, but I moved quite slowly and chose every stepping place with care. Finally, I reached the jagged cliff. I crawled in slowly, testing the wind as I moved, and finally reached the spot. If the buck was in his bed he'd be there, on the other side of the rock, and only 20 feet away.

I lay still to catch my wind. I waited until my heart stopped pounding, then I notched the arrow and slowly raised.

He was there. I could see the long hairs on his back, the black wet glint on his nose and his long ears which flickered at a buzzing deerfly.

I drew the bow with a strength I didn't know I had. The arrow whipped from the twanging bowstring, and then suddenly dived and hit the dirt in front of him. In that instant the buck was up and running, and I heard the rocks roll below where he turned and doubled up another canyon.

I was sick. The built-up anticipation and the bitter reaction and self-accusation was too much. I tried to vomit, but nothing came. So I headed back to camp. I am completely beat from the climb and depressed beyond belief. Never again will I claim to be a hunter. Yes, I used to think I was one. I have killed dozens of bucks in my hunting life. But it wasn't hunting, really. I had always had the help of other brains and muscles. Someone dug the ore and smelted it. Someone designed, built and rifled the barrel. Another craftsman built the lock, calculated the cartridge.

All I have ever done before was pull the trigger.

(9th day, later)

Three great flickering flashes of white lightning ripped the sky above us, and even before I could say, "Look out, kids, here she comes," a tremendous clap of thunder shook the air and seemed to tear the breath from our open mouths.

The wind is tearing down the pass in terrifying gusts. It blows six ways at once, and there is no escaping it.

Now it is raining. The drops fall through our flimsy roof and splash upon us; on the ground and our clothes. The rain is mixed with hail, and in the strange, bronze-colored light, the hailstones look like golden nuggets. But they are cold.

(10th day)

This morning we left our lean-to at the mountain lake. I had made the decision to try living at a lower elevation because we couldn't continue in this lonesome, mountain fastness. . . .

Frankly, we are glad to leave this cliff-rimmed basin. We have known cold, hunger, fear and sickness here. The sickness is a mysterious thing, and I blame it on the water we have been drinking from the snow-fed lake. We have all had serious bouts with chills and fever. Susan has been especially sick, and at times she sits all huddled in the hot sun, and shivers uncontrollably.

My wife, Betty, has been sickest of all. The fever hits her hardest. She also has bursitis in both shoulders, and we blame this on the winds and sleeping on the ground. . . .

We came down the mountainside only about a mile, but we must have dropped a thousand feet in the descent. We followed the outlet from our lake and when we had to cross a field of sleek, round boulders, Betty slipped and fell. She wrenched her knee and within the seconds it took to raise her trouser leg to inspect the damage, the vein across her kneecap had swollen. It puffed out under the skin for a full half-inch.

But we kept going down. . . .

Yes, the "last man on earth" must be a nomad. We have decided to follow the game animals we need to eat. We must live where the weather is kind to our weak bodies. And we must travel with the ripening wild crops. We must find a suitable habitat, just as the animals do.

With this in mind, we've eyed the timber country where we rest right now. It looks good. For the first time I feel that we might make it. . . .

(11th day)

While the family slept, I rolled over on the ground, tried to stretch, then bellied down at the nearby creek for a drink of water, and went down to check my traps. . . .

I ran the last few yards and saw my catch. It was a spotted fawn. It hung limp with the rope cutting into its dainty throat. It had strangled during the night, and it was so tiny that the spring tree had lifted it clear of the ground. There was not a sign of struggle.

This was our first red meat in 11 days.

It was a strange emotional moment. I knew the doe was nearby, probably watching. And for just a moment I felt terribly sorry for the doe and fawn. But survival is a basic need, and my thoughts turned quickly to Betty and the children who were hungry. I pictured the look on their faces when I'd bring this meat to camp. So I cleaned it quickly, placed the little heart and liver on a rock, and then skinned the carcass where it lay.

Then I headed back to camp and awakened the family. I split the carcass lengthwise with my axe, whacked out the tender back strap and put the chops upon the fire to broil. The meat was almost blue in color. There wasn't an ounce of fat. But we ate as we never did before. We held the sizzling chops in our fingers and gnawed at the bones and munched the blackburned rib tips with our teeth.

I put the rest of the meat inside the hide, wrapped this in my jacket, tied it securely to keep the flies away, and hung it in a tree. But within the hour we were hungry again, and we cooked and ate more meat.

After the meal we felt lethargic. But after we had drunk our fill of water we felt a shot of energy and began to forage for the day. . . .

In our excitement we had failed to watch the weather. Even while we sought more berries near the creek bank, the sky turned gray with clouds. The rain fell harder as we hiked through the forest. Thunder split the mountain air above us with a boom, and rain fell in a deluge.

We reached camp to find that the fire had gone out. The coals were a soggy, sodden mess, so I grabbed my fire sticks and went to work under the shelter of a tree. I pleaded with the spark, I blew it into flaming life, and while the children fed the fire, I hastily felled three fir trees and we leaned these across the rock and huddled in their shelter.

It is hard to write. We lie close together. Rain drops splash upon us and Betty and the children are huddled beneath our scrap of canvas. Our bellies are filled, but the misery of weather is just as merciless as hunger. Is this all there is to life?

(11th day, later)

I called a family council. We must make a decision: do we stay or leave? Is sheer existence worth the price we pay?

We gathered in a semicircle. In the torment of the moment we were a serious group. Susan was still sick with chills and the drain upon her health was showing. Betty was also ill. I am afraid we overate of the lean, too-fresh fawn meat, and we are paying the consequence with continual belly cramps.

Even Sharon, who has kept our spirits high, realized the despair of our position, and she sat grave-faced waiting for me to speak. Son Bruce, age 8, was also listless. He has known the pangs of continual hunger and cold nights. "The last family on earth" was desperate.

"Let us say that we are truly the last family," I said. "What does the future hold?"

We discussed the prospects and found them terrifying.

"We will never have a decent bath again in our lives," Sharon said.

"And what happens when the first aid kit runs out?" asked Susan.

Betty roused herself to say, "I'm sure the last family could not all live without medical help. Aside from that," she added, "let us list the things we have always taken for granted and which we'll never see again."

So we counted the many, tiny things. None of us will ever know the comfort of a blanket in the world of night. We might eventually make sleeping robes of a sort from deer hides, but such a task would take years.

Our savage diet of fish, weeds and occasional meat stretched to the infinite future. We must continue to live upon the ground like animals, never know again the wonders of a chair, a table, drinking from a glass, turning on a faucet or throwing an electric switch.

Our life pattern must become a cycle of migration which follows the weather, and the animals, and the ripening weeds.

Our discussion kept straying back to little things. "What happens when the tin can wears out?" asked Betty. Without that we have no vessel for heating water. We have been unable to find a substitute. What happens to us if we lose our knives? When the salt is gone? If the axe breaks? If a bear tears up my snares and we lose the rope? The future is imponderable.

Yet in our imaginations, certain things are inescapable. As parents we shall die and leave our children. What legacy do they have? A life of continual fear, and a fight for sheer existence.

This is the legacy we leave. And the result would be that man degenerates—our religion would be lost in time, and the stories of the Bomb and the Germs and Civilization would become just stories. This is a predictable future and there is no escaping it. . . .

So we discussed these things as a family should. We conclude that mere existence is not living. We decided to return to the valleys, where even if the fallout lingers down low, we will once more know the luxuries of warmth, of sleeping in a bed, of eating foods we've known in other times.

We gathered our pitiful belongings. The five of us walked across the timbered plateau where we've lived. We stood at the edge of the great precipice, above the valley, and looked downhill to the end.

Happily, the Boyd family faced neither fallout nor desolation. The next morning Bud made his way six miles down the side of the mountain to the hunting lodge of J. D. Proctor in the community of Etna in the Klamath National Forest. Together, he and Proctor returned to the campsite with pack mules loaded heavily with foodstuffs, bourbon whiskey, soap, towels and toilet paper. Lunch and washing took so long they all decided to stay for dinner. Then, after highballs for the adults, and another round of steak and potatoes and spaghetti for everyone, the Boyd family mounted up and headed out of the wilderness. The adventure of the Last Man on Earth was over.

★   ★   ★

OUR VERY OWN

When Stanton Delaplane wrote this piece of nostalgia and sweet sentiment he was still new to the column-writing business and fresh out of the Hildy Johnson school of reporting. To read it you would think he had been painting covers for *The Saturday Evening Post* all his born days.

The Chronicle has reprinted this essay in every Thanksgiving Day edition since it first appeared in 1950.

The Gold Was Shinier

Thanksgiving Day, 1950

Walking past the markets this morning and casting an eye on the turkeys which, to my mind, are not as large as when I was a boy. Or is it just that I am getting bigger? Anyway it seems to me that turkeys used to be enormous birds. Bigger than eagles maybe. And I was thinking of Thanksgiving Days of other years. And some were good and some were dull, but just for the remembering of them this day I am truly thankful.

The best Thanksgiving Days are when you are young and when I was a boy (and turkeys were much larger than nowadays) Thanksgiving was the day you spent on a farm in Illinois. With the air turning crisp and maybe even a fall of snow in the smoky twilight evening and the older boys getting out the guns to go rabbit hunting in the morning. And the fields lined up with corn stalks in the shocks and the corn with all the different colored kernels stacked away in the board cribs so that you could see it through the cracks.

Since my great-grandfather had 16 children, there was a terrible number of grandchildren and even more great-grandchildren. And in the morning there was a great squawking and outcry of chickens and turkeys being run down behind the barn, all the little boys running out to see the slaughter and all the little girls running the other way with their hands over their ears.

I remember that the early table was for the children who stood around drooling all morning while roast turkey smells filled the

house and the pumpkin pies were brought up from the cellar where
they had been cooling. And later we could peek through the window while the grownups sat down. My great-grandfather, being a
religious man, but no person to delay the proceedings, would bow
his head and in one breath declare:

". . . Bless this gathering and for what we are about to receive
may the Lord make us truly thankful amen will you have a little
white or dark meat?" And he would tuck a napkin under the beard
and go to work with a big horn-handled knife that was as sharp
as a razor.

Then after dinner we could sit on the floor and he would tell
us how he crossed the plains to dig gold in California. (Like the
turkeys that were bigger, California was much farther from Illinois
in those days.) There was a very high point where he told about
how he was riding far away from the wagon train one day and an
Indian rode up to him "and I whipped out my pistol and pointed
it right at his stomach," said my great-grandfather, "and he kindy
rode away again." And we would all clutch our stomachs in sympathy.

Then he would tell us how he got to California and how his
partner was killed in a mine cave-in and he took his gold and went
back to Illinois to tell his partner's girl about it and stayed there
and married her.

And at the conclusion, he would rise and go to the big glass whatnot in the corner that had the seashell you could put to your ear
and hear the sea roaring. And he would take out a big chunk of
quartz, as big as your fist, and he would say:

"And there's the gold from Californy!"

I can tell you it never failed to bring down the house and I have
handled that gold myself and it seems to me that the gold used to
be shinier and better than the gold they dig nowadays.

The other day I took a young lady of my acquaintance to the
hospital. She is a very close acquaintance and I have known her
for seven years. We have a very fine relationship. She thinks I am
the greatest thing in the world and I think she is the greatest thing
in the world and this is very satisfactory to both of us. It was no
easy thing to leave her at a hospital even though it was a minor
matter of tonsils. It is very hard to watch a 7-year-old being brave
and harder when the time comes when they must be brave all

alone and that is the time when you walk out and leave your heart in the hospital room.

There was a small boy there, too, and he was just coming out of the ether with tears running down his face, but he said it was nothing. It was easy, he said, with tears coming down both sides. He explained that his daddy had to work and his mamma could not be there "because we have a little sister at my house and it's hard for her to get away."

But now today everything is fine and just as if it had never happened. And everybody is eating ice cream (which doesn't seem as creamy or cold as when I was a boy, though). But I suspect that for them the ice cream is cold and creamy and the turkeys are enormous and the gold is shiny and heavy and golden. And for these things today I am truly thankful.

The hawkers of advice on the women's pages used to confine their wares to facial creams, long-lasting nail lacquers and the correct-size paper for thank-you notes. Then, trailblazers entered the more personal fields. There were child-raising experts and marriage counselors. Occasionally, more impudent types have advised in even more private areas, menopause, back-seat necking or hysterectomies. But take even the wildest of these practitioners, put them up against a fellow called Count Marco, and their efforts will look no earthier than a serialization of Elsie Dinsmore.

The Count, who burst upon the women's pages of *The Chronicle* in 1959, chose an obvious, but unexplored thesis. Marriage, he said, involved certain basic relations between the sexes. His column devoted itself to the betterment of those relations.

The Chronicle's promotion of the Count's efforts was handled with tongue-in-cheek dignity, but there was nothing tongue-in-cheek about the hope that the column would provide widespread controversy and amusement. The hope was quickly achieved. The customers read the Count to laugh with him, or at him, or simply to hate him. Some of his fan mail actually saw him as a peril to the American way of life.

Peril or not, **Count Marco** was certainly debatable and attention-grabbing newspaper material, a classic example of the villain with great box-office appeal. The sample chosen here is purposely one of the most flagrant of his early excursions against the established mores.

Marco's Big Tub

August 4, 1959

How long has it been since you had your back washed by your adoring husband as he mops away, slowly, tenderly and soapily, over and over, remarking about that cute little mole he discovered right after your marriage, when he first washed your back?

Today the American woman has lost one of the real arts of enjoyment in marriage and life: bathing *a deux*. By installing a bathtub little bigger than a washbasin, you miss the joy of community bathing, once the most fashionable occupation of nobility and royalty.

The early Roman baths (which were even popular in France, Switzerland and Germany) were great tiled affairs sunk in the floor, complete with hand rail, into which the woman stepped like a sea nymph going home. They were large enough for the husband and wife to soak together, relaxing in the warmth of scented water while they got acquainted again after a day of separation.

Bathing together is having a fashionable comeback in some circles. One famous European actress has two of everything in all her bathrooms because she considers her husband at his wittiest when he is in the bathroom, and she doesn't want to miss a single word.

Surely, you yourself realize that it is while soaking in a hot tub that your thoughts wander into unexplored channels of greatness. Then, why not relax together? Revive in your own house the lost art of romance and take a bath with your husband. It will be lots of fun, full of surprises and one way to get your back washed. I realize that nowadays the typical American household does not boast a tub large enough for both of you.

But we can daydream, can't we?

This essay, then, is my opening fusillade in a one-man campaign to introduce an emperor-sized bathtub into every American home.

There is an art to bathing, just as there is an art to undressing. You just don't wander into the bathroom stark naked. You wear a robe, and while he stands there devouring you with his eyes, you turn your back to him and let the robe slip gently to the floor like a perfumed breeze.

Step daintily into the bubble-filled tub. *Mon Dieu,* this is no time to bend over and test the temperature of the water. Pre-test it for warmth. You want to be able to step in immediately without a lot of caterwauling about how hot it is while you fiddle with the faucets.

Don't offer to his horrified eyes the ungainly sight of a bare bottom that will only remind him of a blimp struggling through a storm.

Once in the tub, stand momentarily like the girl in the painting, "September Morn." Your shoulders should be hunched slightly forward, arms crossed in modesty. Even if it gets a laugh (which it probably will, if he hasn't by then fallen down hysterically), you will be getting him in the mood.

Lower yourself gradually into the water. Don't just plop in like a baby whale.

Then it is his turn to get into the tub. He'll have his own techniques for this, having watched you. It should enthrall you, and no doubt will.

Think how pleasant it will be stretched out side by side in a bathtub built for two, chatting softly away about the birds and bees, as the water swallows all your problems. The hour is late and you can both relax your cares and troubles away.

Pass the soap, dear.

★ ★ ★

The television critic faces a strange and difficult assignment. He must write for people who have seen the show and at the same time for those who haven't. In either case, his advice and viewpoint can only serve as post mortem. There is only the re-motest chance of a repeat performance.

So, like the good baseball writer, who faces the identical problem, the successful television critic needs to be more than a mere reviewer. He becomes a reporter, a sharer of trade secrets and an intimate of the players. It would be difficult to find a more perfect exponent of this than *The Chronicle*'s Terrence O'Flaherty. With the added ingredient of nothing-sacred sauciness he has shaken his daily report free from the agate channel logs and into a deserving major news position. His column is a highly personal report and commentary on the most popular of our entertainment art forms.

What follows is typical of the O'Flaherty approach to a particular TV show. There is criticism, reporting, a helping of gossip, and a lot of O'Flaherty.

The Silver Screen

January 12, 1960

Now we can all die happy, including Ed Sullivan. "Hedda Hopper's Hollywood" has come and gone. The famous faces glittered briefly on the screen and were paid their $210 for a million dollars worth of free personal advertising apiece.

There were some good moments and many bad ones and, considering the possibilities, it was a disappointment. But I'd be deceiving you if I give the impression that I didn't enjoy every minute of it. Even Ed Sullivan stayed home from his own show so he could see it. (His replacement said he had "a bad cold.")

The show opened with Hopper sitting on an abutment overlooking the foothills of Hollywood at a spot just above the old "HOLLYWOODLAND" sign. She was wearing fox furs, a black lace picture hat and a choker of diamonds and rubies that would have dropped a jewel thief at 60 paces. Just the right costume for tramping through the foothills on a winter afternoon.

Miss Hopper looked over the chasm and invited us to take a look at "some of the people in MY town." (If you heard a cry of anguish at this moment, I suspect that it came from the general vicinity of her arch enemy, Louella O. Parsons, who also lays claim to the same piece of real estate.)

Hopper saved her most flattering introduction for Marion Davies, which must have puzzled many viewers. But there's a solid basis for their friendship. In the days directly following the death of William Randolph Hearst many of Miss Davies' friends dropped her. Among them, they say, was Miss Parsons, who by that time was probably tired of having to write about her. But in those two long weeks before Miss Davies discovered she had inherited an empire, Hedda was one of the few to stick by her.

"Marion loved big parties and you could always count on finding an ex-President or a Prime Minister among the guests. . . . And now let's go into her home to accept a gracious welcome from a great lady. . . ."

The cameras moved in cautiously on a full shot of Marion and I suspect that people all over Hollywood gasped in disbelief. For once, the old Parsons line, "Marion never looked lovelier," really applied. The fragile star, who usually looks a beat 65, turned into a 25-year-old doll.

Over the years Hollywood has been a glorious monument to the delicate myths of youth and beauty. So it was no accident that the Westmore family of makeup artists was lined up for Hedda's show looking like the Nuremberg judges. One of the Westmores had the best line of the evening—possibly the best line of the season. "I had the privilege of shaving the head of Bette Davis as Queen Elizabeth," he said soberly. That's all. These privileged moments come so seldom, even in Hollywood, that I suppose that one hates to talk too much about them.

The youngest-looking people on the show were Miss Davies, Gloria Swanson, Janet Gaynor and Hopper herself. Put them all together and they spell "grandmother"—but you'd never know it. As Bob Hope said:

"Makeup artists have done more for Hollywood women than anything since Community Property."

Of course, these people were beautiful women to begin with—and that's 90 per cent of the battle. The makeup bit restores beauty, but doesn't bestow it.

At considerable effort I have learned the actual makeup secret that turns many of the aging Hollywood beauties into ravishing young women before the camera. I may be shot for giving this secret away, but here goes.

A strip of strong, finely woven net (the kind used for hair pieces) is glued along the temple and down almost to the middle of the ear. Tiny hooks are secured to the lace and then the face is made up, hiding everything.

The hair on the front of the head is combed down over the face, rubber bands are looped over the hooks and tied together on the top of the head. The tighter the tie, the less skin dangles at the chin line. The hair is combed back over the rubber bands and voila! When the jowls disappear, 20 years go with them and madame is a chicken once more. As long as the rubber bands hold out.

Miss Davies liked her rubberized finish so much that she toured the nightspots before removing her makeup, thus startling everyone on the Sunset Strip. At 3 in the morning she called Hedda asking how to get out of the contraption. Miss Hopper sent glue remover.

I have just looked at myself in the mirror and I think that by keeping the hair long in front and growing sideburns to cover the laceworks I might just date Marion myself. With a bottle of glue remover for a night cap, we could have danced all night. . . .

★   ★   ★

Allan Temko's first brush with journalism occurred at *The Chronicle* where, as a copyboy, he demonstrated a natural talent for criticism, more often than not of the efforts of those in higher echelon. So the young Temko was banished to a garret in Paris. For years he slaved at studying various arts, concentrating perhaps on writing and architecture. A result of these labors was a mighty, prize-winning history of the cathedral of Notre Dame.

Temko returned in acclaim to the United States, became a contributing editor to *Architectural Forum*, a writer for *Harper's* and joined the faculty of University of California. Thus he was qualified once again for *The Chronicle*.

Temko's *Chronicle* assignment has been to stand as a watchdog over the skyline of the Bay Area. He rails loudly against atrocities already perpetuated and those about to be. On rare occasion he has even deemed a man-made structure worthy of its natural San Francisco setting.

The essay chosen here is typical of Temko lance-tilting. It

matters hardly if his target happens to be a commercial establishment which on the same day might be helping pay the way for the newspaper and for Temko.

Back Street Revisited

August 21, 1961

Maiden Lane, once notorious for its rouged ladies, in recent years has acquired a lively reputation for civic virtue. This dark alley—a typical downtown back street, really, running only two blocks from Union Square to Kearny street—has become a notable example of urban renovation.

As in the Jackson Square area, where the presence of handsome structures of historical importance has made this sort of neighborhood renewal even more striking, the rehabilitation of Maiden Lane shows that San Francisco's narcissistic infatuation with the past, often a lamentable influence in urban affairs, can also be a force for good.

For if we are unable to rebuild the city in an audacious, thoroughgoing and logical way worthy of a great metropolis, which seems sadly the case at present, we can at least try to make the best of what we have.

Such an effort—imperfect enough, but an effort nevertheless—has been made in Maiden Lane. Not all of the Lane's improvements, moreover, may be described as mere refurbishment. Its crowning jewel—Frank Lloyd Wright's V.C. Morris Store—shows the way toward a new order of urban civilization.

None of the other buildings in the Lane approach the Morris store's distinction, but almost all the shops, and frequently the offices above them, have been extensively remodeled. At the same time, with only minor assistance from City Hall, the merchants and other members of the Maiden Lane Association have brightened the entire little street with green sycamores, new sidewalks which have been cheerfully edged with brick, and new lamp posts, including the showy—too showy—white electrical candelabras at the entrance to the Lane.

In a still more significant innovation the roadway has been closed to motor traffic, except for truck deliveries at odd hours, and the Lane has thus become downtown's first pedestrian mall.

This change alone deserves a public vote of thanks. To step off a curb in the heart of an American city, and not risk injury from an onrushing automobile, is a blessing which must be experienced fully. The citizenry has been quick to show appreciation in the way merchants like best.

The Lane is flourishing. Where all had been dull, if not downright disheartening and dingy, there is an unmistakable air of fresh vitality. New tenants have taken over many of the old premises. Not only have designers and architects such as Donald Clever and Welton Becket & Associates who with landscape architect Lawrence Halprin are responsible for the street improvements set up attractive offices, but Brooks Brothers and Saks Fifth Avenue have lent their august—and, alas, architecturally conservative—presences to the intersection of the Lane and Grant avenue.

Physical improvement has undeniably resulted in improved business; and by banishing the automobile, the shopkeepers have actually brought more customers to their doors.

This is a lesson from which the rest of the central district might profit. Indeed, the authors of "The Exploding Metropolis"— fervent advocates of the pedestrians' rights—consider it a lesson for the nation at large, and they claim that the Lane has become one of the country's "finest shopping streets."

Commercially this may be true, but as far as architecture is concerned—with the exception of the Morris store, which may well be the country's finest shop—such extravagant praise is a sad commentary on the general state of the U.S. urban scene. It overlooks the fact that Maiden Lane, partly because it is a back street, was very ugly to begin with (even though it was completely rebuilt after 1906) and it remains fundamentally little changed.

Some ugliness, furthermore, has been added. Earlier I mentioned the flashy lighting fixtures, which seem better suited for a suburban shopping center than for the urban heart of San Francisco. The canned music, which the merchants inexplicably feel compelled to play in the street, falls into the same category. So too, unfortunately, do almost all of the remodeled shops.

In general, again excepting the Morris store, the shops can be described either as traditional pastiches or psuedo-modern still-births.

Of the first, the imitation Georgian pretentiousness of Brooks Brothers and Saks Fifth Avenue—twin establishments which provide a neoclassical formal entrance to the Lane at Grant avenue—can stand as a model.

If these soundly constructed stores are in no way cheap (which alone is something to be thankful for in an age of shoddy commercial architecture), they are nonetheless aesthetically false, and hopelessly unconvincing in comparison with the traditional European architecture which inspired their design—or even with a sensitively detailed older San Francisco shop such as Shreve's.

Not only do they lack meaning for the contemporary world, and indeed revert conspicuously to an age of privilege, but in the case of Brooks Brothers, which provides a needlessly solid base for the lithe, open early 20th Century structure rising above it, the true vigorous elegance of modern American civilization is denied.

Yet the traditionalism of Brooks and Saks (if not of the insufferably coy dress shoppe and the crassly done American Express office which flank the Morris store) is surely preferable to the pseudo-modern of Ransohoff's Maiden Lane frontage, to cite one offender of the other type.

An even more regrettable wall of this kind, perhaps, is the commonplace brick surface with which Sheridan & Bell replaced its charming old facade of white tiles which made it, for me, the most delightful flower shop in town.

Yet a short distance away—quietly resplendent, completely at home in the city even though it makes no concession to contemporary vulgarity—is the Morris store.

My next article will be devoted to this late lesson of the master, designed when Wright was nearly 80, which in some ways is the youngest building in the city.

For more than a decade it has been standing in San Francisco, waiting for study, but the city, strangely indifferent to truly new things, has yet to give it the attenion it deserves.

★　★　★

At issue here, the Sheraton Corp. notwithstanding, was the simple question of "Who owns the Sheraton-Palace Hotel anyway?"

Speaking up squarely against private profit and gain was that noted radical, Lucius Beebe, defender of the citizen's right to four lamb's kidneys in every breakfast portion, and a regular Monday columnist on *The Chronicle*'s editorial page.

This bit of culinary advice to the hotel's corporate fathers in Boston was not exactly a typical Beebe offering. It was one of the few in which the writer espoused a cause likely to have support from the world that, unfortunately, exists outside Mr. Beebe.

Accountant-de-Cuisine

January 16, 1961

The war between the people of San Francisco and the owners and management of the Sheraton Hotels Corp. of America with offices in Boston, 3000 miles away as the Old Crow flies but infinitely farther emotionally and sentimentally, is one in which the owners of the Sheraton-Palace don't stand a chance to win. Nevertheless, they persist in a stubborn rear guard action conducted by an entirely expendable battalion of cost accountants.

When the Sheraton Corp. purchased The Palace from Mrs. William B. Johnston and other heirs to the Sharon estate a few years back, kind friends took Ernest Henderson, president of Sheraton, aside and attempted to tell him that The Palace wasn't just an investment in real estate with convention facilities and permit to sell liquor; it was an institution in the community that had been around for 80 odd years and occupied a position in the community's esteem far different from that of any other hotel properties he might casually acquire in New York, Philadelphia or Chicago. They pointed out that in its primeval years the original Palace had been the wonder and glory of the entire Old West, an oriflamme of San Francisco's pride and splendor and that, over the years, it had come very close to being a private home for many people. Native San Franciscans had, some of them, been born in its private suites; many more had been introduced to society, been

married or spent wedding trips there. All San Franciscans had re-
garded The Palace in its pre-Henderson days with affection and
sentimentality.

No other hotel anywhere was an exact parallel of its peculiar
and unique position of esteem among its patrons.

Mr. Henderson, being a courteous Boston gentleman, listened
attentively to these well-wishers and then, being president of Sheraton hotels, went right about giving The Palace the cost accountant
treatment accorded every other hotel in the absentee-owned
Sheraton string of properties.

As long as Edmond Reider was around in the capacity of manager, there was a bridge across the ever widening gap between the
old Palace and the new ownership. Mr. Reider, a professional Swiss
hotelier with a profound knowledge of food and wine, insisted on
keeping a first-class chef in the kitchen and successfully resisted
the new management's every inclination to install a bookkeeper as
chef de cuisine and a cost accountant as chief saucier. The Sheraton
idea of food is that any short order frycook is good enough especially if he is possessed of the sort of executive genius that can cut
a breakfast order of lamb's kidneys from four to three, as is actually
now practiced at the Sheraton-Palace.

In his book about the Sheraton operations of which he is the
head, Mr. Henderson repeatedly, and both explicitly and implicitly
ridicules the idea that food is of any consequence in the management
of a hotel restaurant. As a result San Francisco is confronted with
a menu at the Sheraton-Palace on which there is no Roquefort, only
blue cheese, and a wine card listing no single vintage champagne
where, in the proper management of any first-class restaurant,
there should be a minimum of 50.

Mr. Henderson is possessed of the curious delusion that he
should make money on food. He should get acquainted with the
record of another and notably successful restauranteur and hotelier
named Fred Harvey who year after year discharged chefs from his
premises because they were not losing enough money on their food.
Harvey died respected as a great man in the history of the American
West and nobody notices any of his heirs around Chicago today as
looking notably seedy.

In justice to the Sheraton management it should be pointed out
that they have accomplished a magnificent job of facelifting in the

public apartments of The Palace. The Garden Court, the main lobby and what used to be the rather gloomy Palace Corner have been expensively reupholstered and redecorated at what must have been staggering cost. The drinks in the Pied Piper and Tudor Rooms are the best this side of the Ambassador in Chicago and the old-time waiters, many of them practically family retainers since Mrs. Johnston's regime, are among the pleasantest mannered people in a mannered and gracious city.

There is nothing wrong with the Sheraton-Palace that a restaurant deficit of half a million annually wouldn't cure. Other hotels know that this can be absorbed by the martinis and old-fashioned department and put their best foot forward to keep pheasant on the menu and Eastern lobster on ice.

It's a pity that the Sheraton management back in Boston doesn't understand that San Francisco is a city that takes food and drink more seriously than Detroit or Chicago. A little imagination and a free hand in the kitchen for the chef could make the Sheraton-Palace the showpiece of all Sheraton hotels and a conversation piece worth a million times that pitiful sum saved by the thrice damned accountants on substitutes for butter and short orders on the lamb's kidneys.

San Francisco hotels and restaurants are crawling with alumni from The Palace. There is a captain or maitre d'hotel who is a Palace graduate in every establishment in town worth mentioning. It would be better, however, if the patrons of the Garden Court did not become alumni, too. Not even all those dreary conventions can keep a hotel in the running if San Francisco itself stays away.

THE FRONT PAGE

Reporter Royce Brier saw war in the streets of San Francisco on Thursday, the fifth of July, 1934.

The day was the fifty-eighth of a strike on the city's waterfront. It was the day chosen to test the strikers' power to throttle the flow of goods at the docks and warehouses. Whoever may have won that bloody test, the day eventually produced the birth of a new and stronger waterfront union.

Brier's "I was there" story tries valiantly to find the word pictures to describe the unbelievable scene of Bloody Thursday. There are times when he is in grave peril of falling over the brink of excitement. He never quite does. The end of the story finds him writing in CAPITAL LETTERS, but still somehow on his feet.

Bloody Thursday

July 6, 1934

Blood ran red in the streets of San Francisco yesterday.

In the darkest day this city has known since April 18, 1906, one thousand embattled police held at bay five thousand longshoremen and their sympathizers in a sweeping front south of Market street and east of Second street.

The furies of street warfare raged for hour piled on hour.

Two were dead, one was dying, 32 others shot and more than three score sent to hospitals.

Hundreds were injured or badly gassed. Still the strikers surged up and down the sunlit streets among thousands of foolhardy spectators. Still the clouds of tear gas, the very air darkened with hurtling bricks. Still the revolver battles.

As the middle of the day wore on in indescribable turmoil the savagery of the conflict was in rising crescendo. The milling mobs fought with greater desperation, knowing the troops were coming; the police held to hard-won territory with grim resolution.

It was a Gettysburg in the miniature, with towering warehouses thrown in for good measure. It was one of those days you think of as coming to Budapest.

The purpose of it all was this: The State of California had said it would operate its waterfront railroad. The strikers had defied the State of California to do it. The police had to keep them off. They did.

Take a San Francisco map and draw a line along Second street south from Market to the bay. It passes over Rincon Hill. That is the west boundary, Market is the north of the battlefield.

Not a street in that big sector but saw its flying lead yesterday, not a street that wasn't tramped by thousands of flying feet as the tide of battle swung high and low, as police drove them back, as they drove police back in momentary victory.

And with a dumfounding nonchalance, San Franciscans, just plain citizens bent on business, in automobiles and on foot, moved to and fro in the battle area.

Don't think of this as a riot. It was a hundred riots, big and little, first here, now there. Don't think of it as one battle, but as a dozen battles.

It started with a nice, easy swing just as great battles in war often start. The Industrial Association resumed moving goods from Pier 38 at 8 A.M. A few hundred strikers were out, but were held back at Brannan street, as they had been in Tuesday's riot, by the police.

At Bryant and Main streets were a couple of hundred strikers in an ugly mood. Police Captain Arthur de Guire decided to clear them out, and his men went at them with tear gas. The strikers ran, scrambling up Rincon Hill and hurling back rocks.

Proceed now one block away, to Harrison and Main streets. Four policemen are there, about 500 of the mob are on the hill. Those cops looked like fair game.

"Come on, boys," shouted the leaders.

They tell how the lads of the Confederacy had a war whoop that was a holy terror. These boys, a lot of them kids in their teens, came down that hill with a whoop. It sounded blood-curdling. One policeman stood behind a telephone pole to shelter him from the rocks and started firing with his revolver.

Up the hill, up Main, came de Guire's men on the run, afoot and the "mounties." A few shots started whizzing from up the hill, just a scattering few, with a high hum like a bumble bee.

Then de Guire's men, about 20 of them, unlimbered from Main and Harrison and fired at random up the hill. The down-plunging mob halted, hesitated, and started scrambling up the hill again.

Here the first man fell, a curious bystander. The gunfire fell away.

Up came the tear gas boys, six or eight carloads of them. They hopped out with their masks on, and the gas guns laid down a barrage on the hillside. The hillside spouted blue gas like the Valley of the Ten Thousand Smokes.

Up the hill went the moppers-up, phalanxes of policemen with drawn revolvers. The strikers backed sullenly away on Harrison street, past Fremont street. Suddenly came half a dozen carloads of men from the Bureau of Inspectors, and right behind them a truck load of shotguns and ammunition.

In double quick they cleared Rincon Hill. Ten police cars stuck their noses over the brow of the hill.

Noon came. Napoleon said an army travels on its belly. So do strikers and police, and even newspapermen.

Now it is one o'clock. Rumors of the coming of the soldiery fly across the town. The strikers are massing down at the foot of Mission and Howard streets, where a Belt Line freight train is moving through.

Police massed there, too; the tear gas squads, the rifle and shotgun men, the mounties. Not a sign of machine guns so far. But the cops have them. There's plenty of talk about the "typewriters."

There they go again into action, the gas boys! They're going up the stubby little streets from the Embarcadero to Steuart street, half blocks up Mission and Howard. Across by the Ferry Building are thousands of spectators.

Boom! go the gas guns, boom, boom, boom!

Around corners, like sheep pouring through a gate, go the rioters, but they don't go very far. They stop at some distance, say a half block away, wipe their eyes a minute, and in a moment comes a barrage of rocks.

Here's the hottest part of the battle from now on, along Steuart street from Howard to Market. No mistake about that. It centers near the I.L.A. headquarters.

See the mounties ride up toward that front of strikers. It's massed across the street, a solid front of men. Take a pair of opera glasses and look at their faces. They are challenging the oncoming mounties. The men in front are kneeling, like sprinters at the mark.

Clatter, clatter, clatter come the bricks. Tinkle goes a window. This is war, boys, and this Steuart street between Howard and Mission is one of the warmest spots American industrial conflict ever saw.

The horses rear. The mounted police dodge bricks.

A police gold braid stands in the middle of the street all alone, and he blows his whistle. Up come the gas men, the shotgun men, the rifle men. The rioters don't give way.

Crack and boom! Sounds just like a gas bomb, but no blue smoke this time. Back scrambles the mob and two men lie on the sidewalk. Their blood trickles in a crimson stream away from their bodies.

Over it all spreads an air of unutterable confusion. The only organization seems to lie in little squads of officers hurrying hither and yon in automobiles. Sirens keep up a continual screaming in the streets. You can hear them far away.

Now it was 2 o'clock. The street battle had gone on for half an hour. How many were shot, no one knew.

Now, it was win or die for the strikers in the next few hours. The time from 2 o'clock to 3 o'clock dragged for police, but went on the wings of the wind for the strikers. An hour's rest. They had to have that one hour.

At 3 o'clock they started again, the fighting surging once more about Steuart and Mission streets. Here was a corner the police had, and had to hold. It was the key to the waterfront, and it was in the shadow of I.L.A. headquarters.

The rocks started filling the air again. They crashed through street cars. The cars stopped and citizens huddled inside.

Panic gripped the east end of Market street. The ferry crowds were being involved. You thought again of Budapest. The troops were coming. Soldiers. SOLDIERS IN SAN FRANCISCO! WAR IN SAN FRANCISCO!

★   ★   ★

It almost seems that Harry Bridges was always there in San Francisco, like the fog, to be for, or against.

Not that Harry Bridges himself was always the issue. As often it was a point of constitutional law, or a shift in foreign policy, or the philosophy of trade unionism, or perhaps even the whole

system of government that was the core of the argument when you chose up sides on Harry Bridges.

Meeting this mighty crucible of ideas face-to-face was usually something of a surprise. On close view the titan assumed ordinary proportions, never altogether the pure demon of radicalism or the heroic champion of the working classes.

For most of San Francisco such head-on meetings with Bridges took place in the newspapers, commonly when he was on public display against a government charge of being a secret Communist. In these two stories by reporter Alvin D. Hyman we meet Bridges in 1950 as he took the witness stand to defend himself against such a charge. Bear in mind that these reports are merely spot coverage of a courtroom proceeding. But random as they are, they capture with keen intelligence the attitude of the aggressive defendant as he painted his own portrait.

The trial, by the way, did not remove Harry Bridges from the San Francisco scene. His conviction in this case was subsequently tossed out on appeal.

Harry Bridges
on the Stand

February 8, 1950

Harry Renton Bridges, the Australian immigrant who became a world-wide symbol to trade unionists because of what he did to the Pacific Coast waterfront, talked about himself yesterday.

He talked under oath, to a jury of eight men and four women in the court of Federal Judge George B. Harris, and what he had to say was of high importance not only to himself, but also to the Government of the United States.

On his words, and on the impression they make on the jury as he continues to pour them out over the next three or four days, will largely depend on the outcome of the trial which has occupied the full time of scores of persons since November 14. If he is believed, he remains free and an American citizen; if disbelieved, he goes to prison and back to Australia.

The Government of the United States alleges that Bridges committed perjury on September 17, 1945, when he became naturalized in the court of Judge Thomas J. Foley and swore that he was not and never has been a member of the Communist party. It charges further that his friends and fellow labor leaders, Henry Schmidt and J. R. Robertson were witnesses in his behalf because of a conspiracy; that they were Communists and knew he was a Communist and conspired to hide that fact from naturalization authorities.

It was a twice-told and thrice-told tale that Bridges began unfolding yesterday in support of his contention that he is a militant, fist-swinging labor leader, that he accepted the help of Communists and anybody else in his struggle to pull down the established order on the waterfront—but that he never became a Communist himself.

Already, in two full-dress hearings, that contention has been put forward, and attacked, and chewed over. Once, it was held that Bridges was no Communist. Once, it was held that he did affiliate with the Communist party—but that finding was later rejected by the U.S. Supreme Court on grounds that the evidence was faulty.

Despite his long, previous tenure of witness stands, Bridges was nervous yesterday as he took his oath and settled into his recital. He stumbled over a matter of siblings. Asked almost immediately to describe his close relatives, he said he had six brothers and sisters—thought a moment—and amended his reply to: "No, four."

Apparently put at ease by getting this verbal misstep out of his system, he thereupon launched into a free and easy account of Harry Bridges, labor leader.

It was an account shot through with sailorman terms picked up in his early years before the mast, cruising between Australia and Sumatra and Java and around the Horn—terms like splicing, reefing, worming and close-hauled.

It was an account shot through with other terms picked up on the San Francisco Embarcadero through his emergence as head of the International Longshoremen's and Warehousemen's Union—terms like fink hall, shape-up, kickback, blacklist and yellow dog contract.

It was an account with no "news" value at all, but it engrossed the attention of the court and jury and the capacity crowd of spectators, because it explained quite clearly how an Australian boy who went to sea at 15 became an American labor leader important enough to be the chief defendant of this most important trial.

Bridges delivered his testimony in the familiar nasal twang, shorn almost completely of the Australian accent that once dripped from his words. He spoke quietly and slowly, except when enveloped in a reminiscence of some ancient waterfront grievance, and then his tongue ran away from him.

Two words crept continually into his discourse. Almost always, in giving a direct, affirmative answer to his attorney, Vincent Hallinan, he replied, "Right." Almost always, he used a question mark in putting a final period to a burst of language. He topped off his declaration with, "See?"

He testified that he was born in Melbourne, Australia, in 1901; had the equivalent of grade school and two years of high school; briefly went to a sort of maritime school, and at the age of 15 shipped before the mast. "I put my age ahead a few years," he confessed.

Even then, he said, he was a union man. He remained a union man when he came to San Francisco in 1920, and he was still a union man when he shifted his allegiance to the "Wobblies" in 1921.

Hallinan interrupted the autobiographical narrative at this juncture to drop a point into the jury box. He had Bridges testify that in Australia, at the turn of the century, labor had made such gains as an eight-hour day, and minimum wages, and old-age pensions—gains which came to the San Francisco waterfront under the Bridges program years later—gains sought by trade unions long before the Communist party took over Russia.

Bridges testified to early disillusionment and increased understanding as a result of his short experience in the Wobblies—the International Workers of the World—the IWW which began as a Socialist union fathered by Eugene Debs. He testified:

"I was a member of the Sailors' Union, and the secretary of the union, a man named Thompson, who was also a member of the IWW, was exposed as being on the employers' payroll. He was on the payroll of the shipowners all the time."

In his references to shipowners, the defendant was obviously torn between his old memories and his recent experiences in which four or five from that once-detested group appeared before that same jury in that same court room to testify that Bridges is a man of good character.

He shrugged and grinned and said, "They've changed. They learned the hard way."

Two devices helped him in his day-long bid for the attention of the jury. One was an eloquent, if awkward, use of his hands to emphasize his points. Another was a barely credible memory for detail—he reeled off names and dates and miniscule happenings without pausing for breath—he knew what barley workers were making in Port Costa in 1923; he remembered that Assemblyman Tom Maloney and Chief Probation Officer George McNulty worked the waterfront in 1924; he knew in what year the IWW lost a strike in San Pedro and in what years there were no Labor Day parades in San Francisco.

In mid-afternoon, F. Joseph Donohue, chief prosecutor, stopped the flow of detail to complain that after three hours the defendant-witness had said nothing bearing on the issue of perjury, that he was not being tried for labor union activities.

Hallinan retorted that the defendant-witness is entitled to refute the "garbage" testified to by Schomaker and others—and Bridges was allowed to go on with his recital. . . .

February 9, 1950

Harry Bridges gave his sworn answer to the big question yesterday.

He said no, he never was a member of the Communist party.

He said he never signed an application to join the party, never carried a membership book, never paid dues to the party. He was solicited many a time, he told a jury of eight men and four women in the court of Federal Judge George B. Harris. "But I never joined," he said.

Having entered his denials in the casual, matter-of-fact, but effective manner that show business calls "throwing away a line," he indulged himself in a little more mild theater. "This is where I came in," he said.

He explained that three times before he had entered the same denial under oath in hearings that looked toward his deportation—but not toward his imprisonment as in the instant trial.

In disowning membership in the Communist party yesterday, Bridges did not deny that he consulted with Communists, took help from Communists, and agreed with some of the aims and principles of Communists. He said:

"When I was asked to join the party, I declined. One reason was that I knew that all alien members of the party were subject to the process of deportation. I was no fool.

"But that was not necessarily the main reason. The waterfront spokesmen, the organizers for the Communist party and other groups, were putting out programs that were utopian, idealistic, revolutionary—but they offered no answer to our immediate problems. Their nice programs didn't fit our problems.

"So I didn't see any need for the Communist party and I had enough sense to see that it would subject me to deportation. That was the reason it was kissed off—it had nothing to offer me."

The defendant-witness then spoke a few kind words for Sam Darcy, the Communist leader who Government witnesses have said put out the orders that Bridges followed in pushing the 1934 strike. Bridges said that Darcy, for his money, was a good man; Darcy came down to the waterfront in the middle of the depression and offered to help the union.

Bridges said waterfront workers didn't like the way Darcy and other Communists were pushed around when they mounted their ladders and made waterfront speeches. "Not ½ of 1 per cent of us agreed with the Communist speakers," he said, "but we didn't like to see the cops beating them up."

In the course of his testimony, Bridges, the sailorman and dock walloper, showed himself adept at spinning an exciting yarn, in either the comic or dramatic style. He sent the courtroom into bursts of tittering with his account of an elaborate "needling" to which he subjected agents of the Department of Justice in New York, 1941—when he discovered that he was being trailed and that there was a "bug" in his room at the Edison Hotel.

"We had a lot of fun," he said. He related that he rented a room in another hotel overlooking the Edison; that he stocked this room with binoculars and spyglasses and telescopes, and installed his friends behind this equipment so they could watch developments in Bridges' room and the room next door.

"We would go into my room and cook up a lot of cops-and-robber stories for the benefit of the agents in the next room who had the tap on my room. They believed everything they heard. I'd get on the phone and call and arrange to meet somebody at the corner drugstore, second stool from the left; I'd say I would be drinking a choc malt with a red cherry, so I could be recognized. We'd go down to the drug store and it would be swarming with agents."

Bridges said the Department never did forgive him for this running gag, which received considerable publicity at the time and made certain agents a laughing stock in New York. He said they have been burned up over it ever since.

By way of contrast, he also told the story of the 1934 strike, the strike that produced "bloody Thursday," put the National Guard on the waterfront, tied up San Francisco in a four-day general strike —and made Harry Bridges a nationally controverted figure.

He told it from the inside and though the telling was manifestly what lawyers call "self-serving," and was directed toward removing the ancient stain of Communism from the strike and its leaders, it had all the occupants of the jury box on the edge of their seats and leaning forward.

Bridges conceded that the Communist party had put out a helping hand to the strikers and that the strikers had grabbed it. He said it would be four-flushing and a display of ingratitude to deny that Communists helped strikers print their pamphlets (but not write them), and helped them to eat.

"But so did a lot of other organizations, not Republicans and Democrats, but minority parties like the Socialists, and the IWW's and the Proletarian party. When help was offered we took it and didn't stop to ask the donor what his political beliefs were."

As a matter of fact, Bridges told the jury, the 1934 strike committee got help from the waterfront employers themselves—"We sent them a bumming letter and they mailed us a check for $25." And the strikers even went so far as to solicit Barbara Hutton, the five-and-dime heiress, for a little help. "We got a nice answer from her," Bridges recalled, "but no money."

The label of Communism, he said, was pasted on the strike by the Industrial Associaton, an organization he described as union-busting and strike-breaking, and which promoted public hysteria by crying out that the strike was the forerunner of "a bloody revolution, straight from Moscow."

"It was a very violent strike," Bridges said, "but we didn't start the violence. I have never yet seen a striker or a picket who took any delight in charging a policeman who had a club or a shotgun or a machine gun or a gas grenade. We don't relish having our men killed. But we lost nine men killed in that strike and had a hundred shot, clubbed and wounded."

There were numerous attempts to frame the union, he said, by having provocateurs hide weapons in union headquarters; there were arm-breakings of union leaders by gangs of vigilantes who toured the city in Marmon automobiles and caught the leaders at home; there was one offer to buy out Bridges.

"The price was $50,000," he said. "The offer was rejected. But I'm not entitled to any credit. I couldn't have done what they wanted me to do even if I tried."

Against this backdrop, Bridges painted his picture of Bloody Thursday—July 5, 1934.

"Early in the morning," he said, "police reserves attacked our picket lines. We had strengthened them that day as a kind of demonstration, not of strength, but of support by the unions.

"The police attacked us. We battled all day. They shot down and clubbed and gassed 400 of our men, not only members of our union but of other unions. We had two men killed. It was a pretty tough day for us.

"So many men were hurt, about 400 of them seriously, gassed and clubbed so bad that they had to be laid out, that we had our entire union hall at 113 Steuart street full of them. A couple of doctors volunteered to help. Our fellows were laid all over the floor and while we were taking care of them, the police shot tear gas and vomit gas into the windows of our hall and gassed us out of there."

A lot of them, he said, found refuge in a building at 121 Haight street. It might have been headquarters of the Communist party—though Bridges thought it was not at that time—but, "We didn't ask. We didn't look around to find out where these people came from when they drove up and volunteered to take our people to a safe place."

★　　★　　★

Some stories are just so big they are full of pitfalls for the earthbound reporter. This is such a story.

The idea of Joe DiMaggio getting married to Marilyn Monroe is still overwhelming. In 1954 it was almost beyond belief.

Reporter Art Hoppe was neither overwhelmed nor underwhelmed. The marriage of the national symbols of sex and muscular coordination was handled with aplomb and perspective.

MM Weds DiMag

January 15, 1954

Joltin' Joe DiMaggio wedded the girl of his and many other men's dreams yesterday afternoon in the San Francisco City Hall.

Marilyn Monroe, who packs no mean jolt herself, said she was very happy. DiMaggio said he was also very happy. Also happy was the battery of columnists which has spent no little time in the past two years running down rumors that the two were already secretly married, were to be married, or were not speaking to each other.

The time and place of the wedding was kept a closely guarded secret and only about 500 people managed to hear about it in time to turn the corridors outside Municipal Judge Charles S. Peery's court into a madhouse.

Marilyn, it seems, had made the mistake of calling her studio in Hollywood yesterday morning and letting it in on her plans to be married at 1 P.M. A studio official casually mentioned it as fast as he could to all the major news services.

Judge Peery's chambers were jammed with reporters and photographers when the couple arrived shortly after 1 P.M. They posed willingly for pictures and politely answered questions.

"Are you excited, Marilyn?"

"Oh, you KNOW it's more than that," she answered, giggling.

"How many children are you going to have, Joe?"

"We'll have at least one. I'LL guarantee that," said the slugger.

When they came in Marilyn looked svelte in a dark brown broadcloth suit with an ermine collar, and Joe looked neat in a blue suit and a blue and white checked tie. By the time they finished kissing each other exhaustively for the photographers' benefit, Marilyn's blonde hair was in disarray, and most of her lipstick had been transferred to the ballplayer's face.

At 1:30 P.M. Judge Peery, an old friend of DiMaggio, threw everybody out of his chambers so the solemnity of the occasion would remain inviolate.

However, reporters hanging over the transom were able to set down for posterity that the Judge began the ceremony at 1:46 P.M. and pronounced the couple man and wife at 1:48 P.M.

With that over, the doors of the chambers were unlocked and several times as many people as possible jammed their way in for a glimpse of the newly married pair.

After posing for more pictures, DiMaggio and a couple of friends formed a flying wedge and with Marilyn hanging to her husband's coattails, they valiantly fought their way through the mob and down the third-floor corridor.

They finally fought their way into the clear only to discover that they had gone the wrong way and had wound up in a cul de sac. So the flying wedge turned around and valiantly fought its way through the crowd again.

This time they reached the elevator. But they found another crowd waiting at the first floor and DiMaggio evolved the strategy of descending to the basement.

"This is a fine thing—dodging your loyal fans like this, Joe," said a member of the crowd who had wormed his way into the elevator. DiMaggio took umbrage and after much this and that shouted: "Don't you tell me what to do!"

Still another telepathic crowd was waiting in the basement and once again the little band had to fight its way through. Out in McAllister street, the couple jammed into a big blue Cadillac.and posed once more.

Miss Monroe has been staying at DiMaggio's sister's house in the Marina since before the holidays. This past month climaxed a two-year courtship that could be described as anything but whirl-wind. Friends report that the pair, neither of them the ebullient type, have been spending their evenings either watching television at home or quietly sitting in a back corner of DiMaggio's restau-rant.

Marilyn told reporters yesterday: "We've been thinking about it for a long time, but we were not too sure until we walked in the door here now."

DiMaggio said he didn't know where they would spend their honeymoon but they would "probably just get in the car and go" tonight.

In the excitement yesterday all sorts of things were forgotten. As Marilyn's flying wedge bore her from the scene, she shouted, "I forgot my coat." And she didn't go back for it. Worse was Judge Peery's oversight. When the excitement was over he announced with a cheerless sigh: "I forgot to kiss the bride."

★   ★   ★

At the news that Ernest Hemingway was dead, reporter Denne Petitclerc wept openly at his desk. During Petitclerc's apprenticeship as a writer in Miami and Havana, he had been a friend and pupil of Hemingway. His grief was a personal thing.

Ever alert to make the most of an emotional opportunity, the City Desk "suggested" Petitclerc put his feelings down on paper. The following is his highly impulsive response, in which he rose to angry defense against those who might dare see any Hemingway weakness in the apparent suicide. Note the writer's strong lapses into the style of the master.

"My Friend Is Dead"

July 3, 1961

Ernest Hemingway is dead. And I have been asked to write something, because he was my teacher and my friend.

The manner of his death, like the manner of his life, was hard and violent and sincere, and there will be critics who will tell that what he wrote was phony because he himself was phony; that his death tends to prove it.

It is not my intent to deprive anyone now of the right to be cynical about Hemingway. It has become intellectually popular. I only wish to tell you about the kind, gentle old man I met six years ago, who was a great writer and a great man.

About the hot, muggy summer night in the hotel in Miami when he sat at the bedside of an old friend from Key West who was dying of cancer; heavy, grizzled, bearded like some patriarch, speaking in his deep, halting voice.

"You know," he said, "I never cared much for *Our* Lord, because dying is not important. —— it! It's like being born, you know? It's the one thing we all have to do sooner or later, so —— it."

The friend, sunken-cheeked and sweating, smiled.

"Ernest," he said, "do you remember that time in Key West when we went to the priest and gave our confessions?"

"Sure," Hemingway said, and smiled, too. "It took four hours and when we were finished the priest fainted."

They laughed and Hemingway poured them both a drink from a vodka bottle and handed one of the glasses to his friend.

"Why did it take so long, Papa?" asked Mary, his wife.

"What?"

"The confession."

The smile faded on the old man's face and his eyes became serious. "It's difficult, you know," he said. "It is a very difficult thing to do, to confess, and it takes a long time when you do it truly."

He turned back to his friend on the bed and raised the glass.

"Don't give it importance, Frank," he said.

"Here's to it, Ernest," his friend said.

"—— it," Hemingway said. And they drank.

Those words are enough of an epitaph for any man who has lived on this earth and suffered it and died from it.

But there is more.

The afternoon at the pool in that quiet, green, sunlit place he lived in outside of Havana. When the old man found a bee struggling in the water and lifted it on the back of his hand and placed it tenderly on the grass at the edge of the pool, and then swam away without saying anything to us. And then later, at lunch in the house, he explained: "I couldn't kill anything now. I guess I respect life too much."

The other things are about his work and they come from letters. This from Cuba:

"I hope things are going better now, and that you don't have to bite so hard on the nail. Things are really very bad now. Nobody realizes how bad, I guess, until you see what crap is being published as writing.

"It is never any comfort but I think everybody has it rough to write now. With me it is more difficult than ever but have had it that way before. Lots of times.

"And if I keep at it and do not worry it is always all right again."

And this from Spain:

"No one can write all the time like the 'Old Man and the Sea', and war is difficult to write of, being compounded of legal murder, stupidity, injustice, extreme efficiency, pompousness, cowardice, bravery, ambitiousness, cupidity and great unselfishness, love and devotion. Most people who can write have one small dose of combat and are through. Tolstoy was the last first rate writer to have any experience of it at all. Stendahl had plenty and you remember the Waterloo part of 'Chartreuse de Parme.'

"I believe the bad words are completely necessary and that you cannot show good without showing reality. There is no great nobility in the Portuguese Man-of-War, in the Galanos of the Old Man. But the mako is a noble shark and that marlin is a very noble fish.

"Don't you see that the good in 'A Farewell to Arms' would be pointless without the bad?"

And this is the last of it.

The twilight of that day in 1958 out in the Gulf Stream east of Havana, with the sun gone and the first stars out in the sky, everything aboard the boat, the Pilar, quiet, except for the smooth sound of the motors, and Hemingway sitting in the fighting chair looking at the white wake spreading out behind the stern; sitting there for a long time watching the last lights go out of the sky and the blue water as if he would never see it again.

And then he got up and came stiffly into the cabin and sat down. His hair and beard showed white in the dim light, and he said quietly:

"We've talked a lot today. I hope it did good. There is only one more thing that I can tell you." He paused for a long moment. "It's almost all I've learned. Don't believe in making excuses. Do what you have to do as well as you can, and be sorry for everybody else, but never yourself."

What happened yesterday in the house in Ketchum happened because it had to be done. He was that kind of a man.

He knew all there was to know about guns and how they were cleaned. You have that and his critics have it. It's just not important. The important thing that Hemingway had is still here and will be long after whatever it was that got him, gets you and me, and whatever comes after us.

★   ★   ★

This is a piece of shop talk. It was shared with *Chronicle* readers after the Leonard Moskovitz kidnaping of January, 1954. It was almost as much an apology for not telling the news as it was a bit of breast-beating over a feat of city-room heroism.

Looking back at the Moskovitz kidnaping, this unusual page-one "confession" survives as the most memorable aspect of a sensational newspaper story that almost never got told.

Trade Secret

January 20, 1954

It can now be disclosed that the well-kept secret of the Leonard Moskovitz kidnaping came perilously close to being spilled on several occasions during the three-day voluntary news blackout.

The first near-slip occurred on Saturday evening, and it was *The Chronicle* that almost made it.

An alert *Chronicle* reporter received a "tip" on the fact that the Moskovitz family had received a ransom note demanding $500,-000. He flashed that news to *The Chronicle* office, half an hour before the first, inadvertent, police radio broadcast at 6:32 P.M.

There had been no request to keep the matter secret at that time, and *The Chronicle*'s city editor was deploying reporters and photographers before the police had time to think about blacking out the news.

An extra edition of *The Chronicle* was in preparation when Chief of Inspectors James English telephoned to ask that *Chronicle* staff men be called away from the Moskovitz home at 2900 Lake Street.

When it became evident that the co-operation of all news media would be given, *The Chronicle* extra was dismantled and no copy of it ever reached the public.

However, with extra policemen being called to duty, and with newspaper, radio, television and wire service men calling their wives to explain why they would not be home on time, there were bound to be leaks.

Out-of-town newspapers and radio stations, who were not informed of the agreement among San Francisco Bay media, were, of course, not bound by the blackout agreement.

A friend of the publisher of the Salt Lake Tribune heard the story in a local club and telephoned Salt Lake. The publisher immediately sent queries to the Associated Press in San Francisco and to newspapers in Los Angeles, San Diego and Chicago with which he has news-exchange agreements.

To the Chicago Tribune, he sent this message:

"We tipped that some wealthy real estate operator in San Francisco kidnaped Saturday, being held for $500,000 ransom. You aware? Anything being developed your end? Seems like many people in Salt Lake know about it. No stories?"

Steve Harrison, the Chicago Tribune Press Service editor to whom the message was sent, replied: "We're checking San Francisco."

Harrison called *The Chronicle* and was told of the blackout.

The Los Angeles and San Diego newspapers who were queried, in turn, sent urgent messages to San Francisco. Again, by long distance telephone, they were informed of the agreement, and they pledged to go along with it.

Of the three principal radio networks, two informed their New York offices of the blackout agreement and one did not.

One network received a tip in New York from an FBI informant and immediately telephoned San Francisco, demanding the facts be broadcast. It was a touchy few minutes, but the New York officials were persuaded to respect the agreement.

An alert teletype operator in the San Francisco office of the United Press made a goal-line save on Monday night.

On the press association's California wire, which serves 69 newspapers in the State, a note started to appear on the machines in the San Francisco office. It began:

"SX (code for San Francisco) CLIENT ASKS STORY SX REAL ESTATE OPERATOR KIDNAPED AND HELD...."

Frank Caunt, a veteran news operator, immediately punched his finger on the "break" button, interrupting the message.

"Who's sending?" Caunt messaged.

"Los Angeles," was the answer.

"Lay off that," Caunt ordered.

The Los Angeles answer was, "? ? ? ? ? ?"

Holding his finger on the "break" key, Caunt called over a wire editor, who put through a hurried call to the United Press Los Angeles office, explaining the situation.

In *The Chronicle* office, the news was gathered and written as it developed and set in type. Photos of the known principals, the scenes of the crime, and the ransom letters were made into cuts for reproduction. Everything was prepared so that the presses could roll within minutes of the first "break."

Radio stations prepared elaborate chronologies. They tape-recorded interviews with police officials and newsmen. KCBS broadcast a half-hour re-enactment of the crime last night, most of which was prepared during the period of the blackout.

All concerned felt the pressure.

Naturally, from copy boy to editor, there was a lot of debate about whether a voluntary news blackout was a good thing.

Some argued that it was a dangerous precedent to suppress news, and that doing so protected kidnapers as well as their victims.

Others argued that it might be worth while to do it this one time. They realized that it probably never would work again. Future kidnapers would know that absence of news about their crime would not mean that the police, too, were laying off the case.

Some said that wide publicity to a crime alerted readers, who might be on the lookout for suspicious people, and so furnish police with useful information. Others argued that the police gained more by secrecy than they lost.

Captain James English, and others in the investigation, thought that secrecy had proved its value. They were joined in that opinion enthusiastically by the grateful members of the Moskovitz family.

Leonard Moskovitz, the victim, disclosed that he and his captors listened to radio broadcasts, after he had been released from his bonds, and the captors went out frequently to buy the latest editions of the newspapers.

Moskovitz related:

"Every time a newscast would start, or one of them went out for papers I'd get pins and needles. Afterwards, with nothing mentioned about kidnaping, it was like a reprieve, and I began to breathe again."

English, gratified, but less effusive, said only that it was "a miracle" that the news did not leak out.

"It was a swell job all around," he said. "Hundreds of people knew about it, perhaps thousands. Yet up to the time they were nabbed, the kidnapers thought they were getting away with it. The press deserves a large share of credit for solving this crime."

★   ★   ★

Newspapers have unselfishly shared with each other the formula for the Important Foreign Visitor story. There is the arrival, the official greeting, the press conference. If possible there is a light touch to the proceedings, a woman's angle, or some unusual food note, or something special to make the familiar business palatable to the local readership.

Edd Johnson's report on the visit of Emperor Haile Selassie to San Francisco in 1954 is made up of almost every one of the classic ingredients. Yet in his very use of the normal techniques Johnson managed to turn each one into comment and criticism. Before he is through, he has taken on the press, officialdom, and the native American boob.

Lion in Our Town

June 15, 1954

Bearing many precious gifts of ivory and of silver and of much fine gold, the Emperor of Ethiopia, together with a very great company, came unto San Francisco yesterday.

He, who is the Conquering Lion of the Tribe of Judah, spoke

with words of flattery for our citizens, and our climate, and our fresh fruits and our Flag.

He, who is the King of Kings, and of the line of Solomon and of Sheba, spoke also with sternness and foreboding, but with hope withal, that peace might come through preparations for war.

Haile Selassie I really made the rounds of San Francisco.

His Imperial Majesty awoke at 6 A.M. in the new Imperial Suite of the Hotel Mark Hopkins, in time for his protracted morning devotionals. Among his titles are those of Elect of God and Defender of the Faith. He adheres strictly to the ancient tenets of the Coptic Christian Church, of which he is titular head.

After devotionals, he drank California grapefruit juice and ate ham and eggs. His son, Prince Sahle Selassie Haile Selassie, who likes jazz records and hot rod cars, and his granddaughter, Princess Sybel Desta, who entertained the press ladies later, had specified California orange juice.

Other members of the entourage, including the Emperor's personal physician, his aide-de-camp, his Minister of War, his hard-working director of protocol and translator, and his Minister of Justice and of the Pen, were called later to be ready at 9 A.M.

The Emperor's first official visitor was unscheduled. He edged past the police guards, identifying himself as a representative of the Voice of America, and he presented himself to His Imperial Majesty as the messenger of a San Francisco restaurant owner. He brought a gift of a box of Halvah, an Armenian candy. The Emperor thanked him in English.

The second official visitor was Major General Earle M. Jones, State Adjutant General, to give welcome greetings on behalf of Governor Goodwin J. Knight. The general said he addressed the Emperor in English and that "he seemed glad to get the greeting."

Next came a press conference, and from then on it was a gallop.

Reporters had been briefed in advance that the first question should be addressed, "Your Imperial Majesty," and that subsequently he might be addressed as "Your Majesty" or "Sir."

A photographer quickly upset the protocol cart on that one. As the Emperor came into the living room of his suite, looking drawn and weary, he was directed to an overstuffed chair, and the Prince and Princess were ordered by the photographers to sit on the arms of the chair.

"Prince, lean forward," a photographer ordered. Then when his order was obeyed, he sought to coax his subjects still further in a sort of baby talk:

"Likee California, huh? Yes? Y-e-e-s-s! Right here now. Nize. Nize."

It is doubtful if anything just like it has been experienced by any member of the Imperial family since the line was established by the union of King Solomon of the Jews and the Queen of Sheba, some three millenniums ago.

The Emperor tugged once at the flap of his jacket pocket, but his expression did not change. He wore the uniform of a field marshal, the fabric the color of U.S. Army sun tans, and his left breast was heavy with decorations and rosettes, including the United States Legion of Merit. He sat on the edge of his chair, so that his feet might reach the floor. He is slightly built, small-boned, and half a head shorter than his granddaughter, who is only slightly over 5 feet tall.

The press conference was conducted through Lidj Endalkatchew Makonnen, director of protocol. The Emperor spoke in Amharic, which is something like Hebrew and something like Arabic. But he demonstrated that he knows idiomatic English.

To kick it off, a reporter asked His Imperial Majesty if he had had any fun on this trip. The answer came in rounded phrases about the inspiration in seeing "the way of life of this great nation" and the "happiness and prosperity" of its citizens.

The reporter persisted that maybe "fun" needed a different translation, and without intervention from the interpreter, Haile Selassie said:

"In answer to the question, the program has been so worked out that there is very little time for diversion."

He went on to say that he has seen Cinerama and Radio City in New York, and that he is fond of eating California fruits, which he gets tinned in his palace.

"His Imperial Majesty would not like to single out any one fruit as his best-liked," the chief of protocol added.

A reporter wanted to know if the Emperor foresaw a third World War, and the initial answer came tartly:

"Is it right that you are asking if another war is coming when all nations are preparing for war?"

Then he went on more diplomatically, to say that he hoped "the strength of the United States will be a preventive of war."

Asked about the recent Supreme Court decision, outlawing segregation by color in American schools, he said:

"That is no new thing to American thinking. It has been in your Constitution. However, the decision will not only strengthen ties between Ethiopia and the United States but also will win friends everywhere in the world."

The Emperor said there was no Communism, as such, in Ethiopia, but "the idea" was known there. He said that big nations could best combat the spread of Communism "by giving economic help to small nations."

The interview was ended at the stroke of 10 A.M. by a State Department man, and next on the schedule was a visit to the Veterans Administration hospital at Fort Miley.

The entourage of five Cadillacs, with motorcycle cops as outriders, went out California street and through Lincoln Park. At the hospital, as throughout the day, the Emperor found himself generally undertitled. He was sometimes called Your Highness (a title for a simple prince of a realm) and sometimes Your Royal Highness (a title for a crown prince). Never was he addressed as Negus Negust (King of Kings) and seldom properly as "Your Imperial Majesty."

The Emperor toured the hospital, and in the auditorium shook hands with Korean veterans, wishing each "good luck" in English. He made a brief speech in Amharic, reminding the veterans that Ethiopian soldiers had participated in the Korean conflict and "the fight for liberty and justice and peace."

To Dr. James G. Donnelly, manager of the hospital, he presented a huge cross of the Ethiopian Orthodox Church, made of silver and plated with gold. He asked that it be placed in the chapel, "where people of all nations come to pray for the mercy of God and the peace of the world." The hospital has no such chapel.

The next stop was at Inspiration Point, overlooking Land's End. The Emperor mounted the bridge of the USS San Francisco, salvaged after the cruiser was hit at Guadalcanal. Fog lay over the Farallones, and when *Chronicle* photographer Bill Young put a dime in the slot, the Emperor trained the binoculars of Inspiration Point on the Golden Gate Bridge and murmured politely in his

accented English about its majesty and beauty. The Emperor's pro-
nunciation of English resembles that of a cultured Frenchman.

Now the State Department men and the police consulted their
watches, and it was time to drive, slowly, so as to arrive at precisely
11:46 A.M., to the City Hall.

In the executive chambers, Mayor Elmer E. Robinson presented
the Emperor with a gavel made of redwood, and told him redwood
trees grow to be 2000 years old. The Mayor said, "I do not know
if you preside over a legislative group or not," and he demonstrated
how the gavel might be used to rap for order, and if that failed,
might be used to rap disorderly legislators on the head.

The Emperor smiled frostily, and the Mayor then gave him a box
which he said contained a Steuben glass goblet, which he should
use to "toast the peace."

The Emperor responded in Amharic, from a written manuscript,
and royal servitors brought in two elephant tusks, tipped with gold
and mounted on a polished wooden base. The base bore a silver
tablet saying the presentation was made on May 27, 1954.

After more picture taking on a City Hall balcony, the party went
back to the waiting Cadillacs. The Emperor walked regally, but
Her Royal Highness limped by now, as if her feet were killing her.

At the Palace Hotel, 1000 citizens had gathered for food and
more speeches. City Attorney Dion Holm was master of ceremonies and eulogisms were offered by Governor Knight and Mayor
Robinson. His Imperial Majesty drank Vichy water during the
meal. He ate in the Continental manner, cutting his roast beef with
his knife in his right hand and forking it into his mouth with the
left.

In his response, read in Amharic through semi-oval, gold-
rimmed spectacles, the Emperor said in part:

"California in many ways resembles Ethiopia, particularly as re-
gards the aspects of its countryside and its unparalleled climate. I
hope that I can lay claim to rivalry in climate without wounding the
pride of Californians." His speech, lasting less than three minutes,
compared other pleasant aspects of California to Ethiopia, with
words of kingly grace for both.

Up to now, the Emperor had not been permitted a moment of
privacy since before 9 A.M.

So back went the Cadillacs to the Mark Hopkins where time was given for a rest stop until 5:15 P.M. The Emperor then received in his suite Governor Knight, Mayor Robinson and Mayor Clifford E. Rishell of Oakland, who had greeted him on his arrival at the Oakland mole Sunday night. A brief ceremony was held during which Knight was presented with a decoration signifying him a Knight of the Grand Cross in the Order of the Star of Ethiopia. Robinson was made a Grand Commander of the Order and Rishell a Commander.

At 5:30 P.M., the Emperor, accompanied by the Prince and Princess, were ushered to the Mark's Peacock Court where some 500 members of the World Affairs Council crowded to get a glimpse of royalty. Dr. Henry Grady, president of the council, introduced the Emperor as a "proven world leader who spoke out for the rights of small countries." He received a similar accolade later from Governor Knight at a dinner and reception in the royal party's honor at the Press and Union League Club.

At 10:30, the Emperor, the Prince, the Princess, members of the Cabinet and aides all went down to the St. Francis Theater on Market street to see "Dial M for Murder."

The movie was not on the intinerary and the idea could presumably have fermented after the question about "fun" in the press conference. The show let out at 12:40 A.M. and the royal party went home to bed.

Men who would be kings might take note that the royal alarm clock was set for 6 A.M. so that everyone could be on their way by car to Southern California at 8 A.M. for another round of handshaking, receptions and speeches.

★   ★   ★

Offered now are two high-style products of the difficult craft of reporting. In each of the two stories that follow the reporter has made maximum use of information, observation and style. In each case there was an imminent deadline at the time of writing. In each case the story had to be written in hectic, unfamiliar surroundings, with a hurry-up travel schedule just ahead.

During the presidential campaign of 1960, reporter Art Hoppe traveled the country as a roving correspondent. His aim was to report not only of the candidates, but also of the mood and flavor of the nation. He was eminently successful. Wherever he touched, people and events took on an intimate proximity for *Chronicle* readers.

Hoppe says the story of Lyndon Johnson's excursion into Rocky Bottom is his personal favorite. But the earlier piece on the first TV debate, with its more complicated approach, is equally deserving. If anyone is tempted to quarrel with the staginess of its format, try to recall that uncertain night of the First Debate, with the whole country nervous for its favorites, and with the backdrop of Illinois summoning images of Lincoln and Douglas. The italics are Hoppe's.

The Great Debate

Chicago
September 26, 1960

It was pleasantly cool this evening in this city of four million people. A soft breeze blew in from the lake.

At 6:30 P.M. a bartender in a tavern on State street wiped his hands on a towel, switched off the air conditioner and switched on the television set. The big, hard, smooth gray eye obediently came to life, reproducing a silvery pattern of flickering blacks and whites that merged into a pretty woman with a bottle of hand lotion.

"About two hours to go," the bartender said.

It was limply hot on the morning of August 21, 1858, in the new prairie town of Ottawa, Illinois. It had been a dry summer, and the dirt roads were choked with wagons and buggies bringing farmers into town. By mid-morning a haze of dust hung in the air.

At 7:22 tonight, Vice President Richard Nixon was driven in a closed convertible down a waxed linoleum-floored corridor right into the heart of the CBS studios here. He waved to the few photographers allowed to be present and was ushered through a door into Studio One, where wrestling matches are usually telecast.

Nixon was greeted by CBS president Frank Stanton, who showed him around the set. The backdrop was a 20-foot-high stone wall that had been built in New York and shipped out here Saturday. It was artificial.

"Am I on this side?" asked Nixon, nodding toward the Danish modern chair stage right.

Stanton said he was.

"We've put the water over there," said producer Don Hewitt, a short, dark, neatly dressed young man, pointing to a table stage right of Nixon's chair.

"If you go for water, you don't have to worry. We'll keep the cameras off you."

"Will they do the same thing if I dab my lips?" asked Nixon. "I tend to sweat."

"Absolutely."

Stephen A. Douglas arrived in Ottawa at 11:30 that morning in 1858. He had come by private carriage from Peru, Illinois. Just out of town he was greeted by several hundred horsemen who whooped it up as they escorted him in. Abraham Lincoln came in at noon on a 14-car special train from Chicago, jammed with his supporters. The Ottawa Federation of Musicians Brass Band and a riotously-decorated carriage were waiting to parade him up to Washington Square.

At 7:26 P.M. Senator John F. Kennedy entered stage left. It was an historic moment. The two men had been skirmishing independently throughout the country. And now, like giant pincers, their two forces had come together, and they were face to face.

Kennedy moved slowly stage center, rubbing his hands together as he often does. Nixon, who had been joking with the press photographers, finished a remark before turning with outstretched hand to the Senator.

"Glad to see you," Nixon said with a broad smile.

Kennedy's answer was inaudible. He was smiling, too, faintly, and his whole demeanor expressed reserve, almost coldness. It is no secret that he has privately referred to the Vice President in reportedly unprintable terms for what he feels have been Nixon's deliberate misquotations of his statements.

"I saw you got a big crowd in Cleveland," Nixon said jovially, referring to Kennedy's expedition there yesterday.

Kennedy nodded.

"You must get your tan the same way I do—riding around in convertibles," Nixon went on. "It's the wind, not the sun."

Neither said anything for a moment. Then Kennedy, in what seemed one of those desperate efforts to make small talk, said: "When are you going out again?"

"I leave first thing in the morning," Nixon said.

"Oh," Kennedy said.

After a few moments, both turned to talk to others, just as you do at a cocktail party when you run out of conversation.

A man with a whisk broom was removing any chance specks of dust from the gleaming stage furniture. Another worker was vacuuming the rug, and a third was sweeping down the artificial wall with a broom.

At 7:38 P.M., the two presidential candidates took their seats stage left and right while the lighting and sound men studied their images.

Kennedy looked deadly serious.

"I think I'd better shave," said Nixon with a grin.

Nixon is plagued by a heavy beard, and it was decided to apply pancake makeup to the Vice President. Kennedy, who has a ruddy complexion, didn't require any.

At 7:45 the candidates retired to their dressing rooms with their handlers to wait. A butler was assigned to each camp to serve coffee.

The platform at Ottawa that afternoon 102 years ago was a simple affair, hammered together for the occasion. Red, white and blue bunting had been draped over the railing, giving it a festive air. The population of Ottawa was 5000. Yet 12,000 men and women stood in the hot sun to yell and stomp for whichever was their hero—Lincoln or Douglas.

At 8.30 tonight, as the "On the Air" sign flashed, scarcely a score of people were present to see the two candidates in the flesh. There were the moderator, the four television newsmen who asked the questions, the cameramen, audio engineers, lighting technicians, floor directors, timekeepers, the two candidates' television advisers and seven newspaper photographers and reporters who were restricted to two small islands chalked off on the floor.

The vast cadre of newsmen following both candidates had been tucked away in two other studios, where they watched the proceedings on monitor sets. The public was barred at the street doors by four city policemen, two special CBS policemen and two secret service agents.

"Let's see your badges, please," one of the officers would ask. The special badges were two inches square and bore only a large eye, symbol of the network. Only those with red symbols were admitted to Studio One. Green was for the reporters in the other two studios.

The photographers' were gold. Blue got you into Nixon's dressing room; gray into Kennedy's. Purple was for the distinguished guests of CBS who had special monitor viewing rooms on the second floor. And lavender was for the Western Union operators and other miscellaneous workers.

The debate began.

Each candidate made his opening speech. Each was impressive in his sincerity and earnestness. Each stared intently and directly into the two-inch-wide cold glass eye of the camera as he stated his case.

Lincoln and Douglas debated for three hours on the sun-baked platform in Ottawa. Their styles were free and easy as they exchanged sharp barbs and witty insults.

At 8:38:29, the green band flashed on above the camera's eye for Kennedy. The band was the uppermost of three on a rectangular glass plate just over the camera's snout.

The green band said, "One minute."

The yellow band in the middle said, "Thirty seconds."

And the red band at the bottom meant, "Cut!"

No less a dignitary than CBS news vice-president Sig Mickelson held the stop watch.

In the question and answer period, Kennedy forgot to stare into the television eye and instead glanced sideways and downward at his questioners.

Nixon, seemingly more relaxed, remembered to talk to the camera throughout.

As the end drew near, it was announced that each candidate had three minutes and 20 seconds to sum up. Nixon finished on the dot. But Kennedy completed his evaluation of the national problems we have and the challenges he feels we face at 9:28:15—wasting a full 30 seconds of national television time on the three major networks.

After that first debate in Ottawa, Lincoln and Douglas held six more throughout Illinois. In the end Douglas won the battle and retained his Senate seat.

"Who won?" asked a reporter tonight as the monitors flickered and went cold and gray and silent once again.

The newsmen in the viewing room looked at each other, none wishing to voice his opinion first.

After that first debate in Ottawa, the New York Evening Post reported: "All prairiedom has broken loose. It is astonishing how deep an interest in politics these people take."

By midnight the carpet, the Danish modern furniture, the lectern, the whole dignified atmosphere had disappeared from Studio One. The stone wall lay in long sections on the floor. Workmen were tacking a protective covering over each section. The painted canvas that once was the stones quivered under each blow of the hammer.

★　　★　　★

LBJ in Rocky Bottom

Rocky Bottom, South Carolina
October 11, 1960

Senator Lyndon B. Johnson, a determined candidate for the vice presidency of the United States, descended from the sky into Rocky Bottom at 4:17 P.M. today.

His hired three-seater Bell helicopter landed in a field of weeds just south of Sugar Liquor Lake. The greeting committee consisted of a solitary farmer who came huffing up to give the Senator the first words of welcome.

"What the hell are you doing on my propitty?"

The Senator's descent had unfortunately missed the spot where all the Rocky Bottom folks were gathered waiting for him by a good two miles, due to difficulties in finding a landing place.

The distinguished Senator was standing there picking cockle burrs out of his trouser legs and wondering what to do next when, happily, Mayor George Coleman of Traveller's Rest, down the road a piece, drove by in his red convertible.

"I knew right away it was Senator Johnson," Coleman told a circle of admiring friends later. "I said perhaps he'd like a ride up to the gathering place if he didn't think I was being forward, and he said that would be mighty fine. He seemed right grateful."

The Senator's arrival for a Democratic supper, gratuitous as it may have been, was undeniably the biggest thing to have happened in Rocky Bottom since the firing on Fort Sumter. The town sits in the shadow of Mt. Sassafras (elev. 3240 feet) in the Blue Ridge country of northern South Carolina. It is about 20 miles from Pumkintown, at the end of a one-lane dirt road. The population, as one resident put it when asked for statistics, is "real small"—perhaps eight families who live in clapboard cabins tucked away amongst the trees.

A small contingent of reporters arrived here three hours ahead of the Senator to collect background data, having been driven in over the winding mountain road by Clyde Bolding, the Sheriff of Pickens County, in which Rocky Bottom is located.

The Sheriff, a cheery, red-necked gentleman, was asked what the major industry in Rocky Bottom was.

"Moonshining," he replied happily. "It's a year-round industry and most of the folks up in the hill country make a nice steady living off of it."

"Is it—ah—approved of?" inquired a lady reporter, delicately.

"Yes, ma'am," said the Sheriff with a grin. "It's illegal."

And then he gave a well-informed dissertation on how to make bootleg whiskey, decrying the sad fact that the demands of mass production had forced the Rocky Bottom artisans to give up making double distilled corn whiskey in favor of the more quickly and cheaply made sugar whiskey.

The national press, looking a little dazed, were greeted in Rocky Bottom by a huge, bald giant wearing a plaid sport shirt, jeans and an impeccable black homburg.

"Everybody in Rocky Bottom calls me Big Nick," said Big Nick, swaying back and forth slightly as he shook hands all around. "You all come down to my cabin and maybe I got a lick or two of white lightning, Real Corn."

The national press trooped down to Big Nick's cabin, gathered in the kitchen and hoisted jelly glasses. One lick of white lightning, which reportedly runs 150 proof, was proof enough. But Big Nick doffed his homburg, raised the quart mason jar, lowered its level a good two inches without batting an eye, sat down on a bench and began singing: "I Had a Little Hen, It Had a Wooden Leg. . . ."

The conversation in the kitchen got around to politics. The local authorities present explained that Rocky Bottom has the only polling place in these parts and folks come down off Sassafras mountain, over from Sugar Liquor Lake and as far as "away over to the next holler" to cast their ballots. In the last election the total number of ballots was 37.

Were all the voters Democrats? "Every single one," said Uncle Tommy Bowen, a short, stout gentleman with a cane, who has spent 36 of his 79 years as Pickens County farm agent. "I never heard tell of a Bowen who wasn't nothing but a Democrat all the way back to my great-great-granddaddy."

A reporter said, somewhat sardonically, that he guessed then that Rocky Bottom would go for the Kennedy-Johnson ticket. "Well, I don't rightly know about that," said Gus Ross, a pleasant young man with fine red veins in his cheeks. "Both in 19 and 52 and 19 and 56 Rocky Bottom went for Mr. Eisenhower."

The political situation here seems to reflect accurately the trouble Senator Kennedy is having throughout the South. On the one hand are the loyal Democrats who, with many a gasp and holding of nose, managed to swallow most of the party's platform. On the other, are the more conservative, who are more Republican in philosophy of government and economics than the most rock-ribbed banker of the North.

"I really don't think we are going to carry this State," said a party leader who was in Rocky Bottom for the festivities. "We couldn't work the split."

Ever since 1948, it should be explained, there have been three tickets on South Carolina presidential ballots—loyal Democratic, Republican, and that of the conservative Democrats, who have backed either a States Rights candidate, or President Eisenhower.

Adlai Stevenson won the State in 1956, but he had less than a majority of the total, the bulk of the votes being split between the Republican and conservative Democratic slates.

"We tried like all get-out to make Strom Thurmond (the former Governor and a leading States Rightist) run on an independent ticket this time," the loyalist party leader said. "But I guess they've smartened up some and they're just setting back waiting for us to fry in our own fat."

Meanwhile Senator Johnson arrived in Mayor Coleman's red convertible for his appearance at the annual "Rocky Bottom Good Will Supper." A large tent, generally used for revivals, had been set up in a glade, and by the time the Senator arrived, 700 people had taken their seats on the unplaned planks under the canvas.

The Senator, enjoying the style of delivery that he has used ever since crossing the Mason-Dixon line, said: "You just don't know how I'd enjoy sitting down here and whittling with you a while." But, he said, he had to catch up with "the LBJ Special" on which he is campaigning through the South.

So he told several very funny jokes, advised everybody to "remember the Golden Rule" and be friends, and wound up re-quoting the tag line of one of his funny stories. "If I ain't your friend, it's just 'cause I ain't got sense enough to be," he said.

Then the Senator, canceling the helicopter, climbed into a highway patrol car for the 30-mile trip back to the train and three more days of whistle-stopping down to New Orleans.

★　★　★

In 1949 a television set was still something "somebody down the block had" around the San Francisco Bay Area. But the big sales push was on, and one of the traditional ways to push was through a "special section" in the daily newspaper, in which advertisements and articles complemented each other.

It was in such a crass arena that we find this piece of clair-voyance—the 24-year-old Pierre Salinger stating unequivocally that television would someday be important in politics, perhaps even forcing an occasional candidate with unkempt hair to go out and buy a comb.

Was this the path to the White House, Pierre?

Cigars Are Out

November 13, 1949

The American politician is going to become a fancy man. No more slouch suits, big cigars hanging from the mouth, or tousled hair. That stuff is out.

From now on, it's going to be pin-stripe suits, well-tied ties, smoothly combed hair—and in some cases, made over faces.

Already out of Washington, D.C. comes the report that politicians by the drove are seeking the advice of plastic surgeons to pretty up their faces for the TV camera.

In a more serious vein, however, there seems little doubt that in the long run—probably within the next five years—television will have a profound effect on American politics. The first indication of this was TV coverage last year of the major conventions and the subsequent campaigns.

TV set owners in the East were given a front-row seat at the party deliberations. They were there. They could see, as well as hear, what their representatives were doing. Such close scrutiny is healthy for the democratic way.

For the candidates themselves, TV will present a challenge. Too often, in our modern political races, the trend is for the candidate to have a well-oiled machine behind him. In this machine will be a group of usually well-paid and prolific writers who will write his statements, radio speeches, etc. A candidate will think twice, how-ever, before he goes before a TV camera reading a script written for him by somebody else. He will have a much more persuasive argument to the voter if he presents a sincere, extemporaneous speech.

In this type of campaign, the politician will have to do a little more speaking for himself, and the result is bound to be a better indication of the real worth of each candidate rather than the worth of his script writers.

It is only a matter of time before television reaches this degree of importance in the American political field.

★   ★   ★

TRIVIA UNSHAKEN...

The spring of 1906 saw San Francisco journalism at its moment of greatest stress. The mighty earthquake and fire struck on the morning of April 18. The *Examiner* and *Call* plants were destroyed. *The Chronicle* building was a burned-out shell, its linotype machines smashed as they fell through to the cellar. But it was a day for newspaper heroics. Everyone went over to Oakland, and on the morning of April 19 delivered the monumental combined four-page paper that told the story of the city's terrible destruction.

The saga of heroic earthquake journalism was not ended with that edition. The feat of the days that followed was equally astounding. With scarcely a stutter, the newspapers bounced back to almost complete normalcy of content and appearance.

The selections that follow are from *The Chronicle* in the month immediately following the fire. In the aftermath of chaos they represent the unbending structure of basic journalism, a calm marvel of information, optimism, humor—and trivia.

Out of the Ashes

April 21, 1906

Item:

At midnight last night the fire was out or under control in all parts of the city except at the base of Telegraph Hill. There the flames were eating southward, and it was feared the docks would go. All vessels were moved into the stream.

April 21

Personal Report:

The richest thing in San Francisco was not shattered by the earthquake. Neither did it shrivel in the fire. Nor did its market value diminish. It is way above par. The spirit of the people of San Francisco today is the grandest and most practically valuable asset which the metropolis ever has possessed.

There is not the slightest doubt that that spirit will consummate the rebuilding of the great city in swifter fashion than any great city has been built or rebuilt before.

This is no vain boast to blow wind into the sails of courage. It is the honest conviction of a homeless man, who has lost everything except his wife, who tramped 20 miles through the stricken city in search of fresh heart, and found it.

April 22

Item:

Every railroad will carry people applying to its ticket agents for transportation to any point within California that is reached by its lines. The railroads ask no payment whatever, only a reasonable assurance that the people applying for tickets have friends in the towns to which they ask to be taken.

April 22

Item:

Weddings in great number have resulted from the recent disaster. Women driven out of their homes and left destitute have appealed to the men to whom they were engaged, and immediately marriages have been effected.

"I don't live anywhere," is the answer given in many cases when the applicant for a license is asked where his residence is. "I used to live in San Francisco."

April 22

Item:

The firm of Goldberg & Bowen, which has done much to aid the suffering in the city in turning its two remaining stores over to the authorities, as well as by caring for the families of its employees, and giving its horses to the service of the relief committee, feels keen regret that their manager at their Haight street store should have raised the prices in some of the sales during the excitemnt of Wednesday.

S. P. Goldberg said yesterday: "Tom Brown lost his head for the moment. One man came in and wanted to buy his whole stock of eggs and he got the idea that the best way to make a fairer distribution was to raise the price. We want people to know that not only was it not ordered, but that we feel keenly sorry that it should have occurred."

April 22

Editorial:

Five babies were born in Golden Gate Park last night. They should make not alone good native sons, but sterling pioneers of newer San Francisco, coming into life as they did with a baptism of earthquake and fire.

April 24

Announcement:

A. P. Hotaling & Co. announce that their store and warehouse containing over 2000 barrels of Old Kirk Whisky are still in business at the same old stand, 429-437 Jackson street. As soon as shipping facilities are resumed they will be able to supply all of their friends and customers.

April 25

Item:

Passing through Colorado Springs, Colo., yesterday on a train bound for Chicago, where her parents reside, was a San Francisco fugitive who said her name was Miss Logan. She wore a bandage on her left hand and said that while she lay unconscious upon the floor of the St. (*sic*) Francisco Hotel in San Francisco after the earthquake last Wednesday the third finger of her left hand was cut off and she was robbed of the rings that she wore there.

April 25

Notice:

The $30,000 due the Bancroft, Whitney book company from San Francisco lawyers who have lost their libraries is canceled. Lawyers outside of San Francisco can help out the situation by remitting at once amounts due.

April 25

Item:

It was agreed by the San Francisco Real Estate Board that the calamity should be spoken of as "the great fire" and not as "the great earthquake."

April 26

Item:

A. B. Bradbury, the aged millionaire who is under sentence to San Quentin, having nothing more cheerful to do the day following the earthquake, put himself on a rent-collecting errand. He called first at one of his homes in Corte Madera which he had rented to Mrs. W. Diggins. As she did not have the ready money to pay, Bradbury ordered her and her family at once to vacate the house. Then Bradbury left for his own handsome house on the opposite hill.

Within an hour a committee of citizens of Corte Madera called Bradbury out of his house and, ordering him into a cart, drove him to an unsettled part of town. They stopped under a eucalyptus tree from which hung a noose on the end nearest the ground. The noose was placed around Bradbury's neck. Then, with this illustration of what would happen to him if he evicts Mrs. Diggins, he was allowed to go. Mrs. Diggins still lives in the house.

April 26

Item:

To the hoboes and tramps that infest San Francisco in large numbers throughout the year the earthquake came as the forerunner of a time of plenty. Amid the general destitution which the country at large is doing its utmost to relieve, the tramps are passing themselves off as sufferers of the disaster, and, in consequence, they are living much better than they usually fare.

An influx of tramps from all parts of the United States may be expected, and it is partly to check this onrush that the lines are being drawn so tightly in regard to the entrance to the city.

April 26

Theater Note:

In "The Girl from the Golden West", David Belasco's latest hit in New York, Blanche Bates has a final line, when with her lover she bids goodby to her home. The line reads: "Farewell S.F.! Oh, my California! Oh, my Sierra!"

As she uttered this line the first night of the earthquake, Miss Bates' voice failed, and she lurched forward into her lover's arms.

He urged her to go on but she could not and the curtain was rung down. As they assisted the actress to her dressing room she exclaimed: "It's my home. I love the town. This is like the going of my best friend. Oh, I can't endure it."

April 27

News Briefs:

Work begun on rebuilding of city on new lines.

Bank vaults investigated and all seem in perfect condition.

Fear of fire caused delay in starting street cars; date still uncertain.

All main sewers in good working order.

Telegrams from Eastern financial centers report that many millions are ready to be poured into the city.

April 27

Item:

Governor George C. Pardee received the following dispatch from Governor George E. Chamberlain of Oregon:

"Many children and some babies are coming through here unidentified and unaccompanied by anyone. Can they not be gathered together at Oakland for identification? As it is, they will be forever lost to their parents."

April 28

Social Notes:

The town is on the level in every sense of the word. No more ghouls are shot because there is nothing to steal. Yet the smashed buildings and desolate streets do not represent the significant leveling. The material loss is overwhelming, but it does not stagger the imagination. A few hundred millions will mend the hurt and there are many people here today who think the shakeup is worth it. The leveling that they are willing to pay for is social. Society is on the ground, face to face, jowl to jowl. Every artificial barrier is swept away. The conventions, the pride, the show and the ease which these people have been erecting for 50 years have been swept away with the same swiftness and finality shown by the flames toward the property.

The loss of life is small; the loss of social position colossal. Now nothing counts but human love. Money has momentarily lost its purchasing power. Servants, luxury, habits, prestige—yes, and enmity, feuds, hatreds, jealousies and contempt have disappeared. Humanity is in the flat and everyone is on the level.

Up and down the streets one can see curbstone fires where the people are cooking their meals in obedience to the municipal order to light no fires in the houses. They bring out big ranges, small kitchen stoves, improvised sheet-iron ovens and the old brick Dutch ovens, from which are turned out some wonderful concoctions. Most of the servants have either run away or been sent away and the people who get their own meals out of doors are among the best in the city. Cooking their dinners in the street may be seen girls who have been educated at Stanford, Berkeley, Vassar and Bryn Mawr. It's a free start, everyone beginning over again, rich and poor alike. . . .

April 28

Public Notice:

A house-to-house canvass will be made for seltzer bottles belonging to the undersigned.

Shasta Water Co.

April 28

Item:

Pedestrians on the streets in the burned districts yesterday had a lively time dodging bricks and debris which had been dislodged from high walls by the strong northwest wind, which howled through the ruins. Several walls collapsed entirely and three or four people were struck by bricks.

April 28

Editorial:

The whole outside world just now is interested in San Francisco, but it must not be imagined that San Franciscans have lost interest in the rest of the universe. Quite the contrary. We have already received complaints because our dispatches are not as full as they were formerly.

April 29

Item:

Enthusiasm was the keynote of the meeting between the Supervisors and architects yesterday afternoon to consider plans for rebuilding the city.

"It is evidently the opportunity and duty of the citizens," said Benjamin Ide Wheeler, "to profit by the recent dispensations of Providence in building up a new and more beautiful city. I never appreciated so much the magnificent situation of San Francisco as today when I walked over it and saw the rectangular slashes of streets obliterated by the removal of disfiguring buildings."

April 30

Social Note:

The 11 P.M. curfew law falls exceptionally hard on San Francisco for San Franciscans have never really learned to sleep. But even the business of finding amusement to the hour of 11 o'clock is a puzzler. The people want something to do. There are no theaters, no cafes, no owl cars clanging across town, and the police whistle is seldom heard. Life is becoming a bore.

May 2

Item:

The cash line supplanted the bread line yesterday. The single file that has tailed daily from the fire stations was strung from the one place in San Francisco where currency was to be had—the Clearing House Bank—and once more coin jingled in pockets that have been all but empty since the day of the disaster.

May 2

Item:

Mrs. Gertrude Atherton, the California novelist, is in Berkeley engaged in writing an account of the earthquake and fire for one of the Eastern magazines. Much of her personal property, including 40,000 words of a new novel in manuscript which was stored in the basement of the Occidental Hotel, was destroyed by fire.

Speaking of her impressions, she said, "I have never known anything more interesting than the psychological result of this earthquake. Not only has it brought out the best in everyone, it has created a new, capable and experienced set of pioneers."

May 2

Theater Note:

A melodrama entitled "The Last Day of San Francisco" is already in rehearsal in New York. As the playwright was busy with the last act he read in the New York papers the misinformation that a heavy rain had caused much suffering and illness among those camped in Golden Gate Park. He at once inserted in the drama a rain storm and several cases of pneumonia.

May 2

Item:

The available supply of intoxicating liquor in San Francisco has never been diminished to its present extent. All liquor in the city is under strict control of the Police Commissioners and the Federal authorities.

Stimulants for invalids are obtainable upon application to the Board of Health. Physicians' prescriptions are not recognized unless the case is known to be one of absolute urgency.

May 2

Item:

Rufus P. Jennings, chairman of the California Promotion Committee, reported yesterday that "the publicity department of the California Promotion Committee is doing excellent work in sending out to Eastern correspondents articles about California and San Francisco."

May 3

Public Notice:

Free burials available at Cypress Lawn Cemetery till further notice. Temporary offices are at 1100 Gough street.

May 3

Editorial:

Naturally there are those who take advantage of such a situation as confronts San Francisco at this time. There is a certain percentage of men who have never worked, and who have no thought of ever working, and who are enjoying life to the uttermost under existing conditions. Steps will be taken at once to persuade men of this type that San Francisco is no place for such as they, and if they will not work after opportunity is offered they will be driven from the city or jailed as vagrants.

May 9

Item:

One peculiar and entirely unlooked for result has attended the proclamation of Mayor Schmitz closing up all saloons and forbidding the sale of liquor. Many habitual drinkers, suddenly deprived of their accustomed stimulant, have been driven temporarily insane. Park Emergency Hospital reports 40 such insanity cases a day.

May 15

Drama Review:

The magnificence of Sarah Bernhardt's performance of "La Sorciere", given last evening at Ye Liberty Theater for the opening of her San Francisco season, transplanted to Oakland, brought the audience to its feet to honor this queen of the stage. When Mme. Bernhardt appeared in the first act, coming in softly and bewitchingly as the moonlight that envelops the scene, she had to pause and be just herself for several seconds while the audience gave her greeting. For herself she would have been cordially welcomed at any time, but coming now, as she does, with loyalty and sympathy to the brave people who are trying to pick up life's interest and go on, she was most royally received. . . .

May 17

Item:

Heretofore much sympathy has been expressed for dwellers on land who suffered from earthquake and fire, but they are not the only ones deserving of commiseration. According to accounts apparently conservative and authentic, there were tragedies other than those recorded at the Coroner's office, for dwellers in the sea and bay are said to have perished miserable deaths. Thousands of succulent bivalves, say the oystermen, were smothered in baths of mud and showers of ashes sifting down through the salt water.

May 18

Item:

An earthquake lasting several seconds occurred on the Oakland side of the bay at 8:15 o'clock last night. It was not heavy enough to do any damage.

June 2

Announcement:

Sambo and his funny noises, Simon Simple and Most, Herr Speigleberger, Uncle Pike, Bobby the Teaser, Tommy Pipp, Weary Waggles and all the other mirth-provoking people of the comic supplement of the Sunday *Chronicle* have come through the earthquake and fire uninjured, and are just bubbling over with fun. They will be glad to see you, and you will be glad to see them, and you will forget all your troubles in the half hour of wholesome amusement which they are ready to afford. You'll miss a treat if you don't look them up at their old address, in tomorrow's *Chronicle.*

★   ★   ★

About the Editors

William Hogan, Literary Editor, *San Francisco Chronicle*, since 1955, has behind him some twenty years of journalistic accomplishment chiefly in connection with *The Chronicle*, where he has acted in various editorial capacities including that of drama-film editor. In World War II, he served on the staff of *Stars & Stripes*, Mediterranean Edition.

William German, News Editor, *San Francisco Chronicle*, has behind him the titles of Copyboy, Reporter, Assistant Foreign Editor and Slot Man for *The Chronicle*. He graduated from Brooklyn College in 1939, studied journalism at Columbia University, was a Nieman Fellow at Harvard, 1949-50.

The editors not only share a long association with *The Chronicle*— they both live with their families in Mill Valley, California. They do not share the same birthplace: William German came West from Brooklyn while William Hogan is a San Francisco Bay Area native.